THE RIPPLE EFFECT

Sleep Better, Eat Better, Move Better, Think Better

GREG WELLS, PH.D.

Collins

Published by Collins, an imprint of HarperCollins Publishers Ltd

First edition

HarperCollins books may be purchased for educational, business, or sales promotional use through our Special Markets Department.

HarperCollins Publishers Ltd
2 Bloor Street East, 20th Floor
Toronto, Ontario, Canada
M4W 1A8

www.harpercollins.ca

Library and Archives Canada Cataloguing in Publication
information is available upon request.

ISBN 978-1-44343-693-9

Printed and bound in the United States
LSC/C 10 9 8 7 6

For Judith, Ingrid, and Adam

Also by Greg Wells

Superbodies

CONTENTS

INTRODUCTION

IT WAS AUGUST and I was sitting on a school bus that was driving down a mountain road. It was a beautiful day. I looked out the window at the clear sky and at the trees, lakes, and mountains around me. The air outside smelled of pine. Healthy, fit, lean people surrounded me. We were on our way to the start line of an Ironman race. Yet I was thinking about dying. Not dying as in "Oh, man, this workout is going to hurt," but really dying. You see, 12 months earlier I had been a patient in the cardiac ward of a hospital.

Life was happening. I had a 2-year-old daughter, whom I love dearly. But anyone who has had kids knows that with the love and happiness come exhaustion and sleeplessness. My wife, finishing grad school, was up studying at all hours. I was launching new research programs at the university where I am a professor and at the Hospital for Sick Children, in Toronto, where I work as a scientist. My first book, *Superbodies*, was about to be published. I was getting ready to go to London, to do sport science analysis for the upcoming Olympic Games TV broadcast. And we were moving houses. As a result, I wasn't sleeping well or eating well, and I certainly didn't have the time or the energy to work out consistently.

I was unfit and unhealthy. To anyone on the outside looking at me, I appeared to be successful. I had a great family, awesome jobs, a book under my belt, and lots of public speaking and media engagements. But on the inside I had become fragile. I was tired. So when my daughter brought home a virus she had picked up at her daycare, I was particularly susceptible to it. It went straight to my heart, causing viral myocarditis—inflammation of the heart tissue. It felt as if I had a deep ache in my chest. Not a good feeling to have when you're only 40 years old. So I checked myself into the hospital. (My daughter was fine—she had only a slight cold.)

Lying in my hospital bed, staring at the ceiling, I wondered, "How did I end up here?" This thought quickly shifted to "How do I get out of here?" and then, more importantly, "How do I make sure I never, ever come back?"

After a few days, a notion began to emerge for me. Each night I was woken by various alarms going off. That there were lights on seemingly everywhere didn't help my sleep either. And the food was about as unhealthy as you can get outside of a fast food restaurant. The more I lay around, undergoing various tests, the worse I felt. I was depressed about my health and state of being: I couldn't sleep or eat healthily, plus I was pretty much immobile. My mental state was deteriorating. I realized that my experience in the hospital, which should be a place of healing, was a metaphor for the health challenges faced by the entire world.

Our world is facing four interrelated grand epidemics—sleeplessness, obesity, inactivity, and mental illness—that are causing people to struggle on a daily basis. Consider this:

- We are in a global "sleeplessness epidemic" that affects close to 20% of the population.[1]
- Non-communicable diseases that can be caused by poor nutrition and physical inactivity such as cancer, type 2 diabetes, and cardiovascular disease are now the leading cause of death in all parts of the world except Africa.[2]
- Almost 60% of Canadians and 70% of Americans are now overweight or obese.[3]
- The World Health Organization has identified physical inactivity as one of the greatest threats to human health.[4]
- One in five Canadians will suffer from mental illness in their lifetime.[5]

What does this mean? That billions of people are missing out on potential creativity, problem solving, ingenuity, inventiveness, and, ultimately, happiness.

These statistics terrified and upset me. So I opened a new window on my iPad and began reading the latest science on how to get healthy and fit, avoid chronic illness, be happy, learn more, and concentrate better. I wanted to be ultra-healthy and to perform at a high level, both physically and mentally. Over and over, the science made it plain: If I wanted to do all these things, I needed to sleep soundly, eat smarter, move more, and think clearly. Most importantly, I had to do all four. Any one of them alone would not be enough. They are all interconnected. And so I began this journey. The first thing I did, lying there in the cardiac ward, was register for Ironman.

Realizing the importance of the four factors and their interconnectedness brought about a fundamental shift in my thinking. I'm an exercise physiologist, specializing in analyzing, understanding, and impacting extreme situations. I work as a scientist and physiologist. I study children with chronic illnesses, elite athletes, and physiology in extreme environments, such as mountains and deserts. I do all this to help me understand how disease, training, and the environment affect us, and how we can adapt to improve our health and reach our potential as human beings. That's my life's work. My team mostly focuses on using exercise in combination with advanced tests such as MRIs to help understand diseases like cystic fibrosis, leukemia, obesity, and congenital heart diseases and to develop new exercise and physical activity therapies. The leap in thinking, which unfortunately took a personal crisis to bring me to, was that if we can combine exercise—powerful and beneficial on its own—with nutrition, sleep, and psychology, we can build an entirely new holistic approach to health and high performance.

And now I had discovered my mission: to solve a billion-person problem.

THE RIPPLE EFFECT

TRADITIONALLY IN WESTERN medicine, sleeping, eating, moving, and thinking are treated separately. If you want to lose weight, your doctor tells you to go on a diet, but not necessarily about the importance of sleep. If you want to sleep better, you're given sleep medication, but you're often not told to exercise during the day. If you have depression, you may not be encouraged to move more as part of your treatment.

We are missing out on a powerful insight that, if applied consistently over time, will result in exponential improvements in your health and in your ability to do the things in life that you care about most. This insight is that sleeping soundly, eating smarter, moving more, and thinking clearly are all interconnected—you can't outrun a bad diet, for example, and a proper diet can't make up for a sedentary lifestyle. These four factors are amplifiers for each other. When you put them together, you end up with much more than the sum of the individual parts.

When you make sure you have a great night's sleep before a big race, presentation, or exam, you're also regulating those hormones that help regulate your appetite and satiety. When you eat foods that improve your energy levels, you're helping prevent cardiovascular disease. When you walk for 15 minutes to activate your brain before sitting down to do your best creative work, you're also reducing your risk of certain types of cancer. Moving from distraction to focus that helps us think more clearly also lowers stress hormones that can cause disease. It's when we combine sleeping, eating, moving, and thinking better that we can make incredible gains in our health and in our lives. I call this the ripple effect.

Here's a real-world example of what happens when you combine these ideas. About 8 months after I gave a presentation at a conference, I received this note from one of the attendees:

Hi, Greg,

I've been meaning to send this note for a little while now—it's a quick thank-you for the message you deliver and the change that it caused in my life.

You might recall that I first saw you during your keynote at the conference last year. I've mentioned to you how impactful that talk was, but I didn't fully explain HOW impactful.

The idea of finding a "high performance" version of myself was intriguing, but it was the way you phrased your message (with relatable references to athletes and mountain climbing) that caused it to resonate with me long after the conference had ended. I spent the next 4 months going through some fairly significant introspection—I watched myself deal with stress, anxiety, depression, fear of failure, fear of success, all of it. I also watched my father pass away in August. What also died with him was the last need I had to meet anyone else's standards—I needed to define my own standards and my own relative "high performance."

The week before Halloween I flipped a switch and started living according to what I saw as my own "high performance" lifestyle. My goal was to live longer, and live better, but also to live more fully and be reconnected with things that I love.

I took steps to manage my stress levels by first identifying consciously when I was stressed;

I stopped flailing at my job by understanding that I'm at my peak when I approach my work from a relaxed frame of mind;

I consciously took steps to manage my sleep and obtain a minimum of 6 hours per night to allow my brain to be flushed of its toxins; and

I started to eat food that I could recognize as food, as opposed to recognizing them by the packaging they come dressed in.

In the 4 to 5 months since I flipped the switch, I've lost 75 lbs. (to date from 315 lbs. to 240 lbs.), I don't snore anymore (which means less chance of apnea), I have lost the pain in my knees and ankles, and I hike approximately 6 hours in the mountains every weekend, regardless of the weather. At work, I feel like I'm more able to cope with the incredibly full job I've taken on, and I've been told I'm more in tune with the broad spectrum of my responsibilities. At home, I'm way more involved in the lives of my three kids and also feel like they know me better than they did before. I've rediscovered my lifelong partner, and my wife and I are planning an epic hike together during our 25th wedding anniversary year (Nepal? Iceland?).

I can imagine that you've given the speech you gave a hundred times. Well, now you know that one speech you gave helped one person and his family (four other people), and those five people will carry the message to others:

"High performance is how you define it as an individual. Find the keys to your personal version of high performance, approach your challenges from a relaxed state of mind, be aware, use the tools that nature provides, recognize your food as food not packaging, and sleep."

I've wanted to send this note for a while now because I wanted to say thanks—so, thank you . . .

DC, March 2016

SIMPLY, THE WAY to improve your health, perform better, and unleash your potential lies in the magical combination of four elements:

- We need to sleep soundly.
- We need to move more.
- We need to eat smarter.
- We need to think clearly.

Together, these four factors lead to remarkable improvements in health, performance, and potential. By applying all these principles to myself, 12 months after being admitted to the hospital, I completed my first Ironman triathlon. I was healthy, fit, and happy. My life was forever changed.

A MANIFESTO AND GUIDE FOR LIVING A GREAT LIFE

IN THIS BOOK, I show you the research and specific simple changes you can make to get healthier, perform to your potential, and live the life of your dreams. We'll look at the foundational concept of sleeping soundly and the powerful impact of eating smart. You'll also learn how and why to move more. And you'll see how sleeping, eating, and moving more will help you learn better and be more creative—in other words, to think clearly. The final chapter provides you with a plan you can use to turn knowledge into action.

This book is about simple, powerful, and scientific ways to improve and amplify your health. Don't feel you need to read the chapters in sequence: each is self-contained, packed with information that will inform and inspire you. The book is both a manifesto and a guide for helping you, and ultimately billions of people, live a life in which you can unleash your health, reach your potential, and become extraordinary.

DR. GREG'S 1% TIPS

As you work through all the information, advice, and suggestions in this book, keep focused on micro-improvements. A 1% change may not seem like much, but each takes you, step by step, farther along the path to optimal health and reaching your potential. You'll find, throughout the book, a series of Dr. Greg's 1% Tips. Practise them, and share them with your family, friends, and community.

1

GETTING STARTED

Our deepest fear is not that we are inadequate. Our deepest fear is that we are powerful beyond measure. It is our light, not our darkness that most frightens us. We ask ourselves, "Who am I to be brilliant, gorgeous, talented, fabulous?" Actually, who are you not to be? Your playing small does not serve the world. There is nothing enlightened about shrinking so that other people won't feel insecure around you. We are all meant to shine, as children do. And as we let our own light shine, we unconsciously give other people permission to do the same. As we are liberated from our own fear, our presence automatically liberates others.   —Marianne Williamson

EVERYONE CAN LEAD a better life. I truly believe this. Everyone can improve, no matter where they are on the scale, whether sick with a serious illness, like the children at SickKids hospital who have had their bodies ravaged by cancer and by the chemotherapy and radiation that helped cure them, or the fittest, highest-performing people on the planet—Olympic athletes. We can all learn the simple, scientific truths to being healthy and living a life in which we reach our potential. Your potential is just that—yours. It does not matter where you are on the health scale, as long as you move the needle and get better.

TURN KNOWLEDGE INTO EXTRAORDINARY ACTION

ON JANUARY 14, 2015, climbers Kevin Jorgeson and Tommy Caldwell finished their 19-day, 915-metre ascent of the Dawn Wall on El Capitan, in California's Yosemite National Park. It is generally considered to be one of the toughest climbs yet completed. To add to the feat, Jorgeson and Caldwell did the ascent by free climbing—that is, they used only their hands and feet to ascend, using ropes only for protection from falls. Jorgeson tweeted about the climb, saying, "This is not an effort to 'conquer.' It's about realizing a dream."

Dreams are powerful. To achieve truly transformational improvement in your health and your life, start by setting your dreams.

WORDS OF WISDOM

"If you can dream it, you can do it. Always remember that this whole thing was started with a dream and a mouse."   —Walt Disney

SET YOUR DREAMS

IN 2010 (AND again in 2012), I attended the Olympic Games as a sport science analyst. I had incredible experiences and saw amazing performances. One in particular is etched in my memory. Early one morning during the Winter Olympics, Slovenian cross-country skier Petra Majdic was warming up. Petra was one of the gold medal favourites in her event. But that morning everything went wrong. She slipped as she came around a corner and fell off an embankment, breaking her ribs. Her Olympic dream was now at risk.

DESPITE HER INJURY, Majdic went on to compete. Each time she took a breath, her broken ribs scraped over each other. Every time she poled to drive herself forward, the vibration forces transferred through her arms and torso. Her latissimus dorsi, a broad back muscle, pulled on her rib cage. The pain must have been torturous. But she persevered. She competed in her first heat, and then her second heat, qualifying for the semi-final, where she was fast enough to make it through to the final. Somewhere along the way, one of the broken ribs punctured her lung and she suffered a pneumothorax—a collapsed lung. Still she kept going. In the final, she skied her way to a bronze medal.

There's an iconic picture of her receiving her medal. Two medical personnel flank her on the podium: she had refused to go to the hospital until she had been awarded that medal.

Once she stabilized in the hospital, the media were allowed to interview her. One of her answers to a question posed to her struck me as being life changing in its importance. The interviewer asked Majdic, "How could you keep skiing through the heats, semi-final, and final, despite all that pain?" Majdic's answer was fascinating. "The pain that I went through today to win that bronze medal," she said, "was nothing compared to the pain that I have gone through training for 20 years to achieve my dream."

She didn't say "achieve my goals," "reach my objective," or even "win a medal." Rather, she spoke of dreams. Why? Because dreams are more powerful than goals—despite goal setting being our traditional method for building self-motivation. I realized when I heard this that athletes, at least the great ones, use their dreams to fuel their passions and to drive action and growth.

The difference between goals and dreams is subtle but significant. Petra Majdic used a skill she had developed as an athlete to overcome incredible obstacles and deliver a medal-winning performance that inspired the world. She thought about her dream when she was faced with the decision of whether to compete. She relied on the big picture—the vision she had created when she was a child that she wanted to achieve. Her dream was to win an Olympic medal. That dream allowed her to compartmentalize the pain of her injury and focus on the performance that ultimately enabled her to successfully complete the competition.

The principle of thinking big and setting dreams applies to almost everything in our lives. By making small adjustments in the way we act, think, and feel—like moving from goals to dreams—we can move from average to iconic, just as Majdic did. We can learn from people who have pushed the limits of human performance, health, and achievement.

Dreams are powerful. They inspire us to new heights. Dreams are our deepest and most dearly held hopes and aspirations. Dreams capture our imagination. Dreams create extraordinary motivation and transformative change. They enable us to live differently.

When Dr. Martin Luther King Jr. stood beneath the Lincoln Memorial at the peak of the civil rights movement and inspired his listeners to action, he repeated a single phrase over and over again: "I have a dream." He didn't say, "I have a goal" or "I have an objective." His dream changed the United States—and the world.

Dreaming BIG, then making small, consistent improvements, can revolutionize your health and your life. If you really want to achieve something, dream yourself into doing it. Dream setting is powerful. And it is the most effective way to change your life for the better.

Unfortunately, many of us believe that thinking of our personal and professional goals as dreams is somehow hokey or silly. It's not. Dreams motivate us to achieve more. And while some dreams are huge—like inventing a new technology or starting an organization from scratch—they can also be as small as you want: running a 10 km race, sleeping more deeply, being more effective in your job, improving your body, overcoming an illness, or learning how to play a particular piece of music.

The key to living a world-class life and getting the most out of this time that we have is to make sure we have dreams. We need something that powers us to do more. We need dreams that can drive us to be better. Dreams give us a flame in our hearts that ignites passion. If you think about what athletes look like when they win—exhilarated, thrilled, excited, energized—you will have an image of what the fulfillment of a dream can do for us all. It gives us a chance to live life at a different level.

Dreams help us overcome challenges and obstacles. In 1987, at the age of 15, I broke my neck bodysurfing in the waves off Florida's West Palm Beach. After spending 2 weeks in traction and 3 months in a halo vest, undergoing surgery (on my 16th birthday!) to repair bones and ligaments, and enduring several months of physiotherapy, I returned to swim training and qualified for Olympic trials—my dream—14 months after the accident. All this after my neurosurgeon told me I'd never swim competitively again. I sent the surgeon a photo of me swimming at the trials.

Dreams can be transformative too. In 2003 I joined up with a group of people who had the dream of setting a Guinness world record for the fastest human-powered crossing of Africa. This expedition became the Tour d'Afrique, an 11,000 km bicycle expedition from Cairo, Egypt, to Cape Town, South Africa. The expedition is now an annual event and the longest bike race in the world.

Cycling through the Sahara Desert, getting very sick in Ethiopia, slowly getting fit and resilient through Kenya and Tanzania, and then getting healthy and psychologically tough through Malawi, Mozambique, Zimbabwe, Botswana, and South Africa completely changed me. I was transformed for the better, physically, mentally, and emotionally.

In each of these experiences I was able to overcome challenges and achieve a result that seemed impossible before I started. I had been told I would never swim again. No one had cycled that route through Africa as quickly as we did. Surviving and arguably excelling through each event transformed me. These events were hard and painful. But they made me better. They changed the way I act, think, and feel. Dream setting, along with the skills and techniques I share in this book, can do the same for you.

What is your dream? What do you want to achieve? What is your passion? What do you love? What do you want to spend your life doing? If it's your work, that's great. If it's supporting your family, that's great too. If it's a health goal, fantastic. Your dream can be anything. It can be big, like running a marathon or completing a triathlon. Or it can be smaller, like running a 5 km race. It might be that you want to lose 10 pounds, permanently. What about that new business you've been thinking of launching? Maybe you just want to be happier every day. It doesn't matter what your dream is or how big it is. Just so long as realizing it will add a powerful spark to your life.

DR. GREG'S 1% TIP: SET YOUR DREAMS

Okay, team, it's time to set some dreams! What passion of yours can become a dream? What vision of the future makes you excited and happy? Develop that idea and it will become something you are likely to achieve. Research shows that by writing down what you want to achieve, you significantly increase your chances of reaching your objective. Research also shows that if you tell someone else about it, your odds of achieving it are even higher. This applies to dreams as well as to goals. Go ahead—jot down some notes about what you want to be or do.

JORGESON AND CALDWELL'S climb included seven pitches (about the length of a climbing rope, or 60 to 70 metres) that were rated 5.14 difficulty (on a scale from 5.5 to 5.15). A single 5.14 climb is a significant career accomplishment for most climbers, so completing seven such pitches in a single push up a route is one of the things that make this such an incredible achievement. Their preparation included not just strength and endurance training but also developing their skills to a point where they could complete these challenging climbs repeatedly.

Once Jorgeson and Caldwell had set the dream of climbing the Dawn Wall on El Capitan, they began to prepare. They scouted the routes. They practised the different pitches. They trained to build the strength and endurance they would need. They refined their nutrition. They slept deeply to ensure recovery and regeneration. The challenge required that the climbers prepare for seven years—which highlights that it takes time to build capacity, develop skills, and become excellent at whatever it is you are most passionate about.

We live in an age where we have almost immediate access to products, and we are constantly being sold on the latest quick fix. That this expedition captured the world's attention and inspired many is a testament to the power of dreams and long-term commitment. If we can all work on being a little bit better with our sleep, nutrition, exercise, and mental skills, consistently over time, we too can accomplish incredible things. That's the principle— slow, steady, and consistent improvement over time—that I'd like you to adopt when applying the concepts explained in this book.

FOCUS ON BEING 1% BETTER

ONE OF THE best approaches I've seen for turning good into great is focusing on 1% gains. I work with a lot of athletes, from the super talented to the less talented. But it isn't just talent that determines achievement. What sets the best-performing athletes apart from the pack is their dedication to training at a consistently high level, and their equal dedication to aligning their lives with their goals and dreams. And among this group is a factor that sets even the elite athletes apart: a commitment to being just a little bit better each day.

One of my clients, Sophia, is a high-powered executive with a demanding job. When we talked recently, I sensed there was something wrong but couldn't put my finger on it right away. Then she stopped talking and took a long, deep breath before saying, tearfully, "Greg, let me tell you how things are for me right now. I've got a tough job. I work a lot. I love my work, but it's really demanding. I'm a single mom. I have an eight-year-old girl who I barely see, and when I do see her, I'm so tired I can barely deal with her. When I get some time to myself, which is almost never, I go to the bar with friends and drink too much. I want to eat better, but by the time I get home, I'm totally exhausted, so making meals just doesn't happen. I'm not happy with how things are. I can't seem to get myself going. I can't achieve any goals right now, and I need help."

After considering what she had said, I asked her if she could spend 1 hour on the weekend with her daughter in the park. She seemed to be a bit taken aback by the simplicity of my question but agreed that going to the park for an hour on the weekend was something she could manage. When I checked in with her the following week, instead of the tough, resigned look on her face that I had seen the previous week, there was a spark of a smile. She told me about the wonderful walk she and her daughter had taken in the park, how happy her daughter had been, and how the time spent outside had given Sophia more energy— that it was the best thing she had done in years. Over the next several months, that one small change of getting more active had a ripple effect in Sophia's life, and her life had now completely changed. She and her daughter had regular exercise dates on which they went hiking, played tennis, and swam. She had stopped drinking on the weekends and was taking cooking classes. She was not chronically exhausted. Her work performance was more effective.

By simply making one single step toward a healthier, happier life, Sophia created momentum that led to her being, 9 months later, much healthier and happier. This is the key idea of this book: to live a life in which you can reach your potential, improve how you eat, sleep, move, and think one small step at a time. A 1% change might not seem like much, but small improvements in the way you live each and every day will amplify your life. This is exactly what Sophia did, to powerful effect. And it's what I did to bounce back from a broken neck and from a heart infection—ultimately riding my bike across Africa and completing two Ironman triathlons.

WORDS OF WISDOM

"Success is a few simple disciplines, practiced every day; while failure is simply a few errors in judgment, repeated every day."   —Jim Rohn

THE PRINCIPLE OF 1% gains works for large organizations as well. General Electric CEO Jeff Immelt has made "1% better" a mandate at General Electric. His idea is that General Electric can collect data from the self-reporting airplane engines, locomotives, and even power plants that the company builds and then analyze that data to discover how to make micro-improvements in efficiency. Then, using the industrial Internet, updates to operating software can be sent to the equipment to create 1% gains in performance. Over time, the gains have the potential for tremendous returns. General Electric estimates that it can boost productivity in the United States by 1.5%, which over 20 years could raise the average national income of the company by 30%. And, to take airplane engines as an example, a 1% reduction in fuel costs, as the result of improvements to the engines, could save the airline industry $30 billion over 15 years.

What General Electric is doing with machines, equipment, and business processes you can do with yourself. Being just 1% better every day is like compound interest for your body and mind.

LET'S GO BACK to Jorgeson and Caldwell's climb for a moment. At pitch 15 (of 32), Jorgeson was struggling. This was a section of rock where he had to climb laterally between two vertical pitches. He failed 10 times before completing it on the 11th try. Completing the pitch took him 7 days.

Keep in mind that, during the climb, he and Caldwell were sleeping in tents attached to the wall hundreds of metres off the ground. His determination to overcome the challenge of pitch 15 is truly inspirational. The two climbers were putting as much attention and focus into their recovery and regeneration as they were into their climbing. Jorgeson rested for hours between attempts, in some cases even an entire day before trying again.

We are often faced with seemingly insurmountable challenges in our lives. In many cases, it is these challenges that define us. To overcome them, we may not need to try harder, reacting and charging ahead; we may need to step back, rest, recover, regenerate, and respond to the challenge strategically. Sleeping better, eating well, and getting exercise on a daily basis can help all of us improve our performance and health, which is key to overcoming our big life challenges. But it might take repeated attempts using new strategies, tactics, and skills before we succeed.

Climbing El Capitan may not be on your to-do list, but you can still gain inspiration from this incredible accomplishment and glean insights that can help you live a better, higher-performance, and ultimately healthier life.

2

SLEEP SOUNDLY

> I love sleep. My life tends to fall apart when I'm awake,
> you know?   —Ernest Hemingway

WHEN THE *EXXON VALDEZ* oil supertanker crashed in Alaska, 258,000 barrels of oil spilled into the ocean, destroying wildlife and poisoning the environment for years to come. The reason for the disaster? The helmsman had reportedly fallen asleep at the wheel—the crew had just put in a 22-hour shift loading oil. According to the *Anchorage Daily News*, the pilot had had only a catnap in the 16 hours leading up to the crash.[1]

Another disaster attributed to sleeplessness is the space shuttle *Challenger* explosion. Just seconds after launch, the shuttle exploded, killing all seven crew members. Apparently, some of the managers at the flight centre who were involved in the launch had slept for only 2 hours before arriving for work at 1 a.m.[2]

A report of the presidential commission investigating the accident stated, "The willingness of NASA employees in general to work excessive hours, while admirable, raises serious questions when it jeopardizes job performance, particularly when critical management decisions are at stake."[3]

Note that the commission considered the willingness of NASA employees to work excessive hours as admirable—it's exactly the same attitude that exists in many workplaces and schools, even today, almost 30 years after the *Challenger* disaster. But volume of work does not lead to excellence. You cannot perform at world-class levels if you're staring blankly at a computer screen, trying to comprehend words that you could breeze through in a few seconds if you took the time to build a consistent rejuvenating sleep routine.

We live in a 24-hour world, and we're paying the price. For most of history, humans have woken up and gone to sleep based on when the sun came up or went down. When it was light out, we went about our daily activities, and when it was dark, we relaxed and slept (assuming that there were no sabre-toothed tigers in the immediate area). Our current situation is much different. Many of us work indoors and don't have natural light in our workplace or school. We are exposed to fluorescent lights during the day, and in the evenings we're looking at bright TV, computer, tablet, or mobile phone screens. Our internal physiology is no longer matched to the rhythm of the sun, and as a result, we're not sleeping enough and our health and performance are suffering.

THE GLOBAL SLEEPLESSNESS EPIDEMIC

ALMOST 20% OF our population is chronically sleep deprived.[4] Our busy work schedules and home responsibilities leave us with less time to get proper rest. According to the

National Sleep Foundation, people sleep 20% less than those a century ago.[5] Some 70 million Americans have a diagnosed sleep disorder—and that's just the people who actually went to the doctor and got diagnosed. In Canada, one in seven people—or 3.5 million—suffer from insomnia.

Lack of sleep not only impairs our ability to function but also has a powerful impact on our health. With sleeplessness comes increased risk of heart attack, stroke, anxiety, and depression. Not enough sleep is so damaging, it shortens our life. An epidemiological study of over one million Americans reported that sleep duration below 6 hours per night was associated with increased mortality.[6] This is why I believe that the foundation of human health and performance is sleeping soundly. This is where we will start to construct a healthy, high-performance life.

WHAT IS SLEEP?

PEOPLE TYPICALLY THINK of sleep as a time of rest when the body and mind "shut down." Although sleep *is* a dormant state in which the activity of the brain's cortex reduces by 40%, it's not a passive process. While you're asleep, a lot is going on in your body to recover, restore, and rebuild it. Sleep is a highly active metabolic process that helps optimize our brain structure, repair damaged cells in the body, and restore energy levels.

NREM AND REM SLEEP

WHILE WE SLEEP, we cycle through different stages of sleep in approximately 90-minute cycles. Seventy-five percent of our sleep is in the non-rapid eye movement (NREM) stage, where our muscles and other parts of the body relax, temperature and blood pressure drop, heart rate and breath rate come down, and cells and tissues grow and repair. It's in this stage that we recover our energy levels and our nervous systems (brain, spinal cord, and nerves that connect the spinal cord to muscles and organs) recover and regenerate. During NREM sleep, anabolic hormones that encourage cellular growth are released to repair tissues and stabilize our energy levels.

The other 25% of our sleep is the rapid eye movement (REM) stage and is equally important. It's in this stage that our brains are active, energy is supplied to the brain and the rest of the body, and our eyes dart back and forth. It's thought to be the time when we establish new connections between neurons (the individual cells in the brain).

So, as you can see, both stages are critical for the optimal recovery and regeneration of our bodies, including our brains.

WORDS OF WISDOM: THE SCIENCE OF SLEEP

Dr. Charles Samuels, medical director at the Centre for Sleep and Human Performance, appeared recently on my podcast, the Be Better Podcast. He's certified by the American Board of Sleep Medicine, and he had some interesting thoughts on sleep that I want to share with you here:

The fact is that our immune system recovers through [the] night. Our muscles regenerate, so for training athletes who are training hard, the sole purpose of which is to break down muscle, the importance of recovery is absolutely critical, and the sleep state is one of the states during which the muscles recover and actually get stronger.

From a cognitive . . . and executive function perspective, our brains imprint memory, learning, and tasks during sleep and allow us to get better at those tasks. If sleep is disturbed, it becomes harder to retain [imprinted] information . . . and then be able to repeat the tasks.

Thirty percent of the North American population just isn't getting enough sleep, and most people compromise sleep, so while you feel that there's a great interest in sleep, I would still argue that the average person out there does not put great emphasis on sleep [and will] compromise sleep for some other activity, whether it's school or work or fun or kids.

Getting more sleep is important, and if you do, you're going to feel better. If you're struggling with your sleep, you should get help. . . . There are a multitude of resources online. . . . [See] your doctor [or] your health care provider to get help with sleep, [and recognize] that sleep is not a passive state. It's an absolute requirement to maintain good, normal health.

YOUR CIRCADIAN RHYTHMS: USE THEM TO BUILD YOUR ULTIMATE DAY

WE HUMANS HAVE developed what are known as circadian rhythms, which include the sleep–wake cycle, changes in body temperature, and regular times over the 24-hour cycle where various hormones are released into the blood.[7] Our circadian rhythms are regulated by a pair of structures in the brain called the suprachiasmatic nuclei (SCN). These master circadian pacemakers are so powerful that they can control your behaviour and even your genes. They control the release of melatonin (the hormone that regulates your wakefulness and sleep) and of cortisol (a stress hormone). They can also be overridden by the light or dark in our environments—that's what happens when we fly across time zones and become jet-lagged, since we are naturally attuned to the 24-hour cycle of light and dark, meaning naturally awake during the day and asleep at night.

We also experience times of the day when we're more or less alert, hungry, energetic, and fatigued. These states are in many cases influenced by our circadian rhythms, the natural changes in the body's internal chemistry. Once aware of these natural rhythms, we can take advantage of them to improve health and performance.

Here's the typical person's energy and performance pattern during the course of a day:

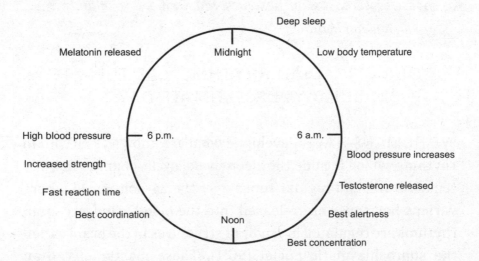

What does *your* circadian rhythm look like? When are you at your best mentally? When do you have trouble concentrating? When do you feel most energetic or lethargic? To figure this out, keep a daily log and note your energy levels each hour throughout the day. Once you have answers, you can craft your ideal day, aligning your tasks and schedule with your body's natural rhythms to take advantage of your high mental and physical energy times. You'll perform better and you'll also be much healthier because aligning your tasks to your circadian rhythms can dramatically reduce your negative stress levels.

One way to manipulate circadian rhythms slightly is by increasing or decreasing body temperature, since it's the SCN that controls body temperature and is sensitive to changes—like a self-adjusting thermostat. If you want to increase your alertness and concentration at a time of the day when you normally feel sluggish, increase your body temperature by doing 5 to 10 minutes of light cardiorespiratory exercise, such as a brisk walk. If you can do the exercise outdoors in natural light, you'll feel even better.

SLEEP AND YOUR HEALTH

WORDS OF WISDOM

"Pulling all-nighters isn't a badge of honor. It's the enemy of intelligence, patience, and creativity."
—Jason Fried, founder of Basecamp

OPTIMAL HEALTH AND performance start with sleep. You can set yourself up for success in all aspects of your life by sleeping soundly and sleeping enough. Since it's during sleep that the immune system recovers and regenerates, sleep helps us fight off disease and illness—it can even help us survive cancer. As well, it helps manage chronic pain. Sleeping well also decreases the risk of heart attack. And it can help us lose fat, recover faster from training (it's during sleep that our muscles repair and grow), remove waste products from our brains, and be better at solving problems. We consolidate memories while we sleep, so it's actually during sleep that we learn. Sleeping better will improve mood and energy.

Imagine if someone developed a drug that could do all that! The drug would be hailed the miracle of our lifetime. Whoever developed it would win a Nobel Prize. Regardless of whether you're an elite athlete, brilliant student, superstar parent, or titan of business, sleep is the foundation of your healthy, high-performance life. Let's explore the relationship between sleep and health in more detail.

SLEEP AND CANCER

THE IMMUNE SYSTEM is the body's main defence against cancer, so it's not surprising that sleep is related to the risk of getting cancer. The amount of sleep you get also affects whether you will survive cancer, should you have it, and your risk of recurrence after treatment.

A 2012 US study found that women who don't get enough sleep are at a higher risk of developing breast cancer and of developing more aggressive tumours than are those women who do get adequate sleep.[8] Another study shows that women who sleep longer and more efficiently (measured as less movement during sleep) survived advanced breast cancer for 68.9 months on average, as opposed to only 33.2 months for those who slept less efficiently. The study's authors suggest that sleep helps the immune system work better and keep cancer cells under control.

In 2011 Dr. Li Li, of Cleveland's Case Western Reserve University School of Medicine, published his research in the journal *Cancer*, showing that people who slept fewer than 6 hours each night had a 50% greater chance of having colorectal adenomas—precancerous tumours in the colon—when compared with those who slept more than 7 hours.[9] To quote Dr. Li: "A short amount of sleep can now be viewed as a new risk factor for the development . . . of colon cancer."

Here's the physiology behind the sleep–cancer link: Each night when it gets dark outside, the body naturally releases the hormone melatonin. Melatonin regulates our sleep and wakefulness cycles: when it is released at night, you get drowsy, and when it is not released—in the morning and throughout the day—you feel awake and alert.[10] Researchers have discovered that this same hormone, melatonin, also helps enhance the immune system, which fights off disease.[11] Disturbed sleep leads to the disruption of melatonin, which leads to the suppression of the immune system, and, in turn, to higher levels of cancer-stimulating cytokines. Cytokines are tiny proteins that circulate around the body and carry signals between the various cells. Think of them as little mail carriers running around your body with letters from one cell to another. Lack of sleep leads to the mail carriers getting confused and dropping off the signals at the wrong cells, thus wreaking havoc in your body.

Bottom line: Make sure you're sleeping enough. If you have been diagnosed with cancer, make sure enough sleep is part of your treatment plan.

DR. GREG'S 1% TIP: CREATE A TRANSITION RITUAL

A transition ritual will help you make the shift from working to not working. What activity will help you make that shift? For me, it's walking from work to the park near my house and relaxing on a bench for 5 minutes before continuing home. Take a few minutes to walk, listen to music, or make a call to a friend on the way home from work. The key is to make sure that when you arrive home, you're not mentally still at work. If you work at a home office you can leave your house for 10 to 15 minutes to create that transition even if you're already at home.

SLEEP AND INFLAMMATION

INFLAMMATION IS THE body's mechanism for healing and repairing tissues. The inflammatory response has several effects in the body, including expanding blood vessels to increase blood flow to an injured or infected area, a signal for more immune-system cells to come help repair tissues or fight off an invader (like bacteria or a virus). For example, if you get a cut, the inflammatory process heals your skin. You can see it at work if you look closely: there will be some redness around the cut, and you might also feel pain from the swelling. For acute injuries, this process is critical for healing. However, if the inflammatory process stays turned on or elevated for a long period, serious problems can develop. This is termed *chronic inflammation*. Chronic inflammation of the body's systems is now being linked to the development of asthma, arthritis, cancer, cardiovascular disease, type 2 diabetes, and depression, among other health problems.[12] You'll find more details on this in chapter 3.

Poor sleep is associated with an increased risk of inflamma-tory diseases and all-cause mortality. All-cause mortality is *all* of the deaths that occur in a population, regardless of the *cause*. More specifically, research has shown that people with chronic sleep deprivation—6 hours or fewer per night—had higher lev-els of three inflammatory markers: C-reactive protein (CRP), interleukin-6 (IL-6), and tumour necrosis factor-alpha (TNF-alpha).[13] Researchers have suggested that the activation of pro-inflammatory pathways may be the way that sleep is linked to increases in our risk for chronic diseases.[14]

SLEEP AND CARDIOVASCULAR DISEASE

SCIENTISTS AGREE THAT the amount you sleep can either increase or decrease your risk of heart attack or stroke. The risk of a fatal heart attack increases 45% in women who sleep 5 hours or fewer per night.[15] Professor Francesco Cappuccio of Warwick Medical School says: "If you sleep less than six hours per night and have disturbed sleep you stand a 48 per cent greater chance of developing or dying from heart disease and a 15 per cent greater chance of developing or dying of a stroke. The trend for late nights and early mornings is actually a ticking time bomb for our health so you need to act now to reduce your risk of developing these life-threatening conditions."[16]

In addition, a paper presented at the SLEEP 2012 confer-ence by Megan Ruiter, University of Alabama at Birmingham, showed that people who regularly get fewer than 6 hours of sleep have an increased risk of having a stroke—even if they're not overweight, don't have diabetes, and don't have sleep apnea.

Those are significant findings. And we need to pay attention—especially if you are caught in a late-night/early-morning lifestyle habit. You may eat well and you may exercise regularly—two highly beneficial activities—but if your sleep is getting short shrift, you're undermining those benefits and introducing a serious health risk into your life. It's not worth it. You've got to sleep.

SLEEP AND OBESITY

SLEEP AND OBESITY are closely related. Lack of sleep disrupts insulin metabolism, which can lead to obesity, metabolic syndrome, and type 2 diabetes. Insulin is a hormone produced in the pancreas that signals cells to absorb glucose from the blood. Type 1 diabetes is an autoimmune disease in which the immune system attacks the cells in the pancreas and impairs their ability to produce insulin. With type 2 diabetes, cells in the muscles and liver become insensitive or resistant to insulin. According to the Mayo Clinic, metabolic syndrome is a cluster of conditions—increased blood pressure, high blood sugar, excess body fat around the waist, and abnormal cholesterol or triglyceride levels—that occur together and increase your risk of heart disease, stroke, and diabetes.

Frighteningly, even a short period of sleeplessness directly changes the metabolism of our cells: it makes them act as if we have type 2 diabetes. Research by sleep researcher Dr. Matthew Brady and his team, published in the *Annals of Internal Medicine*, shows that after participants slept for only 4.5 hours on each of four sequential nights, their fat cells were acting like the cells of people with full-blown type 2 diabetes.[17] What that means is that the fat cells became insensitive to the hormone insulin. Total body insulin response decreased 16%, and fat cell response decreased 30%. Insulin resistance is one of the hallmarks of metabolic syndrome and type 2 diabetes. Body fat plays an important role in humans. "Many people think of fat as a problem, but it serves a vital function," says Brady. "Body fat, also known as adipose tissue, stores and releases energy. In storage mode, fat cells remove fatty acids and lipids from the circulation where they can damage other tissues. When fat cells cannot respond effectively to insulin, these lipids leach out into the circulation, leading to serious complications."[18]

A similar study by Esther Donga and her colleagues at the Leiden University Medical Center in the Netherlands shows that even one night of partial sleep deprivation causes resistance to insulin in otherwise healthy subjects.[19] They found that when subjects slept less, their livers dumped more glucose into the blood (resulting in high blood sugar) and that their cells had a harder time absorbing the glucose—insulin resistance. This is the same pattern that develops with type 2 diabetes.

SLEEP AND MENTAL HEALTH

SLEEP PROBLEMS ARE common in patients with anxiety, depression, bipolar disorder, and attention deficit hyperactivity disorder (ADHD). Between 50% and 80% of people with psychiatric challenges have chronic sleep problems, compared with up to 25% of the general population. Poor sleep used to be considered the result of mental health problems such as anxiety and depression, but our perspective has changed. Clinicians now believe that poor sleep may *contribute* to mental health problems and psychiatric disorders.[20] Our understanding of the relationship between sleep and brain health is in its infancy, but interesting new research is shedding light on this important topic.

For example, it is only in the past few years that scientists have discovered how the brain gets rid of its waste. In other parts of the body, waste is removed in several ways, including via the lymphatic system, a system of vessels that run in parallel to the blood circulatory system. The lymphatic system picks up waste, broken-down cells, and invaders like viruses, bacteria, and fungi and carries them to the lymph glands, where the immune-system cells deal with them. Despite our well-established understanding of this process, we really didn't know how the brain accomplished the same feat because the lymphatic system had not yet been discovered in the brain. One of the coolest studies I've seen in a long time was released last year by Dr. Maiken Nedergaard, co-director of the Center for Translational Neuromedicine at the University of Rochester Medical Center.[21] Nedergaard's team showed that during sleep, the size of the neurons in the brain is reduced by up to 60%. This creates a lot of space between brain cells. Then, still during sleep, a microscopic network of lymphatic vessels—the glymphatic system—clears the metabolic waste from these spaces between the neurons.

This research shows that you can literally wash your brain of waste products and damage each night, if you sleep well.[22] Dr. Jeffrey Iliff, who works in the same lab as Dr. Nedergaard, has shown that more than half of the amyloid beta, a protein that accumulates in the brains of patients with Alzheimer's disease, is washed out of the brain each night via the glymphatic system. This is important because waste buildup in the brain occurs in nearly all people with neurodegenerative diseases, and this buildup may kill neurons, ultimately leading to cognitive diseases and mental deterioration. (Dr. Iliff's TED Talk "One More Reason to Get a Good Night's Sleep" is a great watch.)

SLEEP SOUNDLY TO PERFORM BETTER

WORDS OF WISDOM

"Society is learning how important sleep is and how dangerous sleep deprivation is. We're teaching our players: Sleep is a weapon."

—Sam Ramsden, director of player health and performance, Seattle Seahawks

BY NOW IT'S clear that poor sleep causes health problems and that a sound sleep can help us live healthy, disease-free lives. Sleep also has a powerful effect on both mental and physical performance. This holds true for exercise, sports, music, academics, business, and most other pursuits. Let's think about the positive effects of sleeping better. Could it help make us superhuman? Can optimal sleep enhance our strength and endurance? What if sleeping soundly made us smarter? Or improved our concentration and memory? The punchline is always the same: more sleep means better everything. That may seem a bit simplistic, but sometimes the simplest truths are the most profound ones.

The main stages of sleep—NREM and REM—each have different effects on our ability to perform at a higher level. Professor Vincent Walsh at University College London has described the deep, slow-wave sleep that happens earlier in the night as being crucial for encoding of information and facts that we encountered during the day. That is, NREM sleep seems to be when we encode memories and learn. When we are in REM sleep, we encode procedural memories, like how to perform a new physical skill or mental process. It is also when we do subconscious creative problem solving. That certain types of recovery, regeneration, learning, and creativity happen during a particular sleep phase means that getting enough sleep is of utmost importance for those who want to consistently perform at their best. Let's take a closer look at how we can optimize our lives by taking advantage of the performance-enhancing benefits of sleeping soundly.

SLEEP SOUNDLY TO EAT SMARTER

IF YOU WANT to lose weight or control your weight, don't ignore sleep. Lack of sleep disrupts the hormones that control our appetite. When we sleep properly, the hormones leptin and ghrelin, which help manage hunger and satiety, are regulated and controlled. Simply, this means that sleeping consistently helps the body manage hunger, minimizing your cravings for unhealthy foods like sugar and "bad" fats. Sleep helps to regulate the levels of leptin and ghrelin in your body, and you'll have a better chance of making good food choices during the day. Just think of the last time you had a bad night's sleep. How did you eat the next day? I'll bet your decisions were less than optimal. When we're tired, we crave high-energy foods like sweets, sodas, and processed foods, which are usually high in calories and low in nutrients, and which ultimately end up damaging our health. Sleep consistently to make sure you have a healthy, lean body.

> ### DR. GREG'S 1% TIP: EAT A PRE-SLEEP PROTEIN SNACK FOR MUSCLE GROWTH
>
> A great biohack for using nutrition to sleep better and vice versa is to eat a small protein snack (like a few mixed nuts, some hummus, Greek yogurt, or roasted chickpeas) right before you go to sleep. Research has shown that ingesting protein before sleep improves protein synthesis (the process of building muscle) by about 22% when compared with a placebo pre-bed snack.[23]

SLEEP SOUNDLY TO MOVE BETTER

SLEEP AND EXERCISE have a reciprocal relationship. All else being equal, if you sleep soundly, you will perform better during your next workout or race. Conversely, if you exercise consistently, you will sleep better. It's a positive cycle and another example of the ripple effect.

Dr. Cheri Mah at Stanford Sleep Disorders Clinic and Research Laboratory conducted a telling research project on the impact of increased sleep on athletic performance.[24] Mah measured the 11 members of the Stanford University men's varsity basketball team for a baseline period of 3 weeks, during which time they slept about 7 to 8 hours per night. Then the athletes deliberately increased their sleep by 110 minutes and tried to stay in bed for 10 hours each night. After the sleep extension phase, the athletes had faster sprint times, improved shooting accuracy (by 9% even from three-point range!), and decreased fatigue. The researchers found that decreased fatigue is a significant predictor of improved performance in competitions. The participants also reported that they had a better sense of physical and mental well-being. Similar results have been seen in tennis players, soccer players, and soldiers.[25]

We know that sleeping well improves our recovery and regeneration after a workout or athletic competition, which helps us adapt to the exercise we're doing, so we get fitter and stronger faster. During sleep, our hearts slow down, our blood pressure drops, and our muscles relax. This provides us with some much-needed rest so that our cardiovascular systems and muscles can repair and rebuild themselves.

One critical restorative process that occurs during sleeping is the release of human growth hormone (HGH). HGH promotes fat breakdown and increases in muscle mass, which allows the body to recover from the physiological stresses that occur during training. If you are sleep-deprived and have relatively low levels of HGH in your system, you will not only restrict your body's ability to recover while you are sleeping but also, it seems, limit your ability to exercise the next day. Lower levels of HGH may decrease the amount of time an athlete can exercise at maximum effort, owing to reduced energy stores in their muscles.[26] So, when you sleep, your body repairs and heals itself—and guess what? You'll be able to exercise well the next day.

DR. GREG'S 1% TIP: DO YOGA FOR A DEEPER SLEEP

Yoga is great for helping us calm down and sleep better. Start with ujjayi breathing—completely filling your lungs with air while slightly contracting your throat and breathing through your nose—for a few minutes to relax and activate your parasympathetic nervous system (your rest and recovery system that calms and relaxes various organs in your body). Then move through standing forward bend, child's pose, legs-up-the-wall pose, reclining bound angle pose, and corpse pose. That sequence works wonders for calming the body and mind and for setting you up for a deep, restful sleep.

SLEEP SOUNDLY TO BE MORE CREATIVE

HAVE YOU EVER woken up in the middle of the night and had a "Eureka!" moment—a deep insight? I certainly have—it's one of the reasons I keep a notebook by my bed. I need to ensure that I capture those insights; otherwise by morning I will have forgotten them. Creative problem solving appears to happen during the REM phase of sleep, which typically occurs more in the second half of your sleep, if you're getting the recommended 7.5 hours.

One of the physiological processes that occur when we sleep is the growth of neurons in our brains and these neurons making connections between each other. There are 80 to 100 trillion neurons in the body, and each neuron has hundreds to thousands of connections to other neurons. It is these patterns of neurons and the connections between them that allow us to encode new learning, movement patterns, and memories. If you want to ensure that you are being as creative as you can, that you can solve difficult problems or come up with new ways of performing a task, put sleep at the top of your list of priorities.

REM sleep has been identified as an incredibly creative state. In a 2009 study at the University of California–San Diego, researchers found that REM sleep "directly enhances creative processing more than any other sleep or wake state."[27] Yes, you read that right: more even than any wake state! One of the study's leaders explains: "We found that, for creative problems that you've already been working on, the passage of time is enough to find solutions. However, for new problems, only REM sleep enhances creativity." In REM sleep, the brain makes new and useful associations between unrelated ideas.

There are two important takeaways here: If you want to remember your learning so you can build on it every day, you need to sleep well. And if you want to solve new problems in creative ways, you need REM sleep in particular.

As always, the sleep news is good. Unless you don't get enough. But this is a situation you can fix, through focus and commitment to the seven keys to improving your sleep, discussed later in this chapter.

DR. GREG'S 1% TIP: KEEP A NIGHTSTAND NOTEBOOK

If you wake up in the middle of the night, stressed about things you need to do, write them down—make a to-do list. That way your thoughts get onto a piece of paper and out of your head. Then trust that you'll deal with them tomorrow, so you can stop thinking about them at 3 a.m. This tactic may seem too simple, but it's amazing how it can help clear the mind so that you calm down and trust in sleep.

SLEEP SOUNDLY TO LEARN BETTER

PULLING AN ALL-NIGHTER studying for exams is common among high school and university students. One principal told me that many students show up to school with an array of energy drinks, after staying up late, studying. This is hardly a high-performance approach. Imagine if we taught all our kids how to sleep better, and created a school system that supported that approach? What would happen to our learning as a nation? How cool would that be?

The good news is that sleep does wonderful things for the brain. We may know intuitively that sleep helps improve memory and learning, but researchers are now discovering how this works at the cellular level. Research is showing that lack of sleep causes decreased alertness, attention, vigilance, perception, memory, and executive function (thinking). Lack of sleep decreases your ability to think, learn, and remember.[28]

Our brains have approximately 80 to 100 billion neurons. And when we sleep, new connections are made between those neurons.[29] These connections are critical because they form the basis for our thoughts, memories, problem solving, decision making, motor patterns (mental "programs" that control how we move), and other important aspects of what makes us human. Scientists in China and the United States have recently, using microscopes, witnessed new synapses being formed in the brain during deep and sustained sleep.[30] What exactly was it they saw? In essence, they saw the brain building memories. We've known for a while that good-quality sleep is necessary in order to remember what we have experienced and learned during the day,[31] but we've not known why. In this study, the brain's work of replaying the day's activity like a movie and building new connections between neurons during sleep was visible. So sleep and get connected!

DR. GREG'S 1% TIP: WHAT TO DO WHEN YOU HAVEN'T SLEPT WELL

Research shows that lack of sleep causes decreased alertness, attention, vigilance, perception, memory, and executive function (thinking). But planning and rule-based reasoning do not seem to be affected. If you're tired from a bad night's sleep, don't try to be creative. Get out your calendar and get organized instead. You can do that just as well as if you had slept for 7.5 hours. But if you need to think of an innovative solution to a problem or if you need to do creative work, then sleep is absolutely critical.

THE SEVEN KEYS TO SLEEPING SOUNDLY

BY SLEEPING SOUNDLY, we can unleash our health and live a world-class life. When we eat better and increase our physical activity, we can improve our sleep even more and strengthen our bodies and minds, enhance our mental and physical health, and reach our potential. To help you on your way, here are the seven keys to sleeping soundly.

KEY #1: SAVE YOUR CAFFEINE FOR THE MORNING

YOUR MOUTH WATERS for morning java, but you don't want the shakes. You crave a mid-afternoon pick-me-up, but you need to be able to fall asleep at night. And you love the whole ritual of a coffee break—from going and getting to chatting and sipping—but you've heard that those fancy store-bought coffees might not be healthy.

Let's start with the bad news. The adrenaline-promoting quality of caffeine gets the heart pumping and the blood racing. Too much of this can promote anxiety and insomnia. Caffeine-rich drinks are also considered to be blockers for nutrients such as calcium and iron because of the absorption competition in the stomach. For this reason, avoid drinking coffee with your meals.

Now the good news. Caffeine does not dehydrate, as we once thought it did, and it does boost brain power. It promotes blood flow to the brain (increasing concentration and memory) and encourages oxygen delivery to the body (making exercise feel easier). The flavonoid compounds in coffee and tea can act as antioxidants (which can keep tissues healthy). Regular caffeine consumers experience lowered rates of brain diseases (such as depression, Alzheimer's, Parkinson's, and dementia) when compared with those who do not drink caffeine.

Caffeine is one of the most powerful known stimulants. It can improve mental and physical performance, which makes it perfect for getting you going in the morning and getting you fired up for important tasks during the day. That is the exact opposite of what you need to be doing in the evenings if you want to sleep well. Caffeine stays in your system for about 6 hours, maybe longer. A good rule to follow if you want to sleep well is to skip the caffeine for 8 hours before you want to fall asleep. So if that's 10 p.m., no more caffeine after 2 p.m.

Because caffeine is such a powerful drug and has performance-enhancing effects, it is often "hidden" in foods and other products. Food manufacturers in North America are not required to list caffeine on labels. So be careful of coffee (even decaf may have up to 20 mg of caffeine—versus 100-plus in regular coffee), teas, soda (which you should never have, anyway, because of how damaging it is for your health), cocoa products like chocolate, weight-loss products (again, which you should not use, unless your doctor prescribes them), pain relievers, energy drinks, and some cold and flu medications—especially the daytime kinds.

The general rule is that up to 200 mg of caffeine a day is safe for most people. That equates to about two coffees, four black teas, or eight green teas (10 ounces each). Remember to pay attention to how you respond to caffeine. If you get agitated, become anxious, or have trouble sleeping, avoid caffeine altogether: you could be one of the few people whose bodies don't break it down well. Sadly, "slow metabolizers" see more health problems from caffeine than the rest of us.

DR. GREG'S 1% TIP: USE CAFFEINE AS A TOOL, NOT A CRUTCH

- Watch what you're putting in your coffee—it's easy to turn it into a 500-calorie treat. Try adding cinnamon or a touch of raw honey to sweeten it up safely.
- Don't get your caffeine from soft drinks, which are associated with health problems.
- It's easy to overdo it—remember that your main fluid source should always be water.
- Avoid caffeine after 2 p.m. so that it doesn't affect your ability to sleep soundly.

KEY #2: DEFEND YOUR LAST HOUR

HAVE YOU EVER had an insane day at the office, come home jacked up and still firing on all cylinders, and then, in the hour before going to bed, found yourself fuming over the day's events while also planning strategies for the next day? How did you end up sleeping that night? Did you fall asleep quickly? No? Did you wake up during the night? Yes? Were you dreaming about work?

Yes? How did you feel when the alarm went off in the morning? Brutal? Once again, you're not alone. Our high-powered lives take a toll on us all. The human cost of our work is huge. I'm okay with your having the passion and drive to change the world and live your best life. But to do so you have to decompress and allow yourself to recover and regenerate.

This means calming down in the hours leading up to when you want to fall asleep. It all comes down to changing your hormone levels so that your body and brain can repair and regenerate instead of breaking down. When you are in a stressed state, your body secretes the hormone cortisol, which increases blood pressure, among other things—such as releasing sugars from the liver into the blood. Cortisol is especially helpful when you are faced with a stressful situation—like meeting a deadline or saving your family from a sabre-toothed tiger—but it inhibits the adaptive processes of your body. It's an activity hormone, not a rest-and-recover hormone. The more cortisol you have, the faster you can run (I hope you don't need to run while you're sleeping), but the worse your recovery. It's important to decrease cortisol before and during sleep. Here's how.

First, do not check your electronic devices within 2 hours of when you plan to go to sleep unless you absolutely have to. Mari Hysing at the Regional Centre for Child and Youth Mental Health and Child Welfare in Bergen, Norway, published a population-based study on 9,846 adolescents, showing a dose-response relationship between the amount of time spent using electronic devices during the day and sleep duration, time to fall asleep, and sleep efficiency (a measure of time asleep versus time in bed).[32] The more the adolescents used their electronic devices during the day, the less they slept and the worse their sleep quality was. You don't need to be activating your brain at night; you need it to wind down and relax. Besides, what often takes you 30 minutes to accomplish at night can usually be tackled in just a few minutes when you're fresh the next morning. Living a world-class life is all about being efficient and effective. I want you to live better, not harder.

Unwind at night by reading, preferably fiction. Reading can calm the mind and activate parts of the brain that help you fall asleep and cause you to dream. And I say fiction because the reading material should have a storyline—something that requires your imagination. Don't read work-related stuff before sleeping. That will just get your brain going. And, of course, I mean for you to read a hard copy—not an ebook, say, which involves a screen. When you're done with a book or magazine, pass it on and share the reading love with other people. Tell them how it's helping you sleep better. Spread word of the ripple effect around the world!

KEY #3: KEEP YOUR SLEEP CAVE DARK

HAVE A PLACE in your home that is your place to rest, recover, and regenerate. Think of it as a peaceful place where you go to crash out after rocking the world all day. This will be your sleep cave—formerly known as your bedroom.

Melatonin (a hormone that helps regulate wakefulness and sleep) is produced by your pineal gland, which is located deep inside your brain and is very sensitive to the light detected by the retina, including light from screens.[33] So it's important to ensure that your sleep space is dark so that the pineal gland can release the right amount of melatonin at the right time. You can also wear an eye mask if that is comfortable for you. I have one I use on flights to help me sleep on the plane.

Make sure to rid the bedroom of any electronic screens. Televisions, tablets, mobile phones—all compromise your ability to fall asleep. You might need to cut out the late-night talk shows or YouTube clips and pick up a good book instead. I realize this can be a huge change for you, but having a massive light that flashes at you at 240 frames per second is a surefire way to make sure you don't fall asleep.

Building on the idea of keeping your room free of flashing lights (TV, iPad, and so on) when you're trying to fall asleep, once you're asleep, you need to stay asleep—and to sleep deeply. To do that you have to keep your room dark. Really dark. Even the light from an alarm clock is enough to reduce your melatonin levels. Since we all lose some melatonin production as we age, the older we get, the more we need to do things to maximize the body's natural abilities. Remember, this book is all about how to live an incredible life. I want you to have great energy, happiness, and success. This means doing the little things right. Little things like covering up the alarm clock light. And getting blackout blinds or curtains for your windows.

There are even night lights for beside the bed that are designed to emit only red light in the evening and blue light in the morning. That will help stimulate melatonin production in the evening (think colours of the sunset) and turn it off in the morning (think bright white light of the morning sun).

A colleague was having a very hard time sleeping. It took him an hour to fall asleep after going to bed, and he woke up constantly during the night. He was exhausted each day at work. He chalked it up to getting older and just being a bad sleeper. But finally, he was at the end of his rope and emailed me to ask if I could help him. The first thing I asked him was what he did in the hour before going to bed. His response was two letters: "TV."

I wrote him back:

> *This weekend, start with sleep habit #1: No more screens at all, including phones, after 9 pm. A 15–20 min hot bath, followed by a cool shower. Then read a book. Nothing related to work. Should be fiction or other light reading. Quiet and calm are the words of the weekend from 9 p.m. on. Let me know how it goes.*

A few days later he told me:

> *The first night after the bath and shower and no TV, I could only read for 5 min. before I fell asleep. I slept better. I am now on to it! Cheers and thanks!*

In just a day, his time to fall asleep dropped from an hour to 5 minutes simply by building a sleep cave routine. I'll soon ask him to remove the TV from the bedroom altogether—we can't have decision fatigue kicking in and bad habits re-emerging.

Finally, if you have to get up at night to go to the bathroom or for any other reason, try not to turn on any lights, in order not to disrupt the melatonin flowing through your brain and body.

DR. GREG'S 1% TIP: TRY LIGHT THERAPY

For most of history, humans have lived in alignment with the daily cycle of the sun. We worked during the day, when it was light, and slept at night, when it was the dark. More recently, with electricity and mobile devices, this pattern has been disrupted. Scientists like Satchin Panda from the Salk Institute of biological sciences in La Jolla, California, are looking into the specific benefits of light for our health. Dr. Panda and his colleagues are finding that bright natural-light environments can increase our alertness and accuracy. Light may help in treating bipolar disorder, decreasing pain after surgery, and speeding recovery from heart attacks.[34] The takeaway here is to make sure you have exposure to natural light each day. For example, if you work in an office with minimal natural light, be sure to get outside for a walk on your breaks. When you wake up in the morning, open the blinds and let the natural light into your home. Try to work by a window. Don't use a computer or device in the hour before bed. Install f.lux software on your computer to reduce its blue-light emissions. If you have iOS, activate the night shift feature, and if you use Android, try the Twilight app.

KEY #4: BE COOL

IN THE EVENING, increased melatonin levels in the body cause the blood vessels in the skin to dilate, releasing body heat into the environment and cooling the body by 0.3 to 0.4 degrees Celsius. This cooling promotes drowsiness and helps us fall asleep.[35] If you are having a hard time falling asleep, have a hot or warm bath to relax, followed by a cool shower to decrease your body temperature slightly, and make sure your bedroom is as dark as possible. This procedure mimics the effect of melatonin and can help you fall asleep.

At night, keep your bedroom cool—at about 19 degrees Celsius. Keeping the room cool should help you stay asleep during the night. If you find yourself waking up because you're too cold or too hot, adjust the room temperature and the blankets until you find the right combination to keep you cool and comfortable all night.

If you need another reason to keep your bedroom cool at night, check out this study.[36] For four months, five male participants slept in a room that changed temperatures each month. In the first month, the temperatures were moderate, then for the subsequent months cool, then moderate, then warm. At the end of the cool month, the participants had better metabolism of insulin (a hormone that regulates blood sugar and is involved in the development of diabetes) and twice the amount of brown fat. Brown fat is very active tissue that burns lots of energy and can help control overall body weight and body composition. The study was small, and more research in this area is needed, but the results suggest that sleeping in a cool room might help prevent diabetes, promote healthy sugar metabolism, and help you get and stay lean.

DR. GREG'S 1% TIP: KEEP IT COOL

Aim to keep the bedroom at about 19 degrees Celsius when you sleep. If you and your partner prefer different temperatures, consider having separate comforters or duvets, each of a different thickness—whatever works for you. Or go high tech with BedJet, a ventilation system that will keep each of you at the perfect temperature.

KEY #5: SLEEP 7 TO 8 HOURS EACH NIGHT

RESEARCH HAS SHOWN that, for adults, sleeping fewer than 6 hours per night is associated with an increased risk of all-cause mortality.[37] The lowest risk of mortality appears to be at between 7 and 8 hours per night. Considering the graph Sleep Stages vs. Time, which shows how we generally cycle through the different levels of sleep each night, we can begin to understand how much we need to sleep and why.

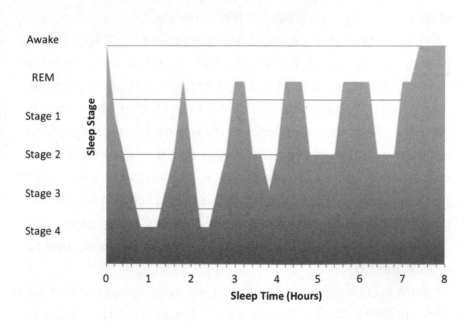

Sleep Stages vs. Time

AS YOU CAN see, it takes about 90 minutes to move through one complete sleep cycle, which takes you through all five sleep stages at least once (four stages of non-REM sleep, plus REM sleep). Which means we need at least four complete sleep cycles (4 × 90 minutes = 6 hours), and ideally five complete sleep cycles (5 × 90 minutes = 7.5 hours), for optimal sleep.

Our sleep requirements change as we age. The US-based National Sleep Foundation has just updated its recommendations; you can check them out here: http://sleepfoundation.org/how-sleep-works/how-much-sleep-do-we-really-need.

As the recommendations show, the younger we are, the more hours of sleep we need. Sleeping more if you're sick, have done a really hard workout, or have had an especially mentally demanding day will help you recover and regenerate.

Even though adults need to sleep soundly for 7 to 8 hours each night, evidence indicates that sleeping on a regular schedule is even more important than the total amount of sleep time. Studies show that when athletes' bedtime is shifted around but the total number of hours they sleep remains the same, there is a measurable decrease in athletic performance. Sticking to a consistent routine is key. Right now, I'm sleeping from 10 p.m. to 6 a.m., which is 8 hours, but I'm planning on decreasing that to 7.5 hours and going to bed a bit earlier so I can be up and working out by 5:30 a.m., before my kids get up.

I want you to get five complete sleep cycles each night. That takes about 7.5 hours. Count back 7.5 hours from the time you want to wake up and aim to be asleep by that time. You'll wake up on time and you'll decrease your risk of obesity, heart disease, and cancer while you're at it. Check out sleepyti.me. It's a cool app/website that calculates best falling-asleep times based on 90-minute sleep cycles. Enter the time you want to wake up, and sleepyti.me will tell you when to try to fall asleep so that you wake up feeling refreshed. You can also set a bedtime alarm in iOS—you can find that in the clock app.

> **DR. GREG'S 1% TIP: TRY PROGRESSIVE RELAXATION**
>
> If you can't fall asleep, or you wake up in the middle of the night and can't get back to sleep, try progressive relaxation, a technique used to relax the body and mind. It will develop your ability to recognize and relieve tension. Muscle tension consumes energy inefficiently and decreases circulation, which results in a buildup of toxins and tension that causes physical aches and pains. Practising relaxation techniques for 5 minutes three times per week, for 3 weeks in a row, can have significant benefits. Positive effects such as improved digestion, improved function of the cardiovascular system, relief from aches and pains, and improved sleep have been reported.

PROGRESSIVE RELAXATION CONSISTS of alternately tensing and releasing different muscle groups. You'll find basic instructions here (as you become more experienced, feel free to develop your own detailed routine). As you do this technique, notice the differences between sensations of strain and calmness, tension and relaxation. This technique can be practised almost anywhere, at any time. Experiment with contracting different muscle areas to relax.

INSTRUCTIONS

- Hold each muscle contraction for 3 to 5 seconds.
- Hold each relaxation phase for 10 to 15 seconds.
1. Make yourself comfortable, ideally sitting or lying down. Close your eyes. Raise your toes as high as possible off the floor/bed, etc., hold for 3 to 5 seconds, then release and let the tension flow out. Point your toes and repeat. Notice the difference between tension and relaxation.
2. Tense the upper part of your legs. Experience the tension. Hold, then relax, feeling your legs against the chair and your feet against the floor. Experience the relaxation.
3. Tighten your abdominal muscles, hold, then relax.
4. Take a deep breath, feeling the tension in your chest. Exhale and relax, while concentrating on how calm you can get.
5. Make tight fists with your hands and hold. Unclench your hands and let the tension flow out, noting how it feels different to relax.
6. Do the same with your upper arms, then your neck, then your face (frown and then relax).
7. Take a moment to notice any other areas of tension, and concentrate on releasing those as well. Take a few deep breaths and open your eyes—you will be alert and relaxed.

KEY #6: NAP GUILT-FREE

LEONARDO DA VINCI reportedly took multiple 20-minute naps throughout the day to help him be more creative and engaged with his work. It's taken hundreds of years, but research now backs up his approach. Naps have been shown to improve energy, productivity, cognitive functioning, and even health.[38] Albert Einstein also napped during the day, to help him think more clearly. Famous politician nappers include former British prime ministers Margaret Thatcher and Winston Churchill and US president Bill Clinton.

These people may have been on to something powerful. Professor Matthew Walker at UC Berkeley has found that a biphasic sleep schedule (sleeping at night and during the day) not only helps with mental recovery and regeneration but can make us smarter as well.[39] Conversely, he found that students who stayed awake longer (those who didn't nap) had more trouble in memory tests than those who followed a biphasic sleep schedule (those who napped during the day).

The neurophysiology of this is interesting. Walker has been working to determine how sleep and the brain interact to help people learn and remember. His team has reported that short-term memories are stored in a part of the brain called the hippocampus, and then are sent to the prefrontal cortex for more permanent storage. When we sleep, the memories that are stored in the hippocampus get cleared out—either discarded or moved to the prefrontal cortex for permanent storage. This opens up the hippocampus for more learning. But if we don't sleep, our short-term memory seems to fill up, and we just don't learn as well.

But there is a catch, and it has to do with how the body cycles through sleep stages. When we sleep, we pass through five stages, from REM sleep, where we dream, down through stages 1 through 4, where deeper sleep happens. We generally pass through REM; then stage 1, stage 2, stage 3, and stage 4; then back through stages 3, 2, 1, and REM. This whole cycle takes about 90 minutes.

That's why sometimes when you take a nap and wake up suddenly, you may feel groggy and sluggish. You might even feel worse than when you fell asleep. When we're woken up while we're in stage 2, 3, or 4, we face "sleep inertia" (a term sleep scientist Sara Mednick uses to describe the inability to shrug off sleep) as the brain is working to recover and regenerate, as opposed to functioning in a waking state. Hence the groggy and sluggish feeling. So if you want to have a rejuvenating nap, go for a short 10- to 15-minute power nap[40] so that you wake up before falling into the deeper levels of sleep, or allow yourself the full 90 minutes to complete all the sleep cycles. Some companies are getting on board—Nike, Apple, Google, and Deloitte Consulting encourage employees to add a power nap to their daily work routines.

Here are a few options for you to consider when you need a nap:

NAP	DURATION	HELPS TO . . .
Micro-nap	2–5 minutes	Decrease sleepiness and improve cognitive performance.
Mini-nap	10 minutes	Improve mental and physical performance, decrease fatigue.
Power nap	20 minutes	Improve alertness, energy, and memory.

| I-feel-like-crap nap | 30 minutes | · Make you feel groggy and foggy. Just go back to sleep. |
| Full-cycle nap | 90 minutes | Improve memory and creativity.* |

*This nap includes all the sleep stages and so is like a mini full-night's sleep. Plus, growth hormone is released, repairing muscle and bones; if you had a hard workout in the morning, this is the nap for you.

KEY #7: WAKE UP NATURALLY

AS YOU NOW know, we naturally cycle through stages during a sleep. We have five sleep stages (REM and stages 1 to 4). Remember, complete sleep cycles take about 90 minutes. Near the end of our sleep, we spend lots of time in REM sleep and will sometimes even wake up. That's when we're likely to remember what we were dreaming about—because dreaming often happens during REM sleep. When you do wake up naturally, it's a great time to get out of bed. Ideally you want to time your wake-ups to get you as close to the end of a 90-minute sleep cycle and that 7.5 hours of sleep. If you check the time and realize it's 30 minutes or less before the time you need to wake up, just get up. Don't hope that getting that extra 15 minutes of sleep will help. It won't. If you go back to sleep at that point, you'll drop down into stage 1 or even stage 2 sleep. And when the alarm goes off, you'll be awakened from a state that you're not physiologically supposed to wake up from. The outcome is that you'll feel groggy and sluggish for hours. If you wake up early enough to get in another complete sleep cycle, then feel free to nod off again.

DR. GREG'S 1% TIP: SET YOUR ALARM STRATEGICALLY

Set your alarm at the latest possible moment for when you have to get up. That way, you get in the habit of not using the snooze button. If you can also get to sleep at a consistent time that allows you to get about 7.5 hours of sleep and those magical five complete sleep cycles, you'll feel better and more energized during the day.

BY SLEEPING SOUNDLY, we can unleash our health. And when we eat better and increase our physical activity, we can improve our sleep even more. It's the ripple effect.

The life dreams you set as signposts for a better, healthier life are the tools you need to transform your life. Setting yourself up to achieve your dreams by sleeping better (and dreaming!) will have a powerful effect. Not only is sleep great for mental stress relief and rebuilding your body, enhancing your mental and physical health, but dreaming during sleep can help with memory and learning too. Get good at sleeping, and you'll get better at so many other things when you're not sleeping. A better sleep means you will eat better, train better, and work better. Ultimately, you'll live better.

It takes attention and it might take some time to figure out what works for you, but keep at it, because when you get a great night's sleep, you'll feel fantastic. And that's how we should feel all the time! If we are well rested, we're able to cope with life's stresses, stronger and more effective in our exercise, sharper in our work, and just simply more fun to be around. And yet, a common attitude is that sleep isn't particularly important. In fact, it's almost the opposite in that getting by on less sleep is considered by many a badge of honour. Which is crazy thinking, and we're getting sick and performing horribly as a result. Plan for a world-class life in which you have an impact on the world, by committing to getting a great sleep, every night.

DR. GREG'S 1% TIP: CREATE BEAUTIFUL BOOKENDS FOR YOUR DAY

You now know what a circadian rhythm is, so let's talk about making the most of the fact that we are naturally designed to repeat daily patterns. Set up great patterns at the beginning and end of the day, and you will feel better during all the parts in between too.

Your body loves consistency. You've learned that going to sleep and waking up at the same time every day is good for your brain, body, and emotional state. Consistent sleep times allow your hormones and other chemicals that your organs release to get into a routine. It takes time for your body to adapt when that pattern is changed. That's what happens when you fly across time zones and get jet-lagged. Changing your sleep-and-wake pattern changes your body's circadian rhythms and gives you micro jet lags every day. You feel awful and your performance drops.

Some of the best performers in business consistently wake up early. Leadership guru Robin Sharma swears by the "5 a.m. Club." Waking up early lets you get a head start on the day. You'll be less likely to be bothered by emails and text messages. The world is quiet. There's less traffic, if you're heading out to the gym. You can run on empty roads. You can read a book in peace. You can meditate or do yoga. Just get out of bed. Win the battle of the alarm clock!

The best part of this early rising is that you can get the important things done for yourself that make you better. And nothing will get in your way. It's a guaranteed method to improve your life. Build your morning routine so that you get up early and do the most important things first.

I love the days that I wake up at 5 a.m. I can take a few minutes to meditate, plan the day, and get some training in all before my kids get up around 7 a.m.

Similarly, I'd like you to work on defending the last hour of your day so you can fall asleep quickly and deeply. Having a routine that allows you to decompress and relax can make a huge difference in your sleep quality. Many of my clients who have trouble staying asleep are those who have stressful days and also work late into the evenings, up until they collapse into bed. Find a calming activity that you love, and do it before bedtime. Protect your time. You will enjoy that hour immensely and will benefit from a regular circadian rhythm.

BIOHACKING SLEEP CASE STUDY: JET LAG

JET LAG, ALSO known as flight dysrhythmia, is characterized by a long list of unpleasant potential symptoms: reduced alertness, nighttime insomnia, loss of appetite, depressed mood, poor psychomotor coordination, gastrointestinal disturbances, fatigue, reduced cognitive skills, and decreased physical as well as mental performance are well-documented examples. The more time zones you cross, the worse your jet lag is likely to be.

Rapid travel across multiple time zones causes a temporary misalignment between biological rhythms and external cues known as zeitgebers, or time givers, which are external factors capable of regulating internal rhythms. Jet lag is essentially caused by a desynchronization between our endogenous circadian clock, which regulates important biological rhythms, and exogenous cues, including geophysical variations like the light–dark cycles in solar days. Simply put, jet lag throws our internal rhythms out of synchrony with our external environment, leaving us with those unpleasant symptoms just mentioned.

The culprits of this desynchronization lie in the brain—specifically the hypothalamus—and are known as the supra-chiasmatic nuclei (SCN). These nuclei regulate circadian oscillators (nerves in your brain that fire rhythmically) by using visual information sent from the retina, which is why external cues, including light and dark cycles, are so important. Information about physical activity and general excitement is also sent to the nuclei. Collectively, these cues set genes throughout the body, known as "clock genes," to 24-hour time. The pathways involved essentially translate external cues into biological rhythms that form our internal concept of time. Without external regulation, our clock genes operate on 24-hour time. The SCN also regulate the secretion of hormones, including serotonin, melatonin, and cortisol; their job is to help regulate our sleep cycles, eating patterns, and cognitive function in concert with the clock genes.

Ideally, in a person who is adjusted to the local time zone, the body's circadian rhythms behave as follows:

- Melatonin secretion peaks at night and decreases throughout the day.
- Cortisol levels peak in the morning and decrease throughout the day.

- Core body temperature reaches its lowest peak in the middle of the night and rises throughout the day.
- Clock genes promote activity in the daytime and recovery during the night.

In a jet-lagged body, these rhythms get mixed up because the external environment has changed and the internal rhythms haven't had a chance to catch up. Rises in core temperature at night will cause premature wakening; melatonin secretion throughout the day will cause daytime sleepiness, and, as we know, lack of sleep is responsible for a large handful of common jet-lag symptoms.

Jet lag can make you feel awful, and it can hang around, sometimes for weeks. Our bodies adjust to new time zones at a sluggish rate of about 1 hour per day after flights. In simple terms, the hourly difference between point A and point B during travel translates into the days required for recovery. I highly recommend planning 1 day of recovery per time zone travelled if you have a performance like a sport event or key business meeting in the new location. For example, I just travelled from the New York time zone to Zurich for a presentation. I planned to travel 3 days (the most I could manage with work—5 days would have been perfect) before the presentation so I could get aligned with the new time zone.

Jet lag can be worsened by travel fatigue and the general difficulties and stresses associated with long trips. Sources of travel fatigue include cramped environments that don't offer much opportunity for exercise, restricted food choices, dehydration from dry cabin air and low oxygen in the air, and disruption of sleep and routine. Travel fatigue has less to do with time-zone transition and more to do with the effects of travelling itself. The good news is that the effects of both travel fatigue and jet lag can be lessened by using a few simple tricks.

1. TACKLE YOUR TRAVEL FATIGUE

Before the trip:
- Anticipate layovers, and arrange for them to be as short as possible.
- Arrange documentation, passports, visas, and so on beforehand.
- Plan to travel early enough to ensure that you are recovered before any performance events.

During the trip:
- Snack on apples, nuts, carrots, and whole-grain crackers.
- Make sure you're drinking lots of water rather than tea, coffee, or alcohol.

Once you've reached your destination:
- Rehydrate with water or herbal teas.
- Exercise on arrival, and get exposed to natural light as much as possible.
- To trigger melatonin release you can take a hot bath/ shower followed by a cold shower. That can help you fall asleep better.
- Take a 20-minute power nap if needed.
- Try to avoid sleeping at your home sleep time if you've travelled to a substantially new time zone, even though it might seem like a good idea. Jet-lag symptoms may be worsened by anchoring sleep patterns to your old time zone.

2. GRAB A BOTTLE OF MELATONIN

RESEARCH SHOWS THAT melatonin can be a helpful tool in overcoming jet lag. Melatonin acts on the body's circadian rhythms by means of the SCN (the culprits of desynchronization that live in the hypothalamus) and promotes sleep, an elusive concept for frequent travellers. Taking 0.5 to 5 mg of melatonin 2 to 3 hours before local bedtime has been shown to help resynchronize circadian oscillators while improving nocturnal sleep and alertness during the day.

3. STRUCTURE YOUR CAFFEINE CONSUMPTION

ALTHOUGH JET LAG can make it very difficult to fall asleep according to the local time, it can make staying awake during the day almost as difficult. Stimulants, namely caffeine, have been suggested to alleviate daytime sleepiness and have shown positive effects in circadian resynchronization when used in combination with melatonin. Both fast- and slow-release forms of caffeine may help counteract daytime sleepiness and nighttime insomnia—tossing a Thermos of green tea in your travel bag for sipping throughout the day may prove helpful in alleviating jet-lag-induced sleepiness and the resulting symptoms.

4. TIME YOUR LIGHT EXPOSURE

LIGHT EXPOSURE PLAYS a massive role in the synchronization of our biological rhythms to external time, by altering our circadian rhythms. Research indicates that critically timed light exposure of sufficient intensity (like getting outside in the daylight early in the day) may help mitigate jet-lag symptoms and speed up circadian synchronization. Ideally it's great to spend time in the daylight on arrival, as exposure to daylight helps to speed realignment of circadian rhythms to the new time.

For eastward travel:

If you are travelling eastward, try advancing your sleep time by 1 hour per night 3 days before travel, and expose yourself to bright light upon rising. Upon reaching your destination, it is suggested that you advance your rhythms by exposing yourself to morning and afternoon light, and avoiding evening light at your destination. Advance the time that you expose yourself to bright light by 1 hour per day at your destination to gradually adjust throughout your trip.

For westward travel:

If you are travelling westward, try delaying your sleep time by 1 hour per night 3 days before travel. Upon reaching your destination, delay your rhythms by exposing yourself to evening light and avoiding exposure to sunlight in the early morning.

5. MAKE TIME FOR PHYSICAL ACTIVITY

EXERCISE HAS BEEN shown to be helpful in alleviating the negative effects of jet lag. Physical activity of any sort that coincides with bright light exposure (ideally daylight) is a zeitgeber (or time giver; an external factor capable of regulating internal rhythms). Working up a light sweat around 2 to 3 a.m. in your home time zone might be helpful—studies suggest that gentle exercise when at your lowest core temperature (typically the middle of the night) in a new time zone may help synchronize your internal rhythms to the local time faster.

6. CONSIDER THE LENGTH OF STAY

OUR BODY CLOCKS aren't easily disrupted by external factors, preserving our biological rhythms even in the face of daytime naps or waking throughout the night. However, it is exactly this resistance that makes it so difficult for our bodies to adjust to new time zones. In other words, our clock genes have substantial inertia that we have not yet found a foolproof way of manipulating. For this reason, it is important to consider the length of stay when travelling to a destination. Adjusting activities to the timing of home may be more appropriate for travel lasting only several days, rather than trying to retrain the circadian oscillator twice.

3
MOVE MORE

> If we could give every individual the right amount of nourish-
> ment and exercise, not too little and not too much, we would
> have found the safest way to health.　　　—Hippocrates

A NEW DRUG has been discovered with such broad-ranging
powers that it may end up being the cure for all human disease.
Early reports suggest it can be used to prevent and treat almost
every chronic illness people face. The list of the benefits of taking this drug are truly amazing:

This drug has been shown to

- lower your risk of certain types of cancer by 24 to 50%,
- prevent and treat cardiovascular disease,
- reverse type 2 diabetes,
- reduce the number of cold and flu infections that you get by
  75%,

- prevent osteoporosis,
- alleviate depression and anxiety,
- delay or prevent the onset of Alzheimer's disease,
- improve memory, learning, problem solving, and concentration, and
- make you happier.

There is only one catch. You have to take this drug almost every day for the rest of your life. You have to be consistent. But if you do that, you're guaranteed to get the benefits. Have you figured it out yet? This "drug" is exercise. It does all of the above and much, much more. Are you in?

THE GLOBAL INACTIVITY EPIDEMIC

THE WORLD IS faced with a grand challenge: the inactivity epidemic. The burden of non-communicable diseases such as cardiovascular disease, metabolic syndrome, type 2 diabetes, and cancers has rapidly increased. Non-communicable diseases account for almost 70% of annual deaths and 55% of the global burden of disease. The World Health Organization has identified this issue as one of the greatest threats to human health.[1] Physical inactivity and unhealthy diets are the leading causes of these conditions. And 80% of our population does not get enough physical activity to prevent chronic disease.[2]

As our nations have become more developed, large percentages of our population have shifted from physical labour to desk jobs, in which we sit immobile for hours and hours each day. We can then add to that inactivity the daily commute—in the car, sitting down. Students are asked to sit for hours in class. We are not moving our bodies enough to prevent disease, much less to get healthy and perform to our potential.

In the United Kingdom, sitting has been called "the silent killer." The media have said that "sitting is the new smoking." Lack of physical activity has crept up the list of global causes of death to fourth place, after high blood pressure, smoking, and high blood sugar.[3] We now know that sitting is an independent risk factor for chronic illnesses, including cancer.[4] Consider that a recent review[5] of 43 studies analyzing daily activity and cancer rates found that people who reported sitting for more hours of the day than their study counterparts had a 24% greater risk of developing colon cancer, a 32% higher risk of endometrial cancer, and a 21% higher risk of lung cancer—regardless of how much they exercised.

Humans evolved as physically active creatures. We walked, jumped, sprinted, and lifted. When we move in these different ways, our genetic pathways are activated, and our DNA signals the creation of new proteins that make us healthier, fitter, and stronger. As little as 15 minutes of exercise a day is enough to decrease our risk of certain cancers by 24 to 50%. Moving more and better even changes the structure of the brain—making it capable of greater creativity, more focused concentration, and better problem solving. Moving even helps improve how we encode memories. So we all need to get back to moving more as part of our daily lives.

WORDS OF WISDOM:
JOHN STANTON, FOUNDER, THE RUNNING ROOM

I've had the pleasure of interviewing John Stanton, founder of the Running Room, on my podcast. His story of transformation and success is inspiring. What did he do to get off the couch and get fit? He received encouragement, started small, and stayed consistent. Along the way, his health and relationships improved. When he followed his passion for fitness, he was able to build a company that has enabled hundreds of thousands of people to follow in his footsteps. Here's an excerpt from the interview.

In some ways, I was a born-again runner, or came into running accidentally. Like many people, I found my career—I had a successful career in the grocery industry—and I was an executive vice-president with a large . . . firm. I had thrown my energies into my family, into my work and community activities, but along the way I kind of neglected my whole wellness and fitness. I'd gotten out of shape. I had two sons, and the older one was going in a 10-mile road race that the local newspaper was putting on, and his younger brother wanted to join him. My wife said, "Sure. You can go in it, but dad goes with you."

This little fun run was my first initiation into running. I didn't know "fun" and "run" could appear in the same line of a sentence. When I finished it, it was a tremendous wake-up call. It made me realize just how badly out of shape I'd gotten, and not intentionally, just had slipped out of shape. Then I reflected on the fact that my father had died young from heart disease, my brother had had a heart condition in his early 50s, and here I was in my mid-30s and I was going to be a perfect candidate for it [too]. I started to train.

Again, you've got to appreciate I was 238 pounds and was smoking two and a half packs a day, so I had to give up smoking, and I had to get the weight down. Along the way, I was able to quit smoking and begin to run, and then started running 5Ks, 10Ks, and then did the marathons and Ironman. People kept asking me how I went through this epiphany and went from being a couch potato to this weekend athlete. I said, "Anybody could do it. It just takes a little motivation and encouragement." When I started, I can tell you, the number one thing that kept me from starting was fear of embarrassment. I got up early in the morning when nobody could see this chubby little guy running around the block. I did it "under the cover of darkness," I called it, just to get away.

Once I did lose the weight, entered some races, and came back home, people said, "How did you do this?" I said, "It's not that difficult." I started the Running Room mainly as a meeting place for people to come, get some encouragement, help foster them along with some of the lessons I'd learned about not overdoing it, not going too far, too fast, too quickly.

JOHN'S STORY IS a perfect example of the type of growth we can bring to the world. What positive impact will you bring?

DR. GREG'S 1% TIP: KEEP YOUR RESTING HEART RATE AT 40 TO 60 BEATS PER MINUTE

In 2016, researchers from the Medical College of Qingdao University in Shandong, China, looked at data from 46 studies to test if there is a link between resting heart rate and the risk of all-cause mortality.[6] They created a database with 1,246,203 patients! After looking at the data, they concluded that higher resting heart rate was independently associated with increased risks of all-cause cardiovascular mortality. If you want to check your resting heart rate, lie down and rest for 5 minutes or so. Relax; do some slow, deep breathing; and calm down. Then take your pulse for 60 seconds and count your heartbeats, or use an app that measures your heart rate. Ideally, your resting heart rate will be between 40 and 60 beats per minute. I just tested mine as I was writing this paragraph, and it was 59. When I wake up in the morning, it's usually in the 40 to 45 range. Relative risk for all-cause mortality increases for each 10 beats above 60 beats per minute. If your resting heart rate is above 80 beats per minute, it would be a good idea to talk to your doctor about stress management and whether it is a good idea to start an exercise program.

WORDS OF WISDOM

"Those who do not find time for exercise will have to find time for illness."   —Edward Stanley

MOVEMENT AND YOUR HEALTH

MOST PEOPLE KNOW that if they exercise regularly, they will be healthier, and this knowledge is becoming more and more mainstream. The research advances in this area have been revolutionary. Medical doctors are starting to write prescriptions for exercise—physical activity is now being used not just to prevent chronic disease but to treat it as well.

Why is exercise so powerful? Because it activates the parts of the body that create movement. Even though that seems simple, it's actually quite complicated, and it triggers a cascade of positive changes inside the body. Because we activate almost all of the body when we exercise, the whole body begins to adapt and improve when we move consistently.

The first thing that happens when we want to move is that our brains activate. That's right—even though we move our legs to walk, and our legs are part of our bodies and are made up of muscles, tendons, bones, and blood, the controller is in our heads. Parts of the brain surge with electricity, motor patterns are activated, and signals are sent down the spinal cord through our nerves, which connect to our muscles. The muscles respond to the signals by contracting in a specific sequence and with a controlled amount of force. The legs move and we walk.

And when we move, the brain and body change for the better. We may be taking many steps, each one not that challenging by itself, but if you add them all up, wonderful adaptations begin to happen inside your body. Your muscles use up much of their stored energy. Blood cells are crushed. Nerves become fatigued and signal-carrying neurotransmitters are depleted. The breakdown of fuels like carbohydrates and fats, which provide energy to muscles, results in the release of waste products such as acids and carbon dioxide.

If we take this to another level and think about picking up something heavy—like a big rock on the beach, or a weight in a gym—things get more interesting. The signals from the brain have to increase so that more nerves are recruited. The nerve fibres connect with and activate muscle fibres, which creates enough force to move that rock or weight. Inside the muscle fibres, energy is broken down more quickly to provide the metabolic power required to fuel the muscle fibres. Waste products are created. Muscle fibres tear. Your nerves release their neurotransmitters (the molecules that carry signals from nerve to nerve and nerve to muscle) and become fatigued. This stimulates even more improvement in your muscles, connective tissues, bones, nerves, and brain.

The magic is that, although in the moment, the physiological stress is tremendous—just think of the micro-tears happening in the muscle tissue, all the waste products being produced, the cellular environment becoming acidic—all those stressors stimulate the muscles and nerves to improve and to get better. More nerves grow, and they fill with more signal-carrying neurotransmitters. Nerve membranes become stronger, and they will need to integrate more omega-3 fatty acids into the myelin sheath that surrounds and protects them as the nerves grow and become stronger. The muscle fibres repair themselves and integrate more proteins to make the fibres bigger and stronger. Metabolically, more enzymes are created that break down food quickly to supply energy quickly.

When you exercise at an intensity that is high enough to cause your body some physiological stress, the body will adapt and improve. You will get stronger, faster, and fitter. You'll also get smarter and happier. You will have more energy.

One of my dreams is that exercise, physical activity, and training become part of life for almost everyone on the planet, and that we are all as healthy as we can be as a result. I'd love to see people in the wards of hospitals walking before, during, and after their treatments. To help make that happen, I want to share some of the latest research on how exercise can exponentially improve health.

EXERCISE AND CANCER

MY RESEARCH TEAM is working on determining how treatments for the blood cancer leukemia cause exercise intolerance in cancer survivors and how we can best use exercise and physical activity to improve outcomes in children who survive blood cancer.[7] We're hoping to clearly establish that exercise can be used as a therapy for patients with cancer.

Fortunately, this is a field of growing interest for scientists and oncologists.[8] We know that exercise is related to lower risk of breast cancer, prostate cancer, lung cancer, colon cancer, and many other types of cancer.[9] We also know it is beneficial for patients with these types of cancer. But in what way are exercise and cancer related? Is there a direct relationship? It turns out that the answer is yes—there *is* a direct relationship, and the link lies in how exercise can help or hinder the immune system.

This is critical because our immune systems are intimately involved in preventing and fighting off cancer.[10] Immune-system cells can target and destroy tumour cells or other types of cancer cells, especially certain kinds of lymphomas. It's like chemical and biological warfare inside the body. When the system works well, we're able to battle invaders and stay healthy. When the system is overwhelmed or ineffective, we get sick. This can happen if we exercise too much or too intensely or if we are chronically stressed.

Moderate exercise that is not too stressful may help prevent and even treat cancer. Several research studies have shown that moderate exercise improves the ability of blood cells called macrophages to target and destroy tumour cells.[11] A study by Line Pedersen and colleagues at the University of Copenhagen shows that exercise reduced the incidence of tumours and growth of tumours by 60% in sedentary mice.[12] These researchers discovered that the hormone adrenaline, released during exercise, was the substance that triggered the mobilization of natural killer cells (white blood cells that can attack tumour cells) and increased their ability to penetrate and infiltrate the tumour cells. Using a firefighter analogy, adrenaline is like the alarm that signals firefighters to race to a fire; the white blood cells are the powerful hoses and fire retardants that will put out the fire quickly.

So, bottom line: Do activities that add a bit of adrenaline to your life! Anything that is fun and exciting will do the trick. Try mountain biking, trail hiking, paddle boarding, or a tennis game with a partner who maybe is just a bit better than you are—the competitive nature will up your adrenaline, and you might learn a thing or two. Lately, I've been taking my daughter to a bike park and learning how to follow her up, down, and over the various obstacles. It's adrenaline central in my cells. Or add something new to your workout routine from time to time.

The key takeaway here is that regular moderate exercise decreases cancer risk. Check with your doctor to see how exercise can help you. Not everyone should exercise, and there are times when exercise is good for you and times when it should be avoided. If you're new to exercise, or if you have cancer and your doctor has given you the okay to go ahead with it, begin very slowly and progress gently. There are many kinds of cancer, and research on the benefits of exercise for cancer patients is new. Take time to work with your doctor to find the exercise that makes you feel better and that you can incorporate into your life.

DR. GREG'S 1% TIP: BOOST YOUR IMMUNE SYSTEM AFTER YOUR WORKOUT

Dr. Brian McFarlin of the University of North Texas has done research on runners.[13] He and his research team found that supplementing with 250 mg of beta-glucan (found in baker's yeast) per day for 10 days after a marathon improved immune function in runners, and also after a 50-minute high-intensity bike ride in a laboratory. After the marathon, the runners who took beta-glucan had a 37% decrease in the number of cold and flu symptoms, compared with members of the placebo group (who took rice flour). After the cycling test, taking beta-glucan was associated with a 32% increase in salivary IgA, an antibody found in saliva that tags invaders like viruses and bacteria and makes it easier for other immune-system cells, such as white blood cells, to find the invaders and destroy them. So if you have a race coming up, why not try supplementing with beta-glucan for 10 days to keep yourself healthy postrace? Always work with a health care professional when you're trying to figure out what supplements to take and when.

EXERCISE AND INFLAMMATION

INFLAMMATION IS THE body's natural response to injury or infection. Acute (short-term) inflammation can happen when we're injured—like when we get a cut, burn, or bruise. It can also happen when we have a bacterial or viral infection. Or, say, when we sprain an ankle and it swells up—that's the inflammatory response in action. It's important to remember that tissue inflammation is helpful for healing and repairing our injured or infected tissues. But it can be very bad for our health if we have inflammation in our bodies for long periods.

Let's use the sprained ankle as an example to explore how the inflammatory process works. When you roll over on your ankle and sprain or tear the ankle tendons, inflammatory cells rush to the area to clean up the damaged tissue and stimulate new fibres to regenerate. Gaps in the damaged cell walls open, allowing fluids and immune-system cells to rush in and heal the tissue. This is what causes swelling. Some of the inflammatory cells that rush into the injured area are macrophages, which digest the damaged tissue.

While the macrophages and other immune-system cells do their work to repair the affected tissue, a substance called insulin-like growth factor-1 (IGF-1) is released and begins circulating throughout the body. The IGF-1 signals for a special cell called the satellite cell to build new tissue. The benefit of this healing process is that it stimulates new and stronger tissues, like tendons and muscles. The drawback is that it is very painful, and it takes some time—as long as 72 hours for muscles and even longer for tendons and other soft tissues. But this is still considered short-term (acute) inflammation, and it's good because it helps repair and regenerate our tissues.

Long-term (chronic) inflammation is much more of a problem. It's a situation where the inflammatory response and your immune system are on high alert all the time. Chronic inflammation appears to play a role in many diseases, including cardiovascular disease, cancer, cystic fibrosis, asthma, obesity, type 2 diabetes, Alzheimer's disease, and depression. Chronic inflammation in your body can cause all sorts of damage to your heart, lungs, brain, nerves, and muscles.

In my research on patients with cystic fibrosis, I found that chronic inflammation had affected the function of mitochondria in their muscles.[14] Mitochondria are tiny organs inside cells that create energy; the impaired mitochondria seem to cause patients with lung disease to have slower recovery times after a bout of exercise. In the real world, that translates into, for example, situations that keep children with chronic illnesses from participating in sports and other physical activities. Think about it. If you had 30% slower recovery time after exercising, and you and a friend were playing soccer and you both sprinted for a ball, it would take you much longer to recover after that sprint than your friend. Sadly, this results in kids not wanting to participate because they can have trouble keeping up to their peers. With patients with cystic fibrosis, we know that physical activity can slow the rate of lung function decline, so anything that impairs or enhances exercise ability can have profound effects for them. If we can find better exercise and nutrition therapies, we can give these kids back their health and also give them back the chance to experience all the benefits of playing with their friends.

Just like with cancer, when it comes to exercise and inflammation, moderation is key. Exercise is a good thing when it causes acute inflammation and we can heal our tissues with rest and nutrition, but it can be a bad thing if the workouts are too intense or if we train too hard too often and inflammation gets out of control.

Extreme exercise can increase inflammation.[15] The physiology works like this: When we exercise, we burn nutrients such as carbohydrates and fats to produce energy for the contraction of our muscles. The fat and carbohydrate molecules are broken down into acetyl CoA, which enters our mitochondria (those tiny organs in our cells that produce energy), where the molecules are burned or broken down in the presence of oxygen. This creates compounds called reactive oxygen species (which are what cause rust on metal and browning of apples when the flesh is exposed to air). At low or moderate levels, reactive oxygen species can promote healing and the inflammatory response, which stimulates positive changes in the body (including more muscle proteins and stronger mitochondria). Too much inflammation and reactive oxygen species have the opposite effect and can play a role in the development of cancer and cardiovascular disease. This all provides an excellent reason to exercise consistently at moderate levels. It is also the rationale for eating vegetables and fruits before and after exercise: to assist the antioxidant system in helping the body recover and regenerate more quickly and become fitter and healthier faster. If you do a really hard workout or play a particularly hard game, that's fine; just make sure to give yourself the time, nutrition, and sleep you need to recover and regenerate.

EXERCISE AND AGING

WE LIVE IN a day and age when our desire to live longer is being fulfilled more and more. From 90-year-old marathon runners to 40-year-old Olympians, everywhere you look, people are pushing the limits of human potential. By understanding the findings of science, you can learn why some people are aging less quickly than others, and more importantly, you'll be able to figure out how to turn back the clock on your own life.

The amazing truth we have discovered is that endurance activities slow the aging process. First, there are the obvious benefits: a stronger heart, more efficient blood flow, and a bolstered immune system, all of which offset some of the negative effects of aging. Exercise even appears to protect the brain from age-related cognitive decline, and elderly people who have high fitness levels have the same brain activation patterns as people who are much younger.[16]

More specifically, exercise can protect the genetic material in our cells. This genetic material—DNA—is what our cells use to replicate and stay healthy. When people engage in regular aerobic exercise, they maintain telomere length. Telomeres, repeating sequences of DNA at the end of a DNA strand, are the protective caps on our DNA. Think of them like the aglets, or caps, on your shoelaces that keep the laces from fraying. Since your DNA generates the proteins and machinery that make your body work effectively, preventing aglets from "fraying" keeps your body going, and that is exactly what endurance activities seem to do.[17] Staying fit helps keep your DNA young and healthy.

The long-term benefits of exercise give new meaning to the phrase "act your age." By shifting your mindset about exercise so that you include regular fitness in your daily experience, you can offset the aging process and help ensure that you are healthy and active throughout life. You only need to exercise for 20 to 25 minutes a day for a few days per week to get the benefits.[18]

EXERCISE AND OBESITY

THE WORLD IS faced with an overweight and obesity epidemic that affects a growing number of people. Along with obesity come metabolic syndrome and type 2 diabetes. Type 2 diabetes causes premature mortality and a host of other health complications.[19]

Fortunately, physical activity and exercise can help people with these conditions. The benefits are more powerful when combined with nutritional changes—another ripple effect—but exercise alone will help.[20] Exercise has been shown to improve physiology and health in people with obesity even if they don't lose any weight. The risk is that exercise makes you hungrier and tired, so you might start exercising and end up eating more and resting the remainder of the day, ultimately sabotaging any progress you made. The key is to start slow and build slowly.

I understand how hard it is to put this into practice. But remember, overweight and obesity don't happen overnight. It takes a long time to end up in that health crisis. Getting out of it can also take a long time. That's an important point. Rapid weight loss almost never works. Fad diets usually fail. But if we take the long view and approach weight loss as a slow, gradual process that we push forward through permanent lifestyle changes, we can overcome this grand challenge.

Simple changes such as going for a short walk every day, or taking a flight of stairs instead of an escalator, or doing five knee push-ups can add up to huge changes over time. Remember that your body is changing for the better, even if you don't see changes on the scale. If you can add sleep, exercise, and nutrition together, the ripple effect will kick in, and you'll see tremendous changes.

EXERCISE AND MENTAL HEALTH

A STAGGERING NUMBER of people struggle with mental illness. Approximately 20% of Canadians will be affected by mental illness in their lifetimes.[21] And yet, mental health challenges are often "invisible," not obvious to an onlooker. We can see a broken arm or when someone has a cold or many other conditions (although not all, of course), but sadly, we can easily miss it when someone has depression.

Last year as I was nearing the end of a school presentation on how exercise, nutrition, and sleep can positively impact our mental performance and health, a girl sitting at the front of the auditorium started crying. I finished the talk quickly so I could go make sure she was okay. She told me that she wished I had been there a year ago, because it was around then that her friend had committed suicide—and maybe she could have been saved. Right then and there, I silently committed to always talking about mental health and opening up this issue for conversation at every opportunity.

We don't understand mental health well, we don't treat mental illnesses effectively, and even worse, people with mental illnesses are stigmatized—kind of like how people with cancer were in the 1950s, and people with AIDS in the 1980s.

Fortunately, we are beginning to understand the links between mental health, exercise, sleep, and nutrition.

Dr. Long Zhai in the Department of Epidemiology and Health Statistics at Qingdao University Medical College in China conducted a study of the links between sedentary behaviour and depression.[22] He and his team analyzed results from more than 110,000 participants from 13 research studies and found that being sedentary (sitting or lying down for extended periods), television viewing, and prolonged computer use were significantly related to risk of depression.

I'm a huge fan of technology and all that it can do for our world, but I also believe we have to learn how to use it in such a way that it does not compromise our health. Students need to be given movement breaks during the day at school. In the workplace, we need to stand and stretch for 20 seconds for every 20 minutes of sitting. We need to give ourselves tech-free times during the day. My brilliant colleague Dr. James Rouse has a basket into which he and his family drop their mobile devices when they come home. Or, the bedroom could be designated a tech-free space. There are lots of options.

If physical inactivity may be a contributor to mental illness like depression, can the mind–body connection work in a positive way as well? The answer is yes: exercise and physical activity, in addition to medication and/or psychological therapy, can be an effective treatment for some people who are struggling with depression.[23] When we look at review papers that summarize the growing body of individual studies that have explored the links between depression and exercise, interesting observations emerge: Research shows that exercise is about as effective as traditional psychological treatments and antidepressants.[24]

When exercise is added to antidepressant therapy, a moderate additional benefit is seen. But if the exercise stops, the benefits don't appear to last. So, if you want to be mentally healthy, exercise has to be a part of life, forever.

When you're depressed, it can feel like the weight of the world is on your shoulders. Simply getting out of bed can be a challenge. Exercising in those moments might feel almost impossible. But remember, you don't need to do much. Try to get outside for a 5-minute walk. Or do a few push-ups. It's amazing how good it feels to vent some anger into your muscles, where it seemingly dissipates and eventually vanishes. Get as much help as you can from family and friends. Start small by asking someone to go for a walk with you. Use the mind–body connection for your mental and physical benefit.

If you want to amplify the benefits of exercise even more, add meditation to your exercise routine. Meditation is especially beneficial for people with anxiety and depression.[25] It helps people break out of negative patterns of thinking and reduces symptoms of both depression and anxiety.[26] Just like exercise, you need to practise meditation on an ongoing basis to keep the benefits. A new approach called MAP (standing for "mental and physical") training combines exercise and meditation for people with anxiety and depression.[27]

One of the first studies to investigate MAP training involved participants who had gone through some horrific experiences.[28] The researchers worked with young mothers who had been rendered homeless and had suffered physical and sexual abuse, addiction, and depression. The women participated in two sessions per week, at which they sat for 20 minutes and meditated, and then followed that with 10 minutes of walking and

30 minutes of learning a dance routine. After 8 weeks, aerobic fitness had increased, and symptoms of depression had decreased. This is a great example of how we can create the ripple effect by combining exercise and mental-skills training to help us overcome adversity and get healthier, even in some of the worst situations.

WORDS OF WISDOM

"If something stands between you and your success, move it. Never be denied."

—Dwayne "the Rock" Johnson,
professional wrestler and actor

MOVE MORE TO SLEEP BETTER

WE KNOW THAT sleep helps heal the body and amplifies the response to exercise, making us healthier, fitter, stronger, and smarter. We also know it works the other way around too: exercise helps improve the quality of our sleep, even for people with sleep problems.[29] When I was working to overcome the heart infection I told you about in the introduction, the first thing I did was work on sleeping better, and the foundation of that was to use the amplifier of walking to improve my sleep.

Acute-exercise experiments that measured the sleep physiology of subjects who either performed or refrained from daytime exercise indicate that exercise is associated with a small but reliable increase in stage 2 and slow-wave sleep.[30] Exercise may improve sleep quality by regulating body temperature, though the exact physiology to explain how exercise improves sleep is still being explored.

Exercise is a powerful mechanism for improving sleep. Exercise acts just like insulin in that it moves carbohydrates and large amino acids into muscle, thus removing them from competition with tryptophan, a small amino acid that induces sleep, to get into the brain. Exercise also improves fatty acid metabolism, which helps increase the available tryptophan that can be moved into the brain. Try an evening walk after dinner or yoga to help you create the physiological conditions for falling asleep quickly and sleeping deeply.

In the short term, when you begin an exercise routine or change up your routine to make it more challenging, there may be a period when your sleep actually worsens. This can last for a week or even longer. But once you adapt to the new exercise load, your body and brain get better at handling the exercise stress and your sleep will start to improve. You'll fall asleep faster, and you'll sleep more deeply. It might take you some time to figure out what works for you, but keep at it, because when you get a great night's sleep, you'll feel fantastic. And that's how you should feel all the time!

MOVE MORE TO EAT SMARTER

SURPRISINGLY, THE SCIENCE on how increased exercising impacts healthy eating choices is limited. One study shows that after sticking to an exercise program for 2 months, research participants experienced improvements in a wide range of "regulatory behaviours," including lower stress, less alcohol and caffeine consumption, and an increase in healthy eating.[31] The researchers suggest that exercise amplifies the capacity for self-regulation. I believe that when we make positive changes in any area, ripple effects cascade through our lives. I know this is true for moving more and how it can influence eating.

Adopting an exercise routine or changing a workout will have a powerful impact on your physiology. In the short term, you burn more energy than you otherwise would during your activity sessions, and your body spends more energy helping to refuel, repair, and regenerate itself between workouts. So at first you will feel the need to eat more. This can be a pitfall, so be careful and plan ahead. When you start a workout routine or you change things up to keep it fresh or to increase your workload as you get fitter, make sure you plan on having loads of healthy foods around to fuel your exercise and help your body recover. (You'll find lots of information on this in the next chapter.) This is where many people have trouble, sometimes even gaining body fat upon starting an exercise routine. Remember, you can't outrun a bad diet.

However, once you've got used to your new routine, you'll make better food choices. You'll feel the effects of good and bad foods more acutely. You'll notice when you have eaten well and how that makes you feel better before, during, and after your workouts. You will also become more sensitive to the bad foods you eat. You will feel sluggish or even sick. Your body will send you signals about what is working for you and what isn't. Make sure you listen, and surround yourself with healthy food options. Great nutrition and consistent exercise do not happen on their own—they take planning and commitment. When you put the two together, they amplify results and you'll get healthier and fitter faster.

DR. GREG'S 1% TIP: CHOOSE SUPER HEALTHY FOODS WITH FEW CALORIES

For many years, as a competitive swimmer I was looking to eat as many calories as I could, regardless of where they came from. It has taken me a long time to get over this mindset and to alter my physiology to be healthier and more energetic, even in my 40s. These days I'm always looking for ways to add more nutrients and minimize my calories. Foods that are packed with fibre, vitamins, and minerals while being low in calories include arugula, asparagus, broccoli, Brussels sprouts, beets, cauliflower, grapefruit, mushrooms, tomatoes, spinach, kale, peppers, teas, and berries. So load up on colourful vegetables!

WORDS OF WISDOM

"All truly great thoughts are conceived while walking."
—Friedrich Nietzsche

MOVE MORE TO BE MORE CREATIVE

THE WORLD'S MOST creative people have been known to use exercise to activate themselves before doing mental tasks. Charles Dickens was rumoured to have walked for 30 miles a day. Bob Marley and the Wailers supercharged their creativity and performance in a couple of ways. Before a concert, they would play soccer in the stadium where they were to perform. And before recording sessions, they'd go to the beach to play soccer, then go for a swim before heading into the studio. They found that if they were active in these ways before playing music, they played better and were more creative.

When I read Steve Jobs' biography, it stood out for me that Jobs conducted his meetings while walking around the Apple campus. His biographer, Walter Isaacson, noted that when Jobs took people for a walk, they became more creative, had better energy, and were able to think better than if still in the office. Turns out, Jobs' habit of getting some activity that improved his and others' thinking is backed up by research. Scientists at Stanford University found that walking boosts creative inspiration and that creative output can be increased by an average of 60% while walking.[32] As little as 15 minutes of exercise improves mental performance, so why not add this to your day, before important tasks that you have to do? If you can start your day with a workout, you'll prime your brain for excellence and start the process of remodelling the areas of your brain that will help you think more clearly.

Exercise primes the brain for mental performance. If you have an important thinking-related task to do—for example, a presentation, a major meeting, or an exam—try to take a few minutes and do some light exercise before the task. Go for a walk before that presentation. Do a few flights of stairs before you sit the exam. If you need to solve a problem, block off time to get focused, and walk, stretch, or lift weights in the hour before you settle in to work on the challenge. This exercise will increase the flow of oxygen and nutrients to the brain and improve your mental performance.

You may feel as if you're taking too much time away from the task at hand by doing this, but the physiological science says you'll perform better and get healthier at the same time.

The key is to make exercise part of your daily routine. Not only for your body but for your mind as well.

DR. GREG'S 1% TIP: FOLLOW THE 20/20 RULE

For every 20 minutes of sitting, stand and stretch for 20 seconds—and, if you take public transportation to work, stand instead of sitting. The same goes for meetings or even classes: stand instead of sitting.

MOVE MORE TO LEARN BETTER

FASCINATING RESEARCH HAS shown that our brains function better after we have activated them with exercise. Dr. Art Kramer's lab at the Beckman Institute in Illinois showed that children who did aerobic exercise for 20 minutes before writing math tests had improved scores, and the children who did exercise regularly had different brain structures than those who were less active.[33] The regions of the brain that had larger volumes in the exercise group were related to attention control, cognitive control, and response resolution. These are all centres of the brain that help maintain attention and the ability to coordinate actions and thoughts crisply. These results were confirmed in young adults,[34] meaning it's not just children who benefit from exercise before doing mental tasks.

Another study, by Dr. Josie Booth at Scotland's Dundee University, of 5,000 children in the UK found that 15 minutes of exercise improved performance in math by about a quarter of a grade and that the increments in performance continued right up to 60 minutes, meaning that by doing 60 minutes of activity, it is possible to boost academic performance by a full letter grade (e.g., from a B to an A).[35]

Harvard psychiatrist Dr. John Ratey explains this concept in his book *Spark: The Revolutionary New Science of Exercise and the Brain.* He says, "Physical activity sparks biological changes that encourage brain cells to bind to one another. The more neuroscientists discover about this process, the clearer it becomes that exercise provides an unparalleled stimulus, creating an environment in which the brain is ready, willing, and able to learn."

So if you have mental tasks to do during the day, if your job involves thinking, or if you're a student looking to biohack your way to better grades, do some exercise before your mental task to supercharge your brain and improve your performance. If you do the exercise regularly, you'll change your brain to make it better at cognitive tasks. Imagine that you can do better at calculus without actually doing more calculus homework! I wish I had known that in grade 12 . . .

DR. GREG'S 1% TIP: BOOST YOUR BRAIN FUNCTION WITH YOGA

A study from the University of Illinois at Urbana–Champaign shows that as little as 20 minutes of yoga can improve brain function. It appears that after a yoga practice, study participants were better able to focus, process information quickly and accurately, and also learn more effectively than after performing an aerobic exercise bout.[36] So add yoga to your daily or weekly routine. I have a series of yoga videos on my computer so that I can sneak in 20 minutes when I have a break in the day or in my hotel room while travelling.

THE SEVEN KEYS TO MOVING MORE

THE POTENTIAL FOR improving our lives by moving more is huge. Simply standing up changes the way our bodies use energy and circulates blood; it also changes how we think. Exercise can improve concentration, learning, focus, and memory and can even prevent and treat mental illnesses. But taking advantage of this will require a paradigm shift. We need to incorporate movement into our daily lives. Here are seven keys to making that happen.

KEY #1: BUILD YOUR FITNESS

THE FOUNDATION OF health and performance is our aerobic system, which uses oxygen to create energy that fuels most of the activities in our lives, from walking to running to playing music to writing a test to mentally solving a math problem. Low to moderate physical activity is the key to building up the aerobic system and unlocking the related benefits.

Walking, jogging, cycling, swimming, and hiking will build up the cardiorespiratory system (heart, lungs, blood, blood vessels) and the aerobic energy pathway inside the muscles. All these activities and other similar forms of light-intensity exercise, such as yoga and gardening, will help you develop cardiorespiratory fitness and endurance. These activities enhance the transport system the body uses to get oxygen from the environment to the muscle cells, where it is used to create energy. When you put stress on your muscles, heart, and lungs by pushing them through activities like walking, jogging, running, swimming, or cycling for periods that are longer than they are used to, you stimulate adaptation and make your energy systems more efficient.

Consistent low- to moderate-intensity physical activity completely changes the body. To begin with, forcing your heart to beat more frequently causes the same changes that occur in any muscle you use regularly—your heart gets stronger and can pump blood through the body more easily. You are also increasing the rate at which oxygen is absorbed into your body by your tissues. This happens because you induce a process called angiogenesis, which increases the density of the capillary beds that surround the muscle fibres. Capillaries are the tiny vessels at the end of the chain of blood vessels that begins with your heart and arteries. There are between three and five capillaries around each muscle fibre, and endurance activity ensures that the capillary beds will be at the upper end of that range.

The amount of blood that moves through your body with each beat of your heart is called stroke volume. Regular exercise increases the amount of blood in the body and the amount of blood that can be pumped by the heart each time it beats. In one study, researchers found that although athletes and non-exercisers alike saw an increase in their heart rates during a workout, the athletes were moving 10 litres more blood per minute through their systems.[37] That is a huge difference in the amount of oxygen getting to the muscles!

Aerobic exercise also encourages the growth and development of mitochondria. Mitochondria are organelles (tiny cellular structures) inside your cells that produce energy. Exercise stimulates mitochondria to grow, replicate, and improve their ability to make use of carbohydrates, proteins, and fats in order to generate energy. This does take some time, so be patient when you start a workout routine—the energy boost might take a few weeks in coming as your body produces enough mito-chondria to meet the new demand.

DR. GREG'S 1% TIP: EAT FOODS HIGH IN IRON TO SUPERCHARGE YOUR ENDURANCE

The superstar of your transport systems is the red blood cell, which carries oxygen to the muscles. Endurance exercise improves red blood cells in two ways. First, EPO (erythropoietin), which is responsible for red blood cell production, is naturally increased with endurance training. Second, exercise breaks down old red blood cells and stimulates the body to produce new ones. The newer red blood cells may be more effective at picking up and carrying oxygen than the older cells are. To help your body build new and better red blood cells, you need to focus on eating foods high in iron. Oxygen binds to hemoglobin in the blood, and iron is a key component of the hemoglobin molecule. Foods that are high in iron include red meat—especially organ meats like liver and kidney—dark green vegetables, quinoa, beans, lentils, nuts, and seeds. Also consume foods high in vitamin C, as this helps the body absorb iron.

KEY #2: BUILD YOUR STRENGTH

WHEN YOU DO strength training, you are engaging different energy systems and muscle fibres than you are when doing aerobic training. Strength exercise is more intense and requires us to create more force with our muscles than we need to when doing light- to moderate-intensity aerobic activity. Just think of the difference between hiking in the woods and carrying heavy bags of groceries. One (hiking) requires a little bit of energy over a long time, and the other (carrying) requires a lot of force over a short period. Both types of fitness are critical for health and performance.

The body has two main kinds of muscle fibres: type 1 are aerobic endurance fibres, used to do light activity; type 2 anaerobic glycolytic fibres are used for activities that require strength and speed. By engaging type 2 muscle fibres, you are working both types of muscle fibres (endurance and sprint fibres). This develops your total muscle and prepares your body for situations when you have to pick up the pace—like the final kick when the finish line comes into sight, or sprinting to catch a bus.

Muscle growth occurs when micro-tears in muscle fibres work in conjunction with a molecule called mTOR, produced during a strength session to stimulate the production of new actin and myosin protein chains (the proteins in your muscles that create contraction and movement). In essence, you break them down to build them up. The molecule mTOR doesn't just stimulate your muscles to get stronger; it also does amazing things as it circulates throughout your body during and after a strength session. Its basic effects are that it activates fat, liver, and brain cells and increases general health by making you stronger and more efficient. These effects mean that strength training is as important for our health as cardiorespiratory activities.

Strength training is also great if you want to improve your body composition and lose fat. Of all the body tissues, muscle tissue burns fat most easily. If you can increase your muscle mass, you will have more metabolically active tissue that will burn fat as fuel, even at rest. Remember that when you are strength training, you may gain some weight (in the form of muscle mass), even though you are losing fat. Your focus needs to be on body composition, not the number on the scale. Keep in mind that this kind of weight gain is healthy for you.

Worried that you are going to get big and bulky if you lift weights? Don't be. The reality is that unless you make a decision to get into bodybuilding, you will find that lifting weights for strength simply improves your body composition, helps you feel better, and slows the aging process—all without developing big, bulky muscles.

It is critical to maintain proper form when you're doing strength training. Get guidance to learn the right exercises for you and how to build a training program. See a registered kinesiologist or a certified strength and conditioning specialist (CSCS), or ideally someone with both designations.

DR. GREG'S 1% TIP: FIND YOUR BEST TIME OF DAY TO EXERCISE

If there is one question I get more often than any other, it's about the best time of day to train. The answer is simple: the time of day when you can train consistently. If that is first thing in the morning, that's great. If it's on your lunch break, fantastic. If it's in the evening, brilliant. There are benefits to training at each of these times. By working out first thing in the morning, you're starting your day by increasing your metabolism, and that will help you all day long. Not to mention that you are flooding your brain with all sorts of chemicals and hormones that will help you think better all day long. Lunchtime can also be terrific, as training now will give you a surge of energy that can help you avoid the afternoon blahs. My colleague Robin Sharma, author of *The Monk Who Sold His Ferrari*, calls this "the second wind workout." Afternoon and evening workouts take advantage of the natural increases in strength and endurance that happen with changes in our circadian rhythms and can help to break down all the stress hormone you've built up during the day. Do what works best for you and what you can do consistently.

KEY #3: BUILD YOUR SPEED

ONCE YOU HAVE been training for a reasonable amount of time and have established your basic fitness level, speed training will be a powerful way to improve both your overall fitness and specific fitness in your type 2 muscle fibres and the anaerobic system inside your muscles. With this training, you develop your endurance capacity (aerobic energy system and type 1 muscle fibres) and your strength capacity (anaerobic energy systems and type 2 muscle fibres). When you do that, you teach your body how to process metabolic waste more efficiently, which improves your overall fitness and increases your ability to recover on the fly.

Speed training involves varying your pace from an easy jog right through to a maximal effort. This combination engages both your aerobic energy system and type 1 muscle fibres, which are used for endurance—and anaerobic energy systems and type 2 muscle fibres, which are used for power and speed. The endurance parts of your system are highly efficient and produce very little waste, but they do not generate a significant amount of power. The strength parts of your system produce the burst you need for sprinting or heavy lifting but are highly inefficient and produce a significant amount of waste in the form of lactic acid. By engaging both systems at once, you teach your body how to process metabolic waste while running, which improves your ability to recover after running up a hill or doing a short sprint and enhances your overall fitness.

With speed training, you can do shorter blocks of exercise, usually from 10 seconds to 60 or even 90 seconds, separated by a rest period—for example, 45 seconds at 50% effort followed by 45 seconds at 90% effort, repeated a number of times. As your fitness improves, you can lengthen the amount of time you spend at the higher speeds. You can also adjust the easy-effort portion of the workout to make the training more difficult (less rest) or easier (more rest). The total duration of the speed training can be adjusted from just a few minutes when starting out to up to 60 minutes for highly trained athletes. Make sure you work with a trainer or fitness professional to design the speed training sessions and properly incorporate them into your overall program. And always make sure you warm up properly before speed training.

DR. GREG'S 1% TIP: CHOOSE AEROBIC EXERCISE TO BOOST YOUR BRAIN

There are three main types of exercise: aerobic exercise like running; high-intensity interval training like spinning; and resistance training like lifting weights. Looking at the impact of these types of exercise on the brains of humans is extremely difficult and expensive, so researchers in Finland looked at the impact of exercise on the brains of rats.[38] They found that 6 to 8 weeks of aerobic exercise led to the growth of new neurons in the hippo-campus (a part of the brain associated with learning and memory). High-intensity training had a small, non-significant impact on the brain, and resistance training did not change neural structures in the hippocampus. The researchers explained their results by suggesting that aerobic exercise results in an increase in BDNF—brain-derived neurotrophic factor (a chemical that stim-ulates the growth of new neurons in the brain)—which led to the neural changes in the hippocampus regions in the rats' brains. What does that mean for you? If you want to optimize your brain and keep it healthy, do aer-obic exercise like walking, running, swimming, biking, or hiking regularly!

KEY #4: BUILD YOUR MOBILITY

MOBILITY WORK (ALSO known as stretching or flexibility work) is an incredibly important element of overall health fit-ness that is often overlooked. Yes, there is an ongoing debate about exactly what kind of mobility work is best to do and when, but I'll cut through that and show you what to do. In an era when so many of our activities decrease our flexibility—such as sit-ting for long periods—mobility matters a lot, both for our health and for our mental and physical performance.

The most important thing you need to know about mobility is this: it is good for you. Done properly, stretching can help you decrease muscle tension; reduce pain; and improve your range of motion, performance, and health. The second most important thing to know is that the word *stretching* refers to many types of exercises that do many different things to the body. We just need to understand what to do, how to do it, and when. The ongoing debate in the scientific and athletic communities about how to approach mobility work is sometimes taken as a sign that there are no significant benefits to increased flexibility. That just isn't true. The truth is that mobility is a complicated topic, but understanding and applying the science of movement through range-of-motion exercises and proper warm-up techniques is essential if you are to improve your health and performance.

There are two major categories of stretches: static stretching and dynamic activation. Static stretching refers to traditional stretches, where you put a muscle on stretch and hold it for a length of time. Dynamic activation refers to any motion that extends your muscles while moving. This is what people are doing when they swing their legs or arms, or do lunges before a workout. The two types of stretching have opposite effects on the nervous system—knowing this can help you understand what to do and when. The emerging opinion about stretching in the scientific community is that we should engage in dynamic activation before a workout and use static stretching during the cool-down.

Before you exercise, mobilize your body with dynamic activation. Dynamic activation causes excitatory signals to be sent from your brain to your muscles ("Woo-hoo, let's run!"), whereas static stretching creates an inhibitory response ("Chill out, man"). Also, dynamic activation increases range of motion, blood flow, and muscle temperature, all of which help with exercise. This is what to do when you want to warm up before your workout. This also works wonders if you want to bring your brain to life during your workday but don't want to break a sweat, since you're in your work clothes!

Static stretching is best done when you are cooling down or when you're just stretching to feel good and relax. Static stretching helps align muscle fibres and reduces tension by relaxing the muscles and nerves. It's also fantastic for calming down the nervous system and decreasing stress, so you may want to do this at home after a tough day at work.

Studies show that static stretching before activity limits your power output and results in a neuromuscular inhibitory response in the muscles, which is counterproductive when you are trying to prime your body for activity. In simple terms, static stretching reduces muscles' power output for a period after the stretch. Researchers are not sure how long the inhibition lasts. Research also shows that static stretching before exercise does little for injury prevention. The largest such study involves military recruits and found that those who performed static stretches before exercise were just as likely to get injured as their cohorts who did not stretch at all.

If you want to integrate mobility training into your workouts in a way that is supported by the scientific evidence, follow this progression: Begin by warming up for 5 to 10 minutes with light activity (around 50% of your maximum heart rate) so that your muscles have sufficient blood flow, oxygen, and temperature to work optimally. Then find a place to do dynamic activation exercises. Make sure you get your coach or trainer to show you activities that are appropriate for you. Select dynamic activation movements that replicate the kind of movements you will perform during your workout (e.g., shoulder rotations before swimming and walking lunges before running; runners could also include the famous A and B drills that get blood flowing through the quadriceps and hamstrings by kicking at your butt or lifting your knees toward your chest). Then move on to the main part of your training.

Once your workout is complete and you've done a proper active recovery with at least 10 minutes of light activity, the benefits of static stretching will be significant—relaxing your muscles and calming your nervous system. By performing static stretches for at least 20 seconds per stretch, you can reduce tension in your muscles. You can tell how long to hold a static stretch by placing a muscle on stretch and holding the stretch until you feel the muscle relax and lengthen. This often takes 20 to 30 seconds, and the relaxation and lengthening happen when your nervous system reflexes, which are designed to protect the muscle from rapid lengthening, decrease their firing.

Of course, no conversation about mobility is complete without a comment about yoga. We are fortunate to live in a day and age when the ancient art of yoga has achieved international popularity and we have widespread access to yoga studios. Yoga is a deeply meditative and spiritual practice that will help you develop mindfulness and get in tune with your body—habits of great benefit to all of us. From stress reduction to various forms of emotional release, yoga has side effects that will improve your fitness and help you live the vital and healthy life you crave. If you have never tried yoga, see if you can fit a class into your exercise routine to experience what it is all about. The physical benefits of yoga are immense because the techniques promote improved flexibility and have been tested during a 3,000-year process of trial and error. Most anyone will benefit from attending a yoga class—even if only once a week. I prefer flow Ashtanga yoga classes but encourage you to try out a few types to see what works for you.

DR. GREG'S 1% TIP: MOVE MORE TO GET SICK LESS

Research shows that people who exercise at a moderate level consistently get sick the least. So build in exercise to your everyday routine. If you're thinking you don't have time, remember that by taking a little time up front, you'll be avoiding days and days of illness down the road. If you think you don't have time to exercise, think again. The reality is that you can't afford not to.

KEY #5: MOVE IN NATURE

IF YOU ARE increasing your exercise and activity, great! More physical activity will benefit your muscles, blood, heart, and lungs—pretty much everything in your body. Doing your activity outside is even better.

First, what's amazing is that simply looking at a picture of nature can lower blood pressure, stress, and mental fatigue.[39] That's how powerful nature is. Try changing your desktop background to a nature scene! And preferably a nature scene that includes water—research has shown that images containing water are more restorative than those without.[40] See how that photo makes you feel!

But if you can get outside, by all means get out there. Exercising in nature has benefits that go above and beyond the benefits gained by exercising indoors. Research has shown improvements in mental well-being, self-esteem, and even depression.[41] Which explains why my wife kicks me out of the house to go on a trail run when I'm stressed out from a crazy day at work. Trail running and mountain biking seem to help me decompress much better than running on a treadmill or even on city streets, and the research would seem to back up this feeling. Being exposed to plants decreases levels of the stress hormone cortisol, decreases resting heart rate, and decreases blood pressure.[42] It's clear that exercise can be just as good for our brains as our minds, and getting outside and exercising in nature might amplify the benefits.

One challenge we often face is staying motivated to exercise. About half of people who join a gym don't stick with it beyond the first year. Yet people who exercise outside tend to stick with their exercise programs more consistently than those who train indoors.[43] So if you're having trouble being consistent, consider adding an outdoor workout to your routine.

Another perhaps surprising thing about getting outside and into nature is that exposure to plants and trees can also improve your immune system. As you know, your immune system helps fight off illnesses and keep you healthy. Scientists think that airborne chemicals (called phytoncides) that plants emit to protect themselves from fungi, bacteria, and insects may also benefit humans. In a study published in 2007, people who took 2-hour walks in a forest had a 50% increase in the levels of their natural killer cells. These cells may sound scary, but they're the good guys—the cells that circulate through your body and kill bacteria, viruses, fungi, and other invaders.[44] The benefits of exercising outdoors appear to last for at least a week, and maybe even up to a month. So once per week (or at least once a month), spend some time outside doing something fun. Go hiking on a trail, go skiing, go cycling—and the more you can immerse yourself in nature, the better.

And if you prefer walking and light activity to running or more intense activities, you're in luck. It appears that walking in nature improves measures of revitalization, self-esteem, energy, and pleasure and decreases frustration, worry, confusion, depression, tension, and tiredness far more than light activity indoors does. Running outdoors does not seem to have a greater impact on emotions or mood than does running inside—maybe because running and more intense activities cause the release of endorphins that can cause feelings of elation and exhilaration regardless of where you run. If you want to feel better, get outside and don't worry about whether you walk or run.

WORDS OF WISDOM:
WALLACE J. NICHOLS, AUTHOR OF *BLUE MIND*

I've had the pleasure of interviewing Dr. Wallace J. Nichols on my podcast. He's a swimmer, and his research on our connection to water really resonated for me—I think it will with you too. Here's an excerpt from the interview.

It turns out if you exercise outdoors rather than indoors, it can be better for you depending on your environment; and if you exercise in blue space near water, it's even better than green space, so going for a run by the river or the lake or on the beach is even better for you, and one of the reasons is it's calming, it's simplifying, it's kind of a visual, an auditory blank slate, if you will. But it also holds our attention, so there is this concept of soft fascination . . . just a blue room with white noise would be relaxing in a way but after a couple of minutes will be kind of boring. It would not hold your attention. You get fidgety and bored, whereas just being by the water is relaxing because it's a simple auditory, visual environment, but it holds our attention. That holding of our attention keeps us in that calm state longer.

Contrast that to going to the gym and working out and putting on, say, CNN or some bad news for an hour on a treadmill. You're stressing your body and you're stressing your mind. You're watching terrible news, which is just about all they report on these days, and you're stressing your mind, you're stressing your body. What if you could relax your mind while you're exercising your body? Perhaps the performance would be better. Perhaps the benefits of that exercise would be deeper.

DR. GREG'S 1% TIP: TRY MUSCULAR MEDITATION

Muscular meditation is any activity in which you move in a repetitive, rhythmic pattern. Examples include walking, swimming, cycling, jogging, rowing, and paddling—any type of exercise where your muscles are contracting in a consistent pattern over a period. This form of movement helps put the brain in a state in which it can relax and your mind can wander. If you do this regularly, it can be powerful for stress reduction, as well as for decreasing symptoms of depression and anxiety.[45]

KEY #6: BE A 24-HOUR ATHLETE

WANT TO KNOW one of the greatest secrets to being stronger, swifter, and fitter? Hint: it's not about lifting more, running faster, or adding extra workouts. One of the great advances in the health and sport sciences in the last decade has been the realization that what we do after a workout to help recover and refuel is just as important as what we do during the workout itself, if not more important. That is, the healing and repair process may be more important than the actual training. So, basically, your job isn't over when the workout ends. Here are four steps to getting the most out of your workouts—after your workouts.

STEP 1: PERFORM ACTIVE RECOVERY

LET'S ASSUME YOU'VE just finished your workout. Good job. You've pushed your body to the limit. Now it's time to help yourself—as fast as you can!

First, make sure you cool down properly. Take the time to clean your body of waste products that accumulate when you exercise. These can include, among other compounds, carbon dioxide, acids from your muscles, and potassium spillover into your blood. My opinion is that the faster you can remove waste products, the sooner your muscles devote their energy toward refuelling themselves and topping up their glycogen stores.

Help your muscles out by taking 5 to 15 minutes after your workout to do active recovery. Active recovery means moving your body at about 55% of your maximum heart rate, rather than stopping and resting. That means your active recovery is not too easy and not too hard. You shouldn't feel a burn, but you should be moving more than you do when not working out. If you're at the gym, you could cycle or you could walk fast or run slow on a treadmill. If you're doing a sport or an activity, figure out how to dial it down a bit to an easier level before stopping entirely.

STEP 2: REHYDRATE

SO NOW YOU'VE finished your cool-down. Before you do anything else, rehydrate with water. If you've been working out for longer than 90 minutes or in hot, humid conditions, you may wish to add carbohydrates (like a little honey) and electrolytes to your drink, but most of the time for most people, sports drinks are not necessary. Most of all, focus on water. Your body can't properly heal and recover without plenty of H2O.

STEP 3: REFUEL

OKAY, SO YOU'VE had something to drink. Now you need to get nutrients into your system. I differentiate fuel from nutrition. For me, fuels are the foods and fluids used during exercise to power the exercise. Because they're taken during exercise, they can be higher in simple carbohydrates, and you might even take some fats on board if you're experimenting with ketogenic training. I recommend sports gels or other "fuel" only for elite athletes who are training for longer than 90 minutes at a time. Most people most of the time don't need them. Nutrition, at least for me, describes the foods and fluids we need to refuel our bodies and brains. I believe nutrition should help improve your health along with your performance (hence my issue with chocolate milk, which is not healthy). So after a workout, eat foods that help refuel your muscles (complex carbohydrates) and foods that help you repair and regenerate (proteins and fats).

STEP 4: REGENERATE

THE MOST IMPORTANT part of building your endurance, increasing your muscle mass, building stronger bones, creating new blood vessels and more blood, and even building a stronger brain is to allow your body the time and the rest it needs to recover, regenerate, and rebuild. The better you recover and regenerate, the better your body will adapt, the fewer injuries you'll have, and the healthier you'll become.

This is where I need to geek out a bit and talk about physiology. Because if you understand inflammation and its role in helping the body repair and regenerate after exercise, you'll know what type of recovery tool to use and when to use it. Here's the science.

When muscle fibres are damaged, inflammatory cells called neutrophils and macrophages move to the area and help break down and remove damaged tissue. Then a powerful hormone called insulin-like growth factor-1 instructs satellite cells to repair damaged muscle fibres and begin producing new ones. Inflammation is a critical healing process, and if you interfere with it, you can limit your physiological progress.

Anti-inflammation techniques like anti-inflammatory medicines (non-steroidal anti-inflammatories, or NSAIDS), cold baths that constrict blood vessels, and compression clothing are gaining popularity because they may reduce postworkout soreness and pain. But they also may slow your progress because they block or impair the inflammation process that signals the body to rebuild itself in response to the training stress. Your body needs the process of breaking down, experiencing inflammation, and making the repairs in order to develop and improve. That said, compression clothing and cold baths can be useful as you approach a race, say, to decrease pain and to blunt the inflammatory response when you are not in the development phase of your training. They can also be helpful if you are planning two workouts on the same day, or if you are planning on two hard training days back to back. This can be complicated, so work with your coach to determine when it's best for you to use, or not use, techniques that speed recovery from intense exercise.

Allow yourself adequate time after your workouts to regenerate. For light workouts that are pretty easy and not stressful, you won't need much time—8 to 12 hours is enough. The harder and more intense the workout, the longer you need for regeneration. Strength workouts that make you sore normally require about 48 hours to recover from. The same length of time holds for interval sessions where you're producing lots of lactic acid. Long cardio sessions that drain your glycogen stores require about 24 to 48 hours. Pure speed and sprint training sessions take 48 to 72 hours to recover from. Work with a coach or trainer to help you set up your weekly training schedule, or you can check out my book *Superbodies* for lots more info on this topic.

DR. GREG'S 1% TIP: EAT WATERMELON TO PREVENT POSTWORKOUT MUSCLE SORENESS

Having watermelon within the hour before exercise may reduce muscle soreness after exercise.[46] Watermelon is high in L-citrulline, which is thought to improve exercise performance because of its effects on synthesizing nitric oxide and increasing sugar transport in muscle. It has also been shown to be a potent antioxidant. And it may help remove lactic acid, potentially allowing for better performance and improved recovery. Interestingly, the form of L-citrulline found in watermelon appears to be more bioavailable than other forms. Watermelon may provide additional carbohydrate and hydration and might be a great pre-exercise snack for those who like something light before their workouts. Watermelon juice is an easily digestible carbohydrate to have right before or during exercise.

KEY #7: USE IT OR LOSE IT

THE REASON SHORTCUTS never work for the human body is that physiology is built based on natural principles that have evolved over millions of years. As such, we are designed to change and grow, for better or worse, depending on what sort of stimulus we put on the body. The greater the stimulus, the more the adaptation, so long as it is spread out over time. Short-term bursts of stimulus usually cause problems and make us injured or sick. Spread the same amount of signal over time and the body will get stronger and healthier.

A good analogy is planting a field to grow crops. If you plant all the seeds and then spend the first few days watering the fields non-stop, the fertilizer will wash away, the seeds will become exposed, and few if any plants will grow. If, on the other hand, you water the seeds just a little each day, then over a period of weeks and months you will have a flourishing field of plants (barring any devastations, such as poor seed or a plague of locusts). If a huge rainstorm occurs later in the summer, once the plants have been watered consistently over time, the fields will be able to handle the deluge—no problem.

The same concept applies to the human body. Often I'm asked what to eat the day of a race. My answer inevitably causes raised eyebrows. I tell people that it really doesn't matter. What does matter is what you ate in the 6 months leading up to the event. I'll bet on the athlete who eats well for 6 months over the athlete who has a great race-day plan but weak daily nutrition every time. My colleague Dr. John Berardi calls the idea that you need to eat particularly well on race day the "myth of game-day nutrition."

Eating well and exercising consistently lead to better body composition, healthier bones, stronger muscles, and a powerful immune system. Slowly but steadily, the body will change. You will grow new blood vessels. Your muscles will add proteins to their fibres. Your immune system will create white blood cells with more potent weapons to fight off disease. Consistency is the key.

The body does not maintain structures it does not use. Every tissue in your body requires energy to keep it going. Unless you use that structure—your muscles, your blood vessels, your bones, your brain—the body simply allows the structure to break down and dissolve. The key to long-term health and performance is therefore to stay active, consistently, forever.

As I've mentioned, one of the diseases we study in my lab is cystic fibrosis (CF), a genetic disease that gradually destroys lung tissue and plugs up the digestive tract. We discovered that CF also affects muscle, making it harder to exercise. Simply, CF is a disease that makes it progressively harder to breathe, digest food, and move. But despite these challenges, some CF patients are able to fight the disease, using exercise and nutrition to enhance the medical therapies that are the traditional treatments.

I've met many incredible young people at SickKids hospital during my research. One day, some research participants with a genetic defect that causes CF and its related symptoms came to our lab for their exercise testing. We learned that they were participating in soccer, lacrosse, and pretty much every other sport they could. They knew intuitively what our research ended up proving,[47] that increasing daily physical activity slowed the rate at which lung function declines. Over the years that they came to the hospital for testing, many of these young people managed to optimize their lung function despite the gradual progression of their disease.

Imagine what all of us could do if we followed their lead and took advantage of our ability to achieve better fitness, health, and performance by being consistent despite the challenges we're faced with in our lives.

If you need more inspiration, consider that a 35-year-old man with CF who was on the waiting list for a double lung transplant completed a 5 km walk with an oxygen tank strapped to his back. Or that 100-year-old Fauja Singh completed a marathon (he also holds eight running world records for distances ranging from 100 metres to 5 km), earning a spot in *Guinness World Records* as the world's oldest marathoner—after taking up running at the tender age of 88. Or consider the story of my buddy Ray Zahab, who was a two-pack-a-day smoker before he started running, eventually completing an 8,000 km run across the Sahara Desert (check out www.runthesahara.com). Or Ferg Hawke, who went from being out of shape and prediabetic to finishing second in the Badwater 135-mile running race through Death Valley.

Human potential is unlimited. Anything is possible! Moving more will help you achieve your dreams, whatever they are. But despite most of us being aware of the benefits of exercise, we still have a hard time fitting activity into our lives.

One of the reasons we put off exercise is that the benefits can seem far off. *Yes, exercise prevents cancer, but I don't have cancer right now. But I do have a test tomorrow and a deadline at work, so I don't have time to move.* We need to shift our focus, from the distant future to today. While writing this book, I made it a priority to exercise first thing in the morning by going to the local swimming pool and training with my friends for 75 minutes before starting the day of writing. The benefits of doing this were not in the future; they were immediate. I was happier. I had more energy. My concentration and focus were sharp and clear. The days that I trained were brilliant. The days I missed my swim practice were a struggle.

When we shift our focus to how movement can help us right now, today, it becomes so much easier to justify and rationalize incorporating exercise into our lives. The ultimate benefit is that we are able to achieve our dreams and do so on the foundation of being healthy.

4

EAT SMARTER

> The doctor of the future will no longer treat the human
> frame with drugs, but rather will cure and prevent disease
> with nutrition. —Thomas Edison

RECENTLY, I WENT on an expedition to the Thar Desert, in the northwest corner of India, with my good friend Ray Zahab and his organization impossible2Possible. Our journey through the desert took us into various towns and villages. One morning I went with our medical team to explore the local communities and I saw something extremely telling: two food stalls, side by side, that could not have captured a major cause of the world's health problems more clearly. At one stall was a man who had traditional local foods laid out, which included a lot of fresh vegetables and fruit. All fresh, healthy options that prevent disease. Right next to him was a stall selling bags of chips, chocolate bars, and sugary snacks. This stall was new, and the owner was doing a brisk business selling the foods that cause the grand epidemics.

Even though we were in a rural area far from North America, I saw that the causes of the diseases of the West were showing up there as well. In North America and Europe, people who are overweight or obese comprise up to 68% of the population; in the rural parts of the developing world, fewer people have chronic illnesses, but the numbers are climbing. And with this come other problems such as cancer, metabolic syndrome, and mental health challenges.

Despite the global scale of the challenge and the complexity of the problem, there are solutions available to us today that are powerful if applied consistently over time. Eating healthy, great-tasting food is possible—even necessary—and doing so will dramatically improve our lives. Let's set the stage for making that happen for you and for the rest of the world.

THE GLOBAL OBESITY EPIDEMIC

NEVER BEFORE IN the history of planet Earth have we had access to so much food. Many of us in the developed world can get food anytime we want—you can probably get something to eat within minutes. And you can often get any type of food you want. In any quantity you want. And we do.

Rates of obesity and overweight are skyrocketing around the globe. Obesity is known to cause heart disease, type 2 diabetes, and certain types of cancer. Obesity is also a cause of depression (and vice versa). It's frightening that in Canada and the United States in the early 1980s—only 30 years ago—people who were overweight or obese made up less than 20% of the population. Now that figure is about 58% in Canada and 68% in the United States.

Despite having almost unlimited access to food, we are not healthy. We eat way too many calories: many of the foods we eat are high in calories but very low in nutrients. And no matter how much of the high-calorie, low-nutrient foods you eat, you'll still feel depleted and hungry. Meaning *we are overfed and undernourished*.

Poor nutrition leads to obesity. My research team has shown that obesity damages muscle tissue,[1] which in turn causes exercise intolerance. If it is harder to exercise because your muscles are damaged, you'll become more physically inactive, leading to a greater risk of greater obesity. We end up in vicious circles that seem almost impossible to escape from.

There is hope, though. I love the practical approach suggested by my colleague Dr. Yoni Freedhoff:

WORDS OF WISDOM: DR. YONI FREEDHOFF, FOUNDER OF WEIGHTY MATTERS

Dr. Yoni Freedhoff is an obesity expert, family doctor, and professor at the University of Ottawa who also has a brilliant blog called Weighty Matters. Recently on my podcast he shared his inspiring insights on healthy eating and the approach we can take to eat smarter.

I think we have to approach weight like we do everything else in our lives, and that's with realism. It's weird. When it comes to every other area of our life, we've been taught—and we are pretty darn comfortable accepting—[that] our personal best efforts [are] great. Sporting analogies are really easy, and when people go out for their community races, other than Olympians, most of us aren't winning these races.

Our job is to go out, [to] have a good time, to do our best, and to be proud of the fact that that's what we did. With weight management, it would seem that society has been taught that their best isn't good enough unless it gets them to the winner's circle. That they have to lose everything and be perfect.

I think that has really crippled a lot of people's weight-management efforts, because they feel that sub-total losses aren't a victory, and really they are. That's like finishing the marathon but not placing first. Who cares? The whole point was to enjoy the run in the first place.

ALTHOUGH OUR ATTEMPTS at combating obesity with diets have failed miserably, there *are* approaches that have been proven to work, if you can stick with them. For example, through a regulatory pathway in the brain, vegetables may induce satiety and help reduce the risk of obesity.[2] By making small changes in your approach to eating, you can get tremendous results, especially if you adopt the attitude proposed by Dr. Freedhoff.

DR. GREG'S 1% TIP: FOOD GUIDES ARE NOT CREATED EQUAL

Our government-issued food guide is not only outdated but is influenced by the food industry to such an extent that the recommendations do not necessarily enhance our health—though they do keep people employed. Research suggests that dairy is unhealthy for humans, yet it forms a major part of food guides. We know that added simple sugars found in fruit juice are unhealthy, yet foods high in sugars remain a key part of the nutrition guidelines we are told to follow.

Another problem is that the food guides consider all protein sources (e.g., red meat, poultry, beans) equally healthful, despite processed meat consumption being associated with increased risk of cancer and beans having been shown to improve health, body composition, and resistance to disease.

The first step to getting healthy and performing at your best is to go beyond Canada's Food Guide and the USDA MyPyramid and build a nutrition plan that enhances your health using the keys in this chapter. If you're looking for a food guide that is based on research, check out the Harvard Medical School's Healthy Eating Plate or Brazil's healthy eating recommendations (more on this in the Nutrition and Obesity section).

NUTRITION AND YOUR HEALTH

WHEN I FIRST started doing research at SickKids hospital, I met Dr. Ingrid Tein, one of the world's most prolific researchers in the field of neurology. She treats and conducts research on some of the most debilitating diseases that affect the nervous system and muscles. Her patients are severely affected by these conditions and can become so weak that they are confined to wheelchairs and may even have trouble holding their heads up. They often die at a young age.

Dr. Tein has adopted a revolutionary approach to treating disease. She works in her lab to determine exactly how the disease causes exercise intolerance—or problems in the muscle at the most fundamental level. In many cases, she has identified the exact protein or energy pathway deep inside the muscle or nerve that is not working properly. Then, in addition to pharmaceutical therapy, she determines how to treat these problems with specific activities and vitamins or other nutrients. For example, she uses vitamin C to help treat her patients with genetic muscle diseases. She has also worked with patients to develop exercise routines that bypass the energy systems that are not working. For example, she has found that low-intensity aerobic exercise helps children with McArdle's disease, in which the anaerobic system (the system that breaks down sugars to produce energy quickly for bursts of physical activity like running upstairs or chasing a bus) does not work well.

What Dr. Tein has discovered is that it is possible to treat diseases with nutrition and exercise. This was a total game-changing idea for me early in my career—and I've been pursuing this concept ever since. Other researchers are rapidly discovering how eating better can prevent and treat many chronic diseases.

I mention this because I want you to be aware of the power that optimal nutrition can have in your life and how directly nutrition impacts your health. Let's look at specific examples.

NUTRITION AND CANCER

RESEARCH HAS SHOWN that nutrition can impact people with various types of cancer. Yet the most powerful data relate to how we can use nutrition to prevent cancer altogether.

Foods, compounds, and nutrients have been found to be protective against lung, breast, pancreatic, and skin cancers, among others.[3] Increased consumption of fruit and vegetables has been shown to prevent many cancers because they contain beneficial antioxidants, fibre, minerals, and phytochemicals. Protective foods include citrus fruits, berries, vegetables, whole grains, and foods that are high in flavonoids. Using spices like turmeric (curcumin) can also help prevent various cancers. And data show that there is a small protective effect of drinking green and black tea.[4]

Unfortunately, data also show that certain foods can increase our risk of various types of cancer. For instance, there are links between red and processed meat consumption and risk of cancer, especially if the meat is cooked at very high temperatures.[5] My family has shifted to a mostly plant-based diet for health and ecological reasons, but we will very occasionally have organic, grass-fed red meat, since red meat does contain important nutrients, such as niacin, iron, and zinc, and vitamins A, B1, and B12. My recommendations are to completely avoid processed meats and to eat organic and grass-fed red meat occasionally.

Admittedly, the relationship between nutrition and cancer can be confusing, with some foods increasing your risk and others decreasing it. For example, when it comes to breast cancer, obesity and alcohol can increase your risk. Trans fats, mainly a product of the industrial partial hydrogenation of vegetable oils, have been linked to an increased risk of breast cancer, as have simple carbohydrates like sugar.[6] On the other hand, complex carbohydrates that are high in fibre (whole grains and beans) decrease risk.[7] Further, eating foods high in omega-3 fatty acids (walnuts, sardines, salmon, tofu, shrimp, Brussels sprouts, and cauliflower) can reduce risk by about 14%. Other protective foods include wild cold-water fish (such as wild salmon, sardines, and anchovies), vegetables, and olive oil.[8]

The foods that are protective against cancer seem to be consistent across many types of the disease. Pancreatic cancer is the fourth leading form of cancer, with a 5-year survival rate of less than 5%. Once again, as with breast cancer, foods such as whole grains, sources of folate (fruits, peas, beans, nuts, eggs), foods high in flavonoids (berries, tree fruits, nuts, beans, vegetables, tea, spices), and the spice curcumin seem to play a role in decreasing risk of pancreatic cancer.[9]

Skin cancer (melanoma) is one of the deadliest forms of cancer. Fortunately, eating natural compounds found in healthy foods can help prevent it.[10] Foods that have been shown to be protective against melanoma are fruits and vegetables, tea, and wild cold-water fish. Grapes and grape seed oils are also beneficial. Moderate intake of the nutrient selenium (found in sunflower seeds, fish, and shellfish) may be helpful, though high doses appear to increase risk, so consume this nutrient in moderation. Resveratrol (a compound found in red wine), rosmarinic acid (a compound found in many plants), and lycopene (found in red fruits and vegetables like tomatoes) all have been shown to help prevent melanoma. Of course, the best way to prevent skin cancer is to avoid too much exposure to ultraviolet sun radiation, but having a healthy diet that includes these foods can give you added defence.

Colorectal cancer kills about 600,000 people each year globally. If you drink coffee, you're in luck. Even consuming a moderate amount of coffee decreases your risk of colorectal and liver cancer. Eating red meat and especially processed meat appears to increase risk, while, once again, fish consumption appears to decrease risk.[11] Supplemental calcium, vegetables, dietary fibre, and selenium also decrease risk.[12]

The message here is that by eating specific foods, you can either increase or decrease your risk of getting cancer. The Mediterranean diet has been shown to be protective against many forms of cancer, making it a great template on which to build your nutrition plan. And if you want to decrease your risk of getting cancer, decrease how much of the unhealthy foods you eat—grilled red meats, foods high in trans fats, and foods that are high in simple sugary carbohydrates—and up your intake of cancer-fighting foods and compounds.

> ### DR. GREG'S 1% TIP: EAT TO BEAT CANCER
> Want to eat to beat cancer? Check out the comprehensive list of cancer-fighting foods provided as part of Eat to Beat Cancer, a global campaign that is the brainchild of the non-profit Angiogenesis Foundation. You'll find it at www.eattobeat.org/food.

NUTRITION AND INFLAMMATION

IF MOST OF our physical afflictions that then manifest themselves in our brains and mental health have one thing in common, it's inflammation.

As I mentioned in chapters 2 and 3, inflammation is a powerful process that helps repair and regenerate the tissues in our bodies and brains, but if we don't eat well, are inactive, and sleep poorly, low-grade inflammation develops and inflammation happens consistently over a long period. This is damaging to our health and destroys our ability to perform and reach our potential.

Some researchers suggest that chronic inflammation may be the cause of most of the chronic diseases affecting us.

Neuroinflammation—inflammation in the brain—is believed to play a role in the degenerative cascade leading to Alzheimer's disease and other dementias.[13] People with dementia who show more blood markers of inflammation tend to have more pronounced cognitive deficits than those with lower levels of inflammation.[14] Simply put, chronic inflammation in the brain may be related to the development of Alzheimer's disease and dementia, and the more inflammation that is in the brain, the worse the impact of those diseases.

For better or for worse, eating seems to have a powerful effect on inflammation in our bodies and brains—which means we can impact and control chronic inflammation if we eat smart. Controlling inflammation in our bodies comes down to a few key principles. The first is to address the shift in the consumption ratio between two nutrients that has occurred in the Western diet over the last few decades: the amount of omega-6 fatty acids that we now consume in relation to omega-3 fatty acids. A healthy ratio is about two omega-6 to one omega-3—so 2:1. The typical North American diet now has anywhere from 20 to 60 times more omega-6s than omega-3s. This change in the ratio has caused a shift toward a more inflammatory state of the body, as well as of the brain.[15] Systemic inflammation can lead to increases in many brain diseases and impairments related to aging.

Dietary factors that cause inflammation include high intake of saturated fats, trans fats found in processed foods (e.g., commercial oils, margarine, salad dressings, packaged foods), and omega-6 fatty acids relative to omega-3s (e.g., in grain-fed meats versus organic, grass-fed), as well as low intake of omega-3 fats from fish, low vitamin D status, and a high-sugar/low-fibre diet.[16] Margarine and vegetable oils such as sunflower, soybean, corn, palm, and canola are common omega-6 oil sources in the Western diet.[17]

The good news is that dietary changes such as eating foods high in omega-3s and adding the spice turmeric to foods have been shown to reduce inflammation and, at least in rats and mice, improve the growth of nerves in the brain.[18] Supplementing with omega-3 has been shown to improve cognitive status in younger adults and maintain cognitive function in older adults. Foods such as flaxseed oil, nuts, and green leafy vegetables are rich in omega-3.[19]

Extra-virgin olive oil, which contains mostly monounsaturated fatty acids, or MUFAs, has been shown to have anti-inflammatory effects. One large study showed that supplementing with extra-virgin olive oil led to improvements in both verbal fluency and episodic memory.[20] Olive oil is also rich in polyphenolic compounds (chemicals that protect cells in the body), which have been shown to have anti-inflammatory and antioxidant effects.

Almonds are a good source of MUFAs and also contain an array of phenolic compounds and flavonoids, as well as vitamin E, riboflavin, magnesium, and manganese.[21] Human studies have linked almond consumption to improved markers of oxidative stress and inflammation.[22] Almonds are an excellent addition to your diet in support of your brain health. Avocados are another excellent food source of monounsaturated fatty acids, as well as of a substantial amount of omega-3 polyunsaturated fatty acids.

So, in the simplest terms, by eating an anti-inflammatory diet high in antioxidant compounds, along with foods high in omega-3s, we can give ourselves the best chance of lowering the chronic systemic inflammation in our bodies and minimizing cognitive decline as we age. If we add exercise to the mix, especially aerobic exercise like walking, jogging, and running, we can amplify the benefits. Since our options for treating Alzheimer's and other dementias through pharmaceuticals are so limited, our best bet is to do our best to prevent these conditions from occurring in the first place. We have the knowledge to do that.

DR. GREG'S 1% TIP: PROTECT YOURSELF AGAINST ALZHEIMER'S DISEASE

A high intake of polyunsaturated fat appears to be protective against the development of Alzheimer's disease and other dementias, and this is especially true for omega-3 fatty acids. Omega-3 fatty acids help protect the structural integrity of the brain throughout our lives.[23] Polyunsaturated fatty acids may be involved in the maintenance of cognitive function and have a preventative effect toward dementia through both their antithrombotic (reducing blood clot formation) and anti-inflammatory effects. They are also shown to have specific effects on neural functions. The omega-3 fatty acid DHA (docosahexaenoic acid) in particular may modify genes that regulate functions related to cognitive health, including neurogenesis (growth of new nerves and neurons) and neuronal function. It can affect neuron growth in the hippocampus, a major memory centre in the brain.[24]

NUTRITION AND CARDIOVASCULAR DISEASE

NUTRITION HAS A potent effect on the health of your cardio-vascular system—your heart and the blood vessels (arteries, veins, capillaries) that take blood to and from your organs and tissues. With obesity, type 2 diabetes, and metabolic syndrome, the cardiovascular system can become very badly damaged, and once again, chronic inflammation plays a role in that.

Chronic inflammation damages the cells that make up the endothelia, the lining of the blood vessels, lymphatic vessels, and other tissues in the body, causing the blood vessels to become stiff. This is a concern because vessels need to adjust their size so that they can change the amount of blood delivered to tissues, based on the demand the tissues have for oxygen and nutrients. Further, problems with endothelial cells lead to the production of free radicals—molecules that circulate around the body and cause damage to other cells. Think of this process like rust building up on metal or the browning of apple flesh when exposed to air. This is called oxidative stress. With chronic inflammation comes oxidative stress in our blood vessels.

Nutrients that help alleviate oxidative stress can help improve the health of the cardiovascular system (among other systems). One of the most powerful antioxidant nutrients is lycopene. Lycopene is found in tomatoes and other red fruits and vegetables, as well as in watermelon, papayas, and brown beans. Eating lycopene also has the benefit of improving your cholesterol profile. Diets high in lycopene have been shown to lower the risk of heart disease, as well as prostate, lung, and stomach cancer. Heating up lycopene foods increases their bioavailability, and fats are required for lycopene to be absorbed, so pair your lycopene-rich sources with a healthy oil (e.g., sun-dried tomatoes with olive oil). Other antioxidant foods include many fruits and vegetables, especially those high in carotenoids (like carrots and sweet potatoes), nuts, olive oil, cocoa, and green tea.

Nuts and seeds also help prevent cardiovascular disease. These savoury snacks are rich in unsaturated fatty acids, antioxidant vitamins (especially vitamin E), dietary fibre, and plant proteins. Frequent nut and seed consumption has been shown to combat inflammation by improving total antioxidant activity, improving insulin sensitivity, and modifying cellular signalling. Their consumption has been associated with reduced risk of cardiovascular disease and type 2 diabetes. As a bonus, they are highly satiating, which generally translates to less snacking on sugary, fatty junk foods. Top picks include chia seeds, hemp hearts, Brazil nuts, almonds, and pumpkin seeds.

DR. GREG'S 1% TIP: CHOOSE SAFE, SUSTAINABLE, AND HEALTHY FISH

Eating farmed fish is not a good option, as farmed fish carries both health and environmental risks. Instead, choose fish that is organic, wild, and sustainable. For a list of sustainable seafood, check out Monterey Bay's website at www.seafoodwatch.org. The Safina Center also has an updated list of good seafood choices at http://safinacenter.org/seafoods.

NUTRITION AND OBESITY

HERE'S THE THING about the obesity epidemic. It's happening, it's getting worse, and it's caused primarily by two factors:

our poor nutrition and our lack of physical activity. People say it's a complicated issue that is caused by many things—and it is—but in the end it comes down to those two big factors.

To make things worse, some companies are trying to increase the confusion level. Frighteningly, as was reported in the *New York Times*, makers of sugar-laden beverages have funded researchers who promote the argument that the solution to the obesity epidemic lies in getting more exercise, not in cutting calories.[25] Cutting calories would mean, for many, drinking fewer sugar-laden beverages, which would negatively affect profit margins.

But enough with the negativity. If you can overcome the confusion about what is actually good for you, which foods can improve your health, and how to eat to perform better, you can take action and create a diet that will propel you to new heights. So what can you do? The answers are relatively simple. If you follow the seven keys to healthy eating I propose later in this chapter, you'll be well on your way. But first let's look at some specifics relating to obesity that can be helpful.

NUTRIENT-DENSE FOODS VERSUS ENERGY-DENSE FOODS

THE FIRST STEP is to follow the law of thermodynamics. Your energy intake (food and beverage intake) and your energy expenditure (physical activity and metabolism) determine how much energy your body stores or uses. Ideally, you eat the amount of food that gives you the energy needed to fuel your metabolism and to be as active as you want to be. If you eat more energy than you expend—which is so easy to do, given that we sit too much in cars, on couches, and at desks—you will store the excess energy intake largely as adipose (fat) tissue. Our bodies are very good at this—it's a brilliant survival mechanism that evolution has perfected. So if you want to lose body fat, you must consume less energy than you are using. (But if your energy intake is *too* low, you will get tired or sick.)

That's it. Eat less and move more. It's simple. Or is it? The way we measure energy is by calories. But is a calorie always a calorie? The answer is yes. Energy is energy; it's pure physics. Where some people go wrong is in thinking that because energy is energy, the energy from carbohydrates, fats, and proteins is all equivalent, even when it comes to fat storage and fat loss. And that is not the case. The differences are not owing to the energy itself but to the impact that the different macronutrients have on our metabolism. Carbohydrate, fat, and protein molecules are different, and they have different effects in the body as they are broken down and used to power our metabolism. The most important relationship between the foods we eat and a powerful metabolic response that relates to obesity is the impact that eating simple carbohydrates has on the insulin response and how that stimulates the body to store excess energy as fat.

One thing that happens when we eat foods high in simple sugars—soda pop, white bread, white rice, and the like—or added sugars in foods such as chocolate milk is that when the foods are digested, the sugar levels in our blood go up. That sugar is taken to muscles and the brain, where it could be used for energy, should the need arise. When our blood sugar levels go up, the pancreas responds by releasing the hormone insulin into the blood, which circulates around the body and helps cells absorb the sugars. The end result is a short-term spike in sugar levels, followed by lower blood sugar levels. This can leave us feeling hungry and craving foods with lots more energy—hence the desire for foods high in fat, sugar, and salt—the comfort foods. This is a situation that often results in overeating, despite eating foods with lots of energy.

The opposite occurs when we eat foods relatively high in fibre. These foods take longer to digest, provoke less of an insulin response, and leave us feeling satiated, with nice, even energy levels. This is also true with healthy fats, which is counterintuitive, given what we have historically been told.

The challenge is to recognize this pattern and to remember that our health depends on eating nutrient-dense foods, not energy-dense foods. Here are a few ways to eat nutrient-dense, rather than calorie-dense, low-nutrient foods:

- Eat vegetables at each meal and have cut-up vegetables available for snacks at all times.
- Have a healthy protein with each meal.
- Make sure your diet contains healthy fats, but not too little or too much.
- Stick to complex carbohydrates that are high in fibre, like sweet potatoes, quinoa, berries, legumes, seeds, nuts, and long-grain wild rice.
- Eat fruit but avoid drinking juice, which is basically just flavoured sugar water.
- Avoid high-sugar foods like syrups, candy, junk foods, cereal, fruit juice, pop, foods with added sugars, and refined carbohydrates, including most breads.
- Avoid processed foods, which, because of their high sugar content, can trigger the insulin response.
- Another danger point when it comes to highly processed foods and foods high in added sugar is that they are often

devoid of or lacking in vitamins, minerals, and phyto-nutrients and are high in trans fats. So although we might be eating foods that are high in energy, our actual micro-nutrient intake is low. As a result, we can be overfed and undernourished and experience food cravings, and the cycle of overeating continues. So, again, focus on nutrient density, not energy density.

I've spoken about this approach to healthy eating at many events, and every time I make the argument for nutrients over energy, I get comments from some audience members about how expensive it is to eat healthy foods and how eating the way I suggest is just not practical. I understand this concern, but I don't agree with the ideas behind it.

It is possible to eat healthy foods on a tight budget. It does require more time to prepare fresh foods, and although organic produce may not be in your budget, local in-season vegetables will be. And beans, brown or wild rice, and legumes can all be bought in bulk for reasonable prices. The cost comes in terms of time required to prepare the food. But I would argue that the cost of eating nutrient-deficient foods is much higher, both in terms of dollars and health—fatigue, poor sleep, heart disease, diabetes, cancer, and mental illness. Using the excuse that eating healthy is not practical is only going to hurt you in the long run. You can spend some time now eating better, or you can spend time later on disability leave because you're so sick you can't function.

DR. GREG'S 1% TIP: YOU CAN EAT VEGAN ON $25
Check out the video *Vegan on $25* by author and healthy-eating advocate Rich Roll on how to shop for fruits and

vegetables with only $25. You can find it at https://youtu. be/f1qPgZFN24k.

RECENTLY, THE BRAZILIAN Ministry of Health did something very interesting. It considered the fact that overweight and obesity rates were skyrocketing in Brazil, a developing nation with many people who have significant socioeconomic challenges. It recognized that, much like Canada and the United States, the food guide was not working and that new recommendations were needed. So it did something revolutionary: it created new recommendations based on healthy eating habits.[26] It suggested that people eat real foods, not processed, packaged foods. It asked people to eat regularly and carefully by eating mindfully and slowly, ideally with friends and family. It asked people to develop their cooking skills and to plan ahead to make eating an important part of life. Finally, and perhaps most importantly, it told people to be skeptical of food advertising and marketing. These are principles the whole world should adopt.

HEALTHY FATS

THE NEXT ISSUE to tackle when it comes to obesity is fat. For decades we have been told that fat is the enemy and that saturated fats are especially bad. The latest research helps clarify this notion, which is too simplistic and has resulted in a surge of high-sugar foods that have contributed to the obesity epidemic. I address this in detail in Key #5: Eat Healthy Fats, later in this chapter. Here's my take on the issue. Fats are energy dense, with 10 calories per gram—versus the 4 calories per gram found in carbohydrates and proteins. This means that eating foods high in fats will result in your consuming a large amount of energy. So be careful to control your fat intake if you want to improve your body composition.

Having said that, there are healthy fats you can add to your diet to improve your health. Olive oil, cold-water wild fatty fish, nuts, seeds, avocados, and coconuts all contain fats with loads of health benefits. Unhealthy fats like foods with lots of trans fats, such as commercially fried foods and commercial baked goods made with shortenings, are definitely foods to be avoided, both for weight control and for your health. The takeaway here is not that you should be afraid of fats and of adding healthy fats to your diet but that you should avoid unhealthy fats that can damage your health and metabolism.

THE AGGREGATE OF 1% GAINS

AND FINALLY, KEEP in mind the aggregate of 1% gains that I explained in the introduction. Apply the principle of 1% gains to nutrition and you can make powerful improvements to your health. Simply removing 20 calories a day from your diet (about 1% fewer calories per day) will, over 1 year, help you lose about 2 pounds. If you do that over the next 10 years, you'll lose 20 pounds and end up in a very different life. Examples of small nutritional changes that add up to big gains are not putting sugar in your morning coffee, replacing sugar-laden salad dressings with oil and vinegar, and replacing the sauces you put on your food with spices. The easiest way to make this change is to not eat processed foods, which are often loaded with extra calories, trans fats, and added sugars while being devoid of vitamins and minerals. I discuss how to use the health = nutrients/calories concept in Key #3: Consume More Nutrients, Fewer Calories.

DR. GREG'S 1% TIP: SUGARY FOODS CAN MAKE YOU FEEL HUNGRIER

Eating foods that are high on the glycemic index (a scale that ranks foods from 1 to 100 based on their effect on blood sugar levels), such as refined bread products and snack foods filled with added sugar, will cause higher activity in brain areas related to food intake and reward and craving. Reducing your consumption of high-GI carbohydrates, especially highly processed grains, potatoes, and concentrated sugars, may help reduce overeating.[27]

NUTRITION AND MENTAL HEALTH

THE IDEA THAT the foods we eat can cause mental illness and also prevent and even treat mental illness, resulting in better mental health, is a powerful one. Think about it for a moment. Do you feel different when you eat different types of foods? I certainly do. I've noticed that I'm clear-headed after eating lean protein and vegetables, and I definitely noticed that my thinking was cloudy and that I struggled mentally when I ate baked goods from my local coffee shop (something I no longer do).

The research is now backing up my experiences, clearly showing that what we eat can significantly affect the brain and mental health, for better or for worse. More specifically, changing your diet can have a dramatic effect on mental health conditions like anxiety and depression. Many factors contribute to depression and anxiety, and several of them are uncontrollable, including life stressors, genes, and one's environment. But your diet is an important factor that, for the most part, can be controlled and that can have a significant impact on your mental health without some of the side effects that come with traditional pharmaceutical treat-ments.[28] Green tea, dark chocolate, B vitamins, and omega-3 fatty acids have all been shown to alleviate symptoms of depression. Let's explore each of these in more detail.

Many of the phytochemical compounds in green tea have antioxidant effects,[29] and it is likely that this contributes to the antidepressant effects of the tea. It has also been shown that the polyphenolic compounds in green tea affect the connection between the brain and the hypothalamic–pituitary–adrenal axis (the HPA axis). The HPA axis is the body's stress-control system, and the way in which green tea interacts with the HPA axis may help prevent and alleviate the symptoms of depression.[30]

Another tasty food that has been studied for depression symptom relief is chocolate. Cocoa polyphenols have been demonstrated to have positive effects on mood in humans.[31] More studies on this are needed, but so far, the acute effects of cocoa on mood are promising. Keep in mind that when research-ers suggest that chocolate may be beneficial, they mean dark chocolate with at least 70% cocoa, not milk chocolate. I keep a bar of dark chocolate in my desk and often have a small square after lunch.

Omega-3 fatty acids have a significant impact on neuroin-flammation and brain health. The omega-3 fatty acids eicos-apentaenoic acid (EPA) and docosahexaenoic acid (DHA) are present throughout the brain in lipids and have both structural and physiological roles in the brain. They also influence the neu-rotransmitters dopamine and serotonin, which can impact your ability to concentrate, and affect feelings and behaviours.[32] Low intakes and levels of omega-3 fatty acids have been associated with the onset of depression.[33] So consider eating more cold-water wild fatty fish, ground flaxseeds, and avocados to give yourself the best chance of having good mental health.

The B vitamins also appear to play a role in determining the risk of depression. Studies show that lower levels of B vitamins are associated with an increased risk of developing depression.[34] Folate, B12, and B6 deficiencies and high homocysteine levels appear to be especially important when it comes to modulating our risk for and symptoms of depression.[35] Folate especially has garnered a significant amount of attention. Folate and B12 are important in turning homocysteine into methionine, an important amino acid, but also in the synthesis of S-adenosylmethionine, a compound that appears to play an important role in the synthesis of neurotransmitters in the brain, including serotonin, dopamine, and epinephrine.[36] Lack of folate can also impair the formation of myelin, which increases speed of signal transmission between nerves in the brain.[37] Myelin is a fatty substance that surrounds the axons that branch between nerves. These B vitamins may be essential for maintaining levels of these neurotransmitters and therefore helping prevent depression-like symptoms. B vitamins are present in a wide array of foods, including organic poultry, seafood, bananas, and green leafy vegetables.

DR. GREG'S 1% TIP: USE THE NEW BRAIN FOOD SCALE
Scientists have developed a scale that rates foods based on their impact on symptoms of depression.[38] The research was presented at the American Psychiatric Association's 2016 annual meeting. To develop the scale, researchers led by Dr. Drew Ramsey, an assistant clinical professor of psychiatry at Columbia University, explored the impact of

foods and nutrients on the brain and compiled a list of brain-essential nutrients. They found that omega-3 fatty acids, magnesium, calcium, fibre, and vitamins B1, B9, B12, D, and E were essential for brain health.

The researchers hypothesize that these nutrients improve brain function and health by improving the structural integrity of the membranes of nerve cells (omega-3 fatty acids are known to do this), and through various anti-inflammatory effects.

Foods high in these nutrients include green leafy vegetables, organ meats, game meats, nuts, bivalve shellfish (clams, mussels, and oysters), mollusks (octopus, squid, and snails), and cold-water fatty fish (salmon and sardines). If you are eating meat, I recommend organic, grass-fed meat, and if you're eating fish, it is critical to avoid farmed fish, which has both health and environmental risks. Since most Atlantic salmon is farmed, I suggest wild salmon from the Pacific. Other plants that appear to be helpful for the brain are mustard greens, spinach, bell peppers, and any veggie that contains lycopene (like tomatoes) and carotenoids (like carrots).

EAT SMARTER TO PERFORM BETTER

IN THE PAST when I did presentations on nutrition and health, people politely listened, but I could tell that they were not super interested and that many had an "I've heard this so many times before" attitude. So I changed things up. I began to talk about how nutrition can help us perform better. My next talk was at a high school, so I made reference to foods that could help students do better on exams. Everyone was taking notes and asking questions. I tried it again at a business event, where I was talking about how to eat to concentrate better in the afternoon. Once again, people paid attention and later emailed me, asking for my nutrition protocols. The best part about all this was that I was talking about the same foods I had discussed in the healthy-eating talk. Yet focusing on performance made all the difference in how the information was received.

The takeaway is that we need to link eating smarter to what we care about. So what do you care about most? What motivates you to get out of bed in the morning and take on the world? Answer that, and then eat smarter to help you do that better. Food helps us perform better at sports, academics, business, drama, and music. Eating smarter is how we can experience exponential growth in our lives. To help you make this a reality, let's explore how eating smarter can help you amplify all the great things in your life.

EAT SMARTER TO SLEEP SOUNDLY

YOU KNOW NOW that sleep is a time when physiological processes are taking place that heal, repair, and regenerate your body and brain. A growing body of evidence shows that the foods you eat can improve your sleep. So how can you use food to optimize your sleep? The key lies in the science of neurotransmitters. Neurotransmitters are microscopic molecules that carry signals between nerves and muscles. Simply put, they are chemical messengers that carry information around the brain and body. Numerous neurotransmitters, including serotonin (5-HT), gamma-aminobutyric acid (GABA), orexin, melanin-concentrating hormone, cholinergic, galanin, noradrenaline, and histamine, have been associated with the sleep–wake cycle.[39] You don't need to know all those names, but what you should know is that the foods you eat influence the type and amount of neurotransmitters manufactured in your brain and nerve cells. That's the scientific foundation for how and why we need to eat smarter to sleep soundly.

High-protein/low-carbohydrate meals increase the duration of deep, slow-wave sleep and decrease the number of times you wake up during the night.[40] So if you need to improve your overall sleep quality, try eating meals with more protein.

It's also key to eat foods containing the compounds that nerve cells use to create serotonin and melatonin, two neurotransmitters that help improve sleep quality. The ultimate goal is to increase the amount of available tryptophan, which is taken into the nervous system (brain, spinal cord, and nerves) and used to create serotonin and melatonin.[41] Tryptophan is a small amino acid (amino acids are the components that make up proteins), so high-protein meals will result in lots of available proteins and amino acids in the blood.

A few different combinations of foods can influence tryptophan uptake into brain cells. Larger proteins are taken up preferentially (first) by brain cells. So high-protein meals right before bed are not the best for helping you fall asleep quickly and sleep deeply. Adding carbohydrates to your pre-bed snack or meal changes the game, because when carbohydrates enter the blood, they stimulate the release of the hormone insulin from the pancreas, and insulin increases the uptake of large amino acids into skeletal muscle.

This has two benefits. If you are exercising during the day (and you should be, as you read in chapter 3), moving amino acids into the muscle will help repair the muscle while you sleep—and this makes it easier for tryptophan to move from the blood into the brain and be taken up by the brain nerve cells, where it can be used to manufacture serotonin and melatonin.

Making sense so far? Great. Now on to the nutrition recommendations. Here are specific strategies and tactics that will help you eat smarter to improve your sleep:

- Eat foods that are high in tryptophan, in combination with a small amount of healthy carbohydrate. Foods that are high in tryptophan include nuts, seeds, tofu, chicken, red meat, turkey, fish, oats, beans, lentils, and eggs. These can be paired with carbohydrate sources like figs, air-popped popcorn, vegetables, legumes, and sweet potatoes. Of course, be careful to keep your pre-bed snack small and low in calories if you are trying to optimize your body composition (less fat, more muscle).

- High-fat foods increase available free fatty acids (the components that make up fats). Free fatty acids have the bonus effect of releasing tryptophan that is bound to another compound called albumin. The end result is that more tryptophan is available for transport into the brain from the blood. Healthy fats include nuts, seeds, avocado, coconut, and cold-water wild fish. Be careful to limit fat intake if you are concerned about your body composition, as fats are very calorie dense.

- Meal timing appears to impact sleep quality. Research has shown that eating 4 hours before bedtime was better for shortening the time it took to fall asleep than eating 1 hour before bed.[42] So a healthy dinner is a better option to focus on than a healthy pre-bed snack.

- Tart cherries, melatonin, and valerian (an herb that binds to GABA receptors) have been shown to improve different aspects of sleep, though the research is far from conclusive.[43] Try them and see if they help. If you are going to use valerian root or a melatonin supplement, make sure to consult with a health professional such as a naturopathic doctor or registered dietitian because they can have serious side effects when misused.

The bottom line is that you can improve your sleep quality by eating smarter. Experiment with different options and see what works for you.

EAT SMARTER TO MOVE MORE

SPORTS NUTRITION IS one of the most debated and contested fields in science right now. With the traditional high-carbohydrate approach under siege from the low-carb/high-fat proponents, there has never been more confusion. I think that's a good thing, because sports nutrition needs an overhaul; the traditional approaches have resulted in several products and recommendations that have been damaging to health (such as sports drinks and chocolate milk), rather than helping people perform better.

My approach is based on the principle that high performance is possible only if we are as healthy as possible. I've broken down my approach into three steps, based on what you can eat before, during, and after your workouts to perform great in your movement practice, and to improve your health at the same time. It's a simple approach that works if you stick to it over the long term.

EAT SMART BEFORE EXERCISE

THE MOST IMPORTANT thing you need to do before your workout is provide your blood, organs, muscles, and brain with the fuels you will need to perform. To do your workout at your best, you will need amino acids (protein), glucose (carbohydrate), healthy fats, and a supply of water. Most people most of the time can get everything they need from a well-balanced reasonable meal about 2 hours before the workout.

Protein will help preserve your muscle mass and ensure there are amino acids in your blood when your muscles need them. Carbohydrates will help fuel your muscles and preserve your muscle and liver glycogen stores on which your body will draw during the workout. I recommend eating real foods and not sports drinks and gels. If you are trying to lose fat and increase your muscle mass, you can emphasize protein more than carbohydrates and move the bulk of your carbohydrates to after your workout. Healthy fats help provide your body with vitamins and minerals and can help manage the inflammatory process.

Most people are dehydrated; drinking water before your workout will help you perform at your best during practice. I fill up my water bottle with cold water and the juice from half a fresh lemon or lime, along with a small pinch of sea salt. If I feel like I need an energy boost, I'll add a teaspoon of raw organic honey. If I have a strength training workout, I'll add branched-chain amino acids.

For morning workouts, if you are into performing at a higher level or you have a hard workout planned, it is a good idea to have a pre-exercise snack to make sure you have enough nutrients in your blood and muscles to fuel your activities.

Your preworkout snack should be no more than a cup in volume, eaten 30 to 60 minutes before your workout. Because starches/carbohydrates are easily turned into sugar in the blood, this snack should be carbohydrate-centred. Protein, fat, and fibre take a long time to digest, making them less than ideal just before a workout. (Indigestion will remind you of this—try having fish and chips just before your boot-camp class!) Ideally, the starchy snack will be easily digested and convenient. Examples are fresh fruit, oatmeal, mashed sweet potatoes, rice crackers with organic nut butter, carrots and hummus, quinoa salad, and squash. A pre-workout smoothie is an excellent option, as the blender breaks down the foods, making them easier to digest and absorb.

EAT SMART DURING EXERCISE

EATING SMART DURING exercise is quite straightforward. The number one goal is to stay hydrated. The secondary goal is to provide your muscles with (1) amino acids if you are doing workouts that cause muscle breakdown—like sprinting, CrossFit, or other strength training or (2) carbohydrates if you are doing endurance exercise lasting longer than 90 minutes.

For the vast majority of us, we simply need to stay hydrated, and the best way to do that is to sip water during your workout or practice. Listen to your body and follow your thirst. I try to start my workouts with a few mouthfuls of water and then sip consistently during practice. I use sports drinks only if I'm doing a very hard workout lasting longer than 90 minutes, which for me is a bike ride. I think that for almost everybody, sports drinks are a bad idea.

Did you know that sports drinks have a lot of added sugar— usually the same amount as or more than a can of pop? The difference between the two is that sports drinks are designed to provide us with the right amount of electrolytes to make up for those we lose while sweating during a hard workout. Plus, the lack of carbonation makes sports drinks easy to guzzle. Even given the electrolytes, the added sugars are unnecessary for most people. The exception is elite athletes or people exercising for longer than 90 minutes at a time. Another time when a sports drink might be a good idea is if you're exercising outdoors on a very hot day and you're sweating a lot. And to clarify, we don't actually need a sports drink until we've been exercising for at least 60 minutes at high intensity. If you take an hour-long walk or cycle to work for 30 minutes or do a quick 40-minute workout after you put the kids to bed, avoid rehydrating with a sports drink. Just drink water.

A huge health problem is caused by consuming sports drinks at the wrong time. I see kids drinking them on the bus daily and adults using them during short workouts and even on walks. Sports drinks are not healthy. They have a particular function (providing sugar and electrolytes during long, hard workouts) and may be useful at times, but they should not be a go-to beverage for most people.

I recommend trying healthier options instead of commercial sports drinks. Coconut water, for example, is considered a natural rehydrant because it has potassium, an electrolyte we lose when we sweat. It also contains some carbohydrate. With a pinch of salt and a squeeze of lime, it's even better! Watermelon juice, too, has interesting properties that are worth exploring.

If you are trying to keep to a low-carbohydrate diet, having some branched-chain amino acids (BCAAs) during your workout is a good idea. Unlike all other amino acids, which must be processed by your body before being used as energy, BCAAs are special protein components that can be used as fuel during exercise. BCAA powder can be easily added to liquids to further boost performance. These have been shown not only to delay time to fatigue during exercise but also to help prevent muscle breakdown while working out. Dr. John Berardi has posted good options for BCAAs at www.precisionnutrition.com/supplements. I also recommend Living Fuel SuperEssentials Aminos.

Generally, most of us need only water during our workouts. If you are doing a hard endurance workout, training for a triathlon or marathon, or doing multiple workouts in one day, you can benefit from having some carbohydrates during your practice. If you are doing a strength training workout or want to protect against muscle breakdown, even during an endurance workout, add some amino acids to your fuelling plan.

EAT SMART AFTER EXERCISE

AFTER YOUR WORKOUT, use nutrition to accomplish a few things. First, rehydrate. Second, refuel. And third, regenerate.

Getting rehydrated after your workout is so critical to setting you up to be healthy and to recover as quickly as possible. Getting hydrated will help keep your blood volume at optimal levels, which helps with circulation. Your brain also needs water to function properly, so if you're dehydrated after your workout, you'll have trouble focusing at school or work, or even just in a conversation. Once you're done your workout, drink some water. If you've had a really hard workout, drink coconut water or watermelon juice.

Refuelling means getting carbohydrates and protein back into your system so you can replenish energy stores and repair your muscles, respectively. We used to worry about nutrient timing, recommending that you eat within about 20 minutes of finishing a workout, but more recent research shows that as long as you have a well-balanced and reasonable meal within 2 hours after your workout, you'll be fine. That meal should contain healthy, nutrient-dense foods that have complex carbohydrates and lean, organic proteins.

As someone who is exercising regularly, you have different nutritional needs than the average person. You need to fuel your body for the work it is about to do (sometimes multiple workouts per day!). Throughout your day, you want to make sure you are feeding your body high-quality foods that are dense in nutrients, not just energy. Look for whole foods that are minimally processed and packaged. Eat real, healthy foods.

When choosing carbohydrate sources, consider the nutrient content of that food. Having a slice of white processed bread is not going to provide as many of the vitamins and minerals that are necessary for your health as whole-grain sprouted breads, a cup of cooked quinoa, or brown rice. In the milling and refining processes, grains lose their germ layer, which is rich in micronutrients. Choose whole grains and starchy vegetables and legumes over refined breads and pastas as much as possible when picking your high-carbohydrate fuels.

Eating real food rather than prepackaged or processed foods will make you feel healthier and allow you to perform to your highest potential in both training and daily life. In the United States, 68% of packaged foods and beverages contain caloric sweeteners, and 74% contain both caloric and low-caloric sweeteners. It is well known that excess sugar is associated with a host of cardiometabolic risks.[44] This added refined sugar in processed foods provides no additional nutrients, and you want nutrient-dense foods to fuel your body and brain. As often as possible, stick to whole foods that are unprocessed.

If you are into exercise and training, making wise nutritional choices is vital for success. Not only will good everyday nutrition ensure that your body is healthy and ready to perform, but careful consideration of the timing of that preworkout snack or the composition of that recovery bar after your training could help boost your performance to new levels.

DR. GREG'S 1% TIP: SPORTS NUTRITION AT A GLANCE

Daily

- Eat whole foods, avoiding processed and packaged foods full of refined sugars.
- Include lots of vegetables of different varieties and colours.
- Aim for 6 to 12 grams of carbohydrate per kilogram of body weight, spread out in meals throughout the day.
- Include 1.2 to 1.8 grams of protein per kilogram of body weight throughout the day. Aim for about 20 grams in each meal. Having 0.5 gram of protein per kilogram of body weight before bed could help offset protein breakdown.
- Choose healthy fats and incorporate about 2 grams per kilogram of body weight per day.

Preworkout

- Eat a meal high in carbohydrate 1 to 2 hours before your workout.
- Have a mixed carbohydrate beverage or snack and BCAA solution less than an hour before your workout.

During workout

- For exercise lasting 30 to 75 minutes, a mouthwash of carbohydrate solution may be sufficient for nervous-system benefits.
- For 60 minutes to 2 hours of training, aim for 30 grams of carbohydrate per hour.
- For 2 to 3 hours, increase to 60 grams of carbohydrate per hour.
- For long sessions (more than 2.5 hours), you will require 80 to 90 grams of carbohydrate per hour (a mixture of glucose and fructose will help with absorption).
- Avoid routine use of commercial sports drinks. Instead, consider watermelon juice, coconut water, or simple homemade natural sports drinks.
- Consider adding a branched-chain amino acid (BCAA) solution to any of these options.

Postworkout

- If there are fewer than 8 hours between sessions, consume 1.2 grams of carbohydrate per kilogram of body weight per hour for the first few hours and a total of 8 to 9 grams of carbohydrate per kilogram over the course of 24 hours.
- For more than 8 hours between sessions, refuel according to timing that is comfortable and accessible, as long as you consume adequate energy and carbohydrate.
- Consume 16 to 20 grams of protein as soon after your workout as you can and a further 20 grams every 3 hours for the next 12 hours.
- Include anti-inflammatory foods such as ginger, turmeric, and omega-3s as well as lots of vegetables to reduce the inflammation associated with exercise.

EAT SMARTER TO THINK CLEARLY

FOOD HAS A tremendous impact on your brain and how it functions. The individual cells in your brain are called neurons, and we have about 80 to 100 billion of them. Each neuron has about 2,000 connections with other neurons, which creates trillions of links between brain cells. Those links are gaps between neurons called synapses, and that's where the action in your brain takes place—thinking, learning, creativity, problem solving, and memory building. When the neurons of a particular part of the brain are activated, a given synapse can fire up to 200 times per second! That's a whole lot of energy getting consumed.

The brain uses the glucose found in carbohydrates as fuel. But we need to eat carbohydrates in a controlled way to prevent insulin spikes. Go for complex, slow-digesting carbohydrates packed full of nutrients and fibre to ensure a consistent supply of mental energy. Starchy vegetables (like sweet potatoes), beans, whole fruits (not juice), peas, lentils, brown or wild rice, and quinoa are all good sources of complex carbohydrates. Again, avoid simple carbohydrates (white bread, white rice, white potatoes) and sugary foods and drinks as much as possible.

Also, for optimal brain health and performance, eat foods that provide the building blocks that can be used to keep brain neurons healthy and structurally sound. That's where healthy fats come in. High-quality healthy fats build the nerve structures, like cell membranes and the myelin sheath that protects the nerve, and speed up communication between neurons. Diets high in omega-3s are linked with lower risks of dementia and stroke and with better memory. Here are examples of healthy-fat foods that can improve brain function and health:

- *Fish.* Cold-water fish high in omega-3 fatty acids are great for brain and nervous system health. Examples of healthy cold-water fish include organic wild (unfarmed) salmon, sardines, mackerel, and trout. One habit I've started is to eat wild salmon on nights after a long, hard day at work. It's a great food for mental recovery, and I feel really good the next day.

- *Nuts.* One of the best daily snacks you can have is a handful of nuts. Studies have shown that the healthy fats, vitamins, and minerals in nuts improve thinking and memory and may protect against cognitive decline as we age. So mix together your favourite types and take a portion to work every day, or sprinkle them on cereal, salads, smoothies, or just about anything you consume.

- *Avocados.* The monounsaturated fat in avocados can help improve the cardiovascular system and blood flow to all organs—including the brain. Since your brain has no stored energy and depends on blood flow to deliver the glucose and oxygen that it needs to think, foods that improve your circulatory system can help supercharge your brain.

- *Coconut.* Once avoided because of its high fat content, coconuts have recently been deemed a superfood. The fatty acids in coconut are mostly saturated, which means it is one of the only oils that won't go toxic when cooked at high temperatures. The medium-chain triglycerides (MCTs) inside are special because they can be broken down more easily than other types of fat and can be used as fuel for our bodies and our brains.

- *Olive oil.* One of the cornerstones of the Mediterranean diet, olive oil is rich in heart-healthy monounsaturated fats. The list of benefits seen from regular consumption of this oil includes lowered risk of depression, Alzheimer's disease, stroke, and cancer. The tricky thing about this oil is keeping it fresh. To be sure you're getting the best product, buy extra-virgin oil in a dark glass bottle and consume it in its raw form.

Improve your energy and mental performance with these smart foods. Your supercharged brain will thank you.

Vitamins and minerals, along with other compounds found in our food, can play a significant role in our brain health and cognitive function. Vitamins that are soluble in water (the B vitamins and vitamin C), along with calcium, magnesium, and zinc, appear to be the most helpful for cognitive performance.[45] These vitamins and minerals each play important roles within the body to help our brains, but they also work in symphony. They are important in energy metabolism and synthesis of neurotransmitters in the nerves of our brains.[46]

One of the most important roles the B vitamins play may be their potential function in reducing homocysteine in the brain, which helps prevent vascular disease and is thus crucial for cognitive function and health.[47] Some studies have shown that elderly people with B12, B6, and folate deficiencies and higher homocysteine levels were more susceptible to showing symptoms of depression.[48]

With the current Western-style diet, it is not difficult to develop deficiencies in several of these vitamins. A diet full of processed foods that are high in energy or calories but low in nutrient density will leave you lacking in B vitamins. A stressful lifestyle or one where alcohol consumption is heavy will further increase your risk of deficiencies. Eating a variety of vegetables and whole grains and seeds will help keep your vitamin status up and your brain sharp.

DR. GREG'S 1% TIP: THE TOP THREE SUPPLEMENTS TO IMPROVE BRAIN PERFORMANCE

- *Fish oil.* Research provides overwhelming support for the use of fish oil to improve brain health. EPA and DHA, the omega-3 fatty acids in the oil, are linked with better mood, memory, and mental sharpness. Fish oil also reduces inflammation and pain in general. If you are daring enough to drink liquid fish oil directly, go for it! But you can also sneak it into your morning smoothie or your salads. For an omega-3 supplement, I recommend Living Fuel SuperEssentials Omega and Vega's Antioxidant Omega Oil Blend.

- *Rhodiola rosea.* This is an herb that helps with stress management. It cannot get rid of your stress (now, that really would be a superfood!), but it will support your cortisol-producing adrenal glands and make your stress responses less drastic. This effect can decrease the stall in productivity that happens when tasks pile up and stress shuts you down. Daily use of this supplement can also improve your energy and focus. This herb has been deemed to be safe when taken for a short period of time (6 to 10 weeks), although the side effects are not known at this time. Long-term use has not been studied, and there is no reliable information about if it is safe for women who are pregnant or breastfeeding.

- *Green tea extract.* The health benefits of green tea are widely known, but consuming the recommended 10 cups a day is nearly impossible, so it can be useful to have the convenience of the encapsulated version. Green tea extract (EGCg) boosts energy, burns fat, and improves circulation. It also reduces inflammation, cancer risk, and LDL cholesterol. As one of the world's most potent antioxidants, green tea extract really ought to be on every desk in every office across the country!

EAT SMARTER TO LEARN BETTER

LAST YEAR I did a high school presentation about the Olympics and how students could apply the skills and techniques Olympians use to perform at the Games to get better marks at school. After the talk, one of the students (let's call him John) approached me and asked what he could do to make sure he aced his SAT exam to get into university. The exam was still a couple of months away, so he had time to apply some ideas that I felt could really help him. We started with the foods he was eating, since there are fascinating data on how foods can super-charge your learning.

The first thing we did was to start John supplementing with omega-3s. Omega-3 fatty acids provide the building blocks of the brain, so I wanted to make sure there were lots of those circulating around. As mentioned earlier, omega-3 fatty acids also help with neurogenesis in the brain. They can help improve cognitive processes, promote plasticity in the brain, and aid in long-term memory storage through their effects on the hippocampus.

Eating breakfast has been consistently shown to improve academic performance,[49] so I also made sure John was eating a healthy breakfast every morning, one consisting of protein, healthy fats, and complex carbohydrates. Complex carbohydrates are key, as glucose is the primary fuel for brain neurons.

Another thing we worked on was making sure he got some polyphenols into his system every day. Polyphenols are micro-nutrients found in plants and are powerful antioxidants. They are able to improve memory, learning, and cognition.[50] Polyphenols are found in berries, kiwis, cherries, plums, black grapes, yellow onions, kale, coffee, and green and black tea.[51]

Several studies have shown improvements in cognitive performance with the consumption of flavonoid-rich plants and their extracts.[52] Flavonoids may impact the brain in terms of memory and learning in several ways, including being a trigger for gene expression and protein synthesis to stimulate long-term memory storage.[53] Flavonoids can also facilitate the production of nitric oxide, which not only helps inhibit the production of plaques in the vasculature, which cause inflammation, but also relaxes this vasculature in order to help blood flow and perfusion in the brain to bring in more oxygen and nutrients.[54]

Polyphenols and flavonoid compounds not only help us learn and remember better but also protect against Alzheimer's disease and other degenerative diseases. Anthocyanins in berries can decrease neuroinflammation. Strawberries, blueberries, and blackberries, all rich in anthocyanins, have been shown to slow the cognitive behavioural deficits associated with aging.[55]

Staying hydrated all day long is crucial for brain function. A study looking at the amount of brain activation required to complete tasks when hydrated versus dehydrated found that when dehydrated, subjects exerted a higher level of neuronal activity in order to achieve the same performance level as when hydrated.[56] So if you want your brain to function well and to perform at your best with the least amount of effort, get hydrated and stay hydrated!

I also asked John to keep his calories low ("stop at 80% full") and to avoid saturated fats and sugars, because these nutrients are known to elevate levels of oxidative stress, and they reduce the ability of neurons in the brain to grow and make new connections,[57] which is exactly what needs to happen for learning and memory to be optimized. Think about that when we look at what students are often provided at school: high-fat, high-sugar foods and drinks. That's why I get seriously angry when I hear that students are served chocolate milk at lunch, given that chocolate milk has too many added sugars and about the same amount of sugar as a can of Coke. I also am shocked and dismayed when I walk around an office or school I'm visiting and see cans of pop on desks, or go down to the food court and see people eating fast food. Most people need their brains when they work, yet we don't feed the brain what it needs to be healthy and high performing. When the student put all these ideas in place, he rocked his exam.

We live in a world with an ever-growing volume of things to learn about and explore, but also with a growing number of distractions. Your brain is an incredible organ that can integrate your senses with your feelings, input your experiences into your long-term memory, and learn and create new connections in order for you to have complex thought and reasoning. To build these connections, we need to fuel our brains with all the nutrients and compounds that will keep it functioning optimally. Many of the foods discussed in earlier sections play a factor in learning and cognition, especially those that are important to the hippocampus, a region key to long-term memory storage, and those that can impact neuroplasticity. Neuroplasticity describes the ability of neurons in the brain to reorganize themselves and to make new connections throughout life.

To summarize, for optimal brain function, learning, and memory, do the following:

- Eat breakfast. Ideally, it will contain healthy fats, lean protein, and healthy complex carbohydrates.

- Have coffee or tea before learning or doing major mental tasks. Be careful not to have caffeine for about 6 hours before you plan on falling asleep.
- Eat foods high in polyphenols. I suggest some berries (or other source you like) mid-morning and mid-afternoon.
- Drink water throughout the day.
- Avoid sugars, refined carbohydrates, processed foods, and saturated fats.

You may have noticed that this eating plan looks an awful lot like the anti-cancer, anti-inflammation health plan. There may be some consistencies emerging here!

DR. GREG'S 1% TIP: TRY A SUPER BRAIN-POWERING SMOOTHIE

One way to pack better brain foods into your day is with a morning smoothie. Here's a recipe for one that is brilliant for your brain:

- 1 banana
- 2 handfuls spinach or kale
- 1 tablespoon ground flaxseed
- ½ an avocado
- 1 tablespoon sliced or grated ginger
- ½ teaspoon ground turmeric
- ¾ cup unsweetened almond milk (or a little more or less, depending on your preferred thickness)
- 1 scoop protein powder of your choice (I like Living Fuel and Vega for plant-based proteins)

Put all ingredients into a blender and blend on high for 60 seconds. Pour into a glass and enjoy!

THE SEVEN KEYS TO EATING SMARTER

EATING SMARTER CAN help you in all aspects of your life. The solution lies in building a lifestyle that helps you be healthy, happy, and at your best. Start with a foundation built on healthy foods. Eat the right food at the right time, and you can set the stage for better health and performance. If you add good sleep and exercise to the mix, you can amplify your health and potential. Here are my seven keys to eating smarter.

KEY #1: HYDRATE

QUICK: WHAT'S THE most important thing for health? Breathing? Yes, stop breathing and you'll die in a few minutes. How about the second most important thing for staying alive? Any guesses? Exactly. Water. Water is vital to a body's function and survival. Stop being hydrated for a few days and you stop living. Remember the remarkable story of the Bangladeshi woman who survived 17 days in the wreckage of a collapsed garment building? She managed that near-impossible feat because she had found some bottled water.

There is not a single cell in your body that does not rely on water. Water helps transport the carbohydrates, vitamins, minerals, and other nutrients that your cells need to make energy. When your body works, functions, or moves, it does so because water helped transport the necessary fuel or energy-building components. Reflect on the word *carbohydrate* for a moment. Do you see the word *hydrate* in it? That's not a coincidence. Carbohydrates are basically hydrates of carbon. Carbon. Hydrogen. Oxygen.

Think of your veins and arteries as a city's roads and highways. These roads are used to bring goods into the city but also to transport unwanted materials out. If this transportation is slowed, the eventual result may be a city that is starving for goods and overflowing with garbage.

Continuing with this analogy, think of your body's water molecules as the vehicles on the roadways, transporting the nutrients your cells need to make energy. Water makes up 80% of the blood's volume, so when water is depleted, this has a huge impact on the efficiency of your blood for carrying oxygen and nutrients around your body.

If that was hard to follow, drink a glass of water. Now. Before you read on. Your brain needs water. Your body weight is made up of 60% water, but, incredibly, water makes up almost 90% of your brain. Water lubricates and cushions the brain. It also helps you think, concentrate, problem-solve, and remember. With water, those important cognitive functions . . . well, they function. Without water, they stop functioning properly—or worse. A recent study out of the UK indicates that dehydrated adolescents had structural changes in their brains that were equivalent to those of an Alzheimer's patient over a two-and-a-half-month period or, in a healthy adult, 14 months of aging. In other words, dehydration can cause a person's brain to shrink.[58]

Not a teenager anymore? Water still matters. Mild dehydration—just a 1% loss in body fluids—can impair your mood, concentration, and thinking.[59] With a fluid loss of only 2% (3 pounds in a 150-pound adult), concentration and thinking will become impaired. This 2% loss is incredibly common in a typical day at the office with back-to-back meetings.

DR. GREG'S 1% TIP: DRINK AT LEAST HALF YOUR BODY WEIGHT IN OUNCES OF WATER EACH DAY

This means 75 ounces or 2.2 litres for a 150-pound adult. This requirement needs to be increased when you are under stress (which causes hyperventilation, increased washroom use, and increased sweating), are in extreme temperatures, or exercise (minimum 16 oz. or 500 ml/hr of exercise).

NOW THAT YOU'VE properly hydrated that big brain of yours, do you find it difficult to move it around? Are your muscles and joints sore or not functioning properly? Whether at work or play, staying hydrated is key to lubricating and protecting your muscles and joints. Although the brain has the highest concentration of water in the body, your muscles are still nearly 75% water. Remember the Krebs cycle from grade 10 biology class? No? Maybe that time of your life is a little foggy. Well, the Krebs cycle is the series of steps that take place in all the cells of your body to create energy. No water, no energy. You know that sluggish feeling you get in the afternoon? For most people, the afternoon crash is caused by a combination of dehydration and bad nutrition. So do yourself a favour. Give yourself more energy by drinking some water. Tired? Drink some water.

The heart is one of our most vital organs. Simply drinking water can help keep it beating properly. A constant water balance in the body through regular hydration allows for blood pressure to be maintained within its target range. Dehydration can make it harder for the heart to pump blood throughout the body, which can increase your heart rate and decrease your blood pressure. A lower resting heart rate has been linked to a longer life. And we've all heard about how important blood pressure is to our health—staying well hydrated is one of the ways you can keep your blood pressure in the healthy zone.

Make drinking water part of your daily routine. Get a water bottle and keep it with you, and fill it up a few times every day. Water is just as important at work as it is in the gym. Stay hydrated, stay healthy, and be better.

> ### DR. GREG'S 1% TIP: HYDRATE FIRST THING IN THE MORNING
>
> As we sleep, we naturally lose water (through breathing and sweating) and usually wake up dehydrated, negatively impacting the day ahead. Make one easy adjustment to your morning routine and you'll notice big changes. Place a big glass of water beside your bed each night, and do not get out of bed in the morning until you have finished that glass! Your brain will thank you.

KEY #2: EAT MOSTLY PLANTS

IT CAN BE hard to interpret the results of scientists' published research unless you're an expert in the field and have read most of the studies performed in the area and thus can put the new research in the context of previously published data. An effective form of research analysis called a meta-analysis combines studies into one big data set, so patterns from all the high-quality data in a field can emerge. Meta-analyses are fantastic tools for people trying to make sense of all the research in one particular area.

Dr. Frank Hu's team published a meta-analysis that caught my attention.[60] Dr. Hu works in the Departments of Nutrition and

Epidemiology at the Harvard T.H. Chan School of Public Health. He wanted to determine if there is a relationship between the amount of fruits and vegetables someone eats and dying from cardiovascular disease, cancer, or other causes of mortality.

Dr. Hu's analysis tracked more than 833,000 people. His analysis shows that for each serving of fruits and vegetables you eat, your risk of dying from a chronic disease like cardiovascular disease or cancer decreases. Interestingly, after five servings of fruits and vegetables, the risk does not decrease any more. So if you get five servings every day, you're good to go! The data also show that eating fruits and vegetables helps prevent cardiovascular disease. Another research team took this a step further and found that red, yellow, and orange vegetables, especially carrots, are particularly powerful at reducing the risk of cardiovascular disease.[61]

As long as you don't have a nut allergy, nuts can help prevent chronic diseases. They're full of vitamins, minerals, fibre, and healthy fats. In a study of 70,000 women and 42,500 men conducted by Dr. Ying Bao and colleagues,[62] consumption of nuts was found to be inversely related to mortality, independent of other predictors of death. Inverse associations (the more nuts you eat, the less disease you get) were seen for cancer, heart disease, and respiratory disease. Nuts are very high in calories, so if you are looking to lose weight, be mindful of your overall consumption. When I'm trying to decrease my fat before races, I limit my intake to 8 to 10 nuts per day.

The primary benefit of eating a diet based mostly on plants is an increase in your intake of vitamins, minerals, and other nutrients. These have antioxidant properties that help keep you healthy. Antioxidants are substances that prevent the oxidation of important biomolecules, such as fatty acids, DNA, or proteins, by a reactive oxygen species.[63] Excessive oxidation of molecules in the body can affect their structure and function. Think of how metal begins to rust when it is exposed to oxygen in the air. Or how the flesh of an apple turns brown after it is cut open. The scientific term for this process is *oxidative stress*. Antioxidants slow and minimize this process in our bodies.

One of the best-known antioxidants is vitamin C, but other vitamins, such as those in the vitamin E family, also act as antioxidants. Foods high in vitamin C include bell peppers, leafy green vegetables, broccoli, peas, guava, kiwi fruit, berries, citrus fruits, tomatoes, and papayas. Foods high in vitamin E include tofu, spinach, broccoli, butternut squash, pumpkin, avocado, nuts, seeds, shellfish, cold-water fish, and plant oils (like olive oil).

Foods high in flavonoids and carotenoids are also powerful antioxidants. These foods include sweet potato, carrots, dark green leafy vegetables, squash, cantaloupe and melons, sweet red and yellow peppers, apricots, peas, and broccoli.

The main message here is that plant-based foods are our best defence against reactive oxygen species in our bodies. Along with fruits and vegetables, teas, coffee, spices, and herbs are all great sources of antioxidants, and all of these have been related to lower risk of most chronic diseases and a lower risk of mortality. Research has shown a clear inverse relationship between increasing your fruit and vegetable intake and having a lower risk of cardiovascular disease, stroke, cancer, type 2 diabetes, asthma, COPD (chronic obstructive pulmonary disease), dementia, osteoporosis, certain eye diseases, and weight gain.[64] So if you want to live a long, healthy life, eat mostly plants.

Eating plants will not only help you prevent chronic illnesses but will also help you power up your immune system, which fights off viruses, bacteria, fungi, and other invaders. The immune system is also the primary way the body fights off cancer. An extensive body of research has shown that plants can act as boosters for the immune system.[65] Powerful plants here include garlic, green tea, ginger, the spices cumin and turmeric, licorice, and the herb astragalus. Add these foods to your diet to help stay healthy and prevent colds and flus.

> **DR. GREG'S 1% TIP: BE PLANT POWERED!**
>
> Interested in eating more plant-based meals? Check out Rich Roll's cookbook *The Plantpower Way* for terrific recipes.

KEY #3: CONSUME MORE NUTRIENTS, FEWER CALORIES

I WANT TO give you an easy-to-follow criterion for choosing foods that will give you the most health and performance benefit while helping you avoid the various preservatives, pesticides, genetically modified ingredients, and nutrient-poor crops out there. To get the biggest bang for your calorie buck, you need to *optimize your nutrient-to-calorie ratio.*

Consider this formula: $H = N/C$, which translates as health = nutrients per calorie consumed. Dr. Joel Fuhrman offers this wisdom in his book *Eat to Live*, and it is a great way to think about nutrition. Your goal should be to eat nutrient-dense foods while avoiding calorie-dense foods. For example, skip the muffins and bagels, instead choosing protein and vegetables. An apple has about 90 calories and loads of great nutrients, whereas a blueberry muffin has 350-plus calories and few nutrients.

Water and herbal teas have zero calories and promote health, whereas sugar-laden sodas and flavoured milks are loaded with calories and have minimal nutrient value. The Boston Public Health Commission recently found that the policy of limiting sugar-laden drinks and increasing availability of healthier drinks reduced the intake of unhealthy beverages on city properties by 30%.[66] Of note, beverage prices were not raised, which is good news, because one of the common arguments against eating healthy foods is that they cost too much. We need to follow this example in our businesses, schools, and homes.

To speed you on your way to eating more in line with the H = N/C formula, add superfoods to your diet wherever possible. Superfoods are a special class of food that offers only the very best nutrient density. I define superfoods as foods with very high vitamin, mineral, and other nutrient and antioxidant levels that are also low in calories (think vegetables), or if not low in calories, then powerfully health enhancing (such as fruit, nuts, avocado, and coconut). We should all include these in our daily routine. Here are examples of nutrient-dense superfoods for you to consider:

Leafy greens. Swiss chard, kale, mustard/collard greens, spinach, dandelion, seaweed. These have by far the highest antioxidant density per calorie. Greens are also packed with calcium, iodine, and iron, which are excellent for bone strength, thyroid health, and energy.

Small fatty fish. Sardines, perch, tilapia, salmon, herring, anchovies. The omega-3 fatty acids in fish help with circulation, concentration, and pain relief. Fish is also a source of protein and calcium. To avoid heavy metals, avoid large fish like tuna, swordfish, and shark.

Legumes. Lentils, chickpeas, and black/kidney/navy/cannellini beans. Legumes are the least expensive protein source and are packed with fibre and B vitamins.

Berries. Blueberries, blackberries, cranberries, strawberries, goji, and acai berries. Don't let their sweetness fool you—berries are a superfood full of tissue-healing antioxidants and fibre.

Root vegetables. Ginger, turmeric, garlic, onions, sweet potatoes, radishes, beets. These are disease-fighting, energy-boosting, pain-relieving miracle foods! Besides making our meals burst with flavour, they provide us with an excellent nutrition boost.

Sprouts. Whether talking about lentil, clover, or alfalfa sprouts, eating the plant at this early stage of life is a nutritional bonus. Sprouts have more enzymes, vitamins, minerals, and amino acids than almost any other food on Earth. The fact that they are also cheap, have very few calories, and are easy to incorporate into meals makes them super.

Chia seeds. Yes, these seeds are the very ones we used to spread on pottery and watch grow as kids. A nutritional analysis was done on these tiny seeds. Turns out they are the highest plant source of omega-3 fatty acids in existence, which makes them excellent for brain and heart health.

Spirulina. This nutritional powerhouse is considered part of the algae family. It is packed with minerals, including one of the only sources of the thyroid booster iodine. Sixty percent of spirulina powder is protein by weight (containing every single essential amino acid that humans need). Spirulina also contains four times as much vitamin B12 as liver. Add this to your diet ASAP! I use spirulina in my morning smoothies.

Pomegranate seeds. Research has found that pomegranates

can lower blood pressure and reduce inflammation in our blood vessels, actually reducing the risk of heart attack and stroke.

Turmeric. This mild orange spice is often part of Indian curries, but it can be added to many meals subtly. The benefits of the active ingredient, curcumin, seem endless. Curcumin actually slows down age-related cognitive decline and prevents Alzheimer's disease. It acts as a potent pain reliever, soothes reflux disease, and stops clot formation in our blood vessels. This is certainly a super spice!

Remember, it's all about eating as healthfully as you can. Your common sense should help you put things in context to determine what's good for you and what's not so good for you. Recently, pizza sauce was approved as a serving of vegetables in US schools. Really? If you take some tomatoes, process the nutrients out of them, add loads of sugar and salt, and then put the result on white bread and cover it with high-fat, highly salty cheese, that's not healthy. It's like thinking you're getting your five servings of fruit and vegetables by eating five slices of apple pie. Technically you may be eating five apples, but you're surrounding them with sugar and fatty pastry. Not so healthy. Keep in mind the H = N/C principle and you'll be on your way to unleashing your health and reaching your potential.

> **DR. GREG'S 1% TIP: BRAIN-POWER FOOD: BLUEBERRIES**
> Research has shown that blueberries are packed full of nutrients that help protect the brain from free radical damage and age-related mental decline. They also improve memory and learning. So if you want to keep your brain young, load up on blueberries.

KEY #4: EAT ANTI-INFLAMMATORY FOODS

EATING A LARGE quantity and variety of fruits and vegetables can help optimize your anti-inflammatory and antioxidant status, thanks to their high concentration of various flavonoid polyphenols.[67] Polyphenols, which include flavonoids and tannins,[68] can also help regulate oxidative stress. Flavonoids are the most studied group for brain health.[69] Good fruit and vegetable choices include apples, pears, citrus fruits, red grapes, green leafy vegetables, and onions, which appear to be important for immune-system and overall health.[70] Cruciferous vegetables, which are high in organosulfur compounds—especially broccoli but also cauliflower, bok choy, and cabbage—also have inflammation-reducing properties.[71]

Anthocyanins are flavonoids found in many fruits, especially berries, and they may impact the brain in several ways. The most plausible are through reductions in neuroinflammation and through changes in neural signalling to improve memory and cognition.[72] Other fruits high in anthocyanins have also been examined for their pain-relieving and anti-inflammatory effects.[73] Some examples are blueberries, bilberries, elderberries, cherries, cabbage, and eggplant. The intake of blueberry juice may improve memory performance.[74] Interestingly, the anthocyanins in blueberries tend to circulate in the body for up to 5 days.[75]

Turmeric (curcumin) has been shown to have anti-inflammatory and antioxidant properties as well as the potential to suppress glucose levels. It also has anti-cancer and antibacterial properties.[76] The ability of curcumin to alter inflammation has been quite consistently reported.[77] Curcumin is the primary active ingredient in turmeric and is the compound that gives the herb its yellow colour.[78] A recent study demonstrates that curcumin promotes the synthesis of the omega-3 fatty acid DHA (docosahexaenoic acid) from its precursor alpha-linolenic acid and increases the activity of enzymes that help form DHA in the brain.[79] Curcumin has also been shown to improve cognition through its effect on neuroplasticity.[80] Curcumin ingested alone has fairly inefficient bioavailability because it is quite stable in acidic solutions such as stomach acid.[81] And some data suggest that whole turmeric may be more beneficial than isolated curcumin.[82] Often, consuming a compound in a whole food can provide you with added benefits because of the synergistic effects of other compounds in the food. Turmeric could be added to most meals in some way and may be a less aggressive way of reducing your inflammation than taking a curcumin supplement.

Polyunsaturated fatty acids (PUFAS), which include omega-3 and omega-6 fatty acids, and curcumin have both been targeted as preventing and reversing cognitive deficits with aging.[83] These compounds have been shown to not only reduce inflammation but also improve neurogenesis.[84] Small cold-water fish have high levels of omega-3 fatty acids, particularly DHA and EPA (eicosapentaenoic acid), which help combat inflammation. Compared with bigger fish, smaller ones are lower in persistent organic pollutants (heavy metals, PCBs, pesticides), and their consumption is more ecologically friendly. These omega-3 fatty acids have been linked to healthy aging throughout life and have important roles in all aspects of health and physiology, including fetal development, cardiovascular function, weight manage-ment, and cognitive function. Top picks include sardines, her-ring, rainbow trout, and anchovies.

When you have a diet full of healthy whole foods and lots of vegetables and other anti-inflammatory foods, you will take in a high density of nutrients that can help reduce your inflamma-tion, in turn helping you feel more clear-headed and keeping your memory sharp.

KEY #5: EAT HEALTHY FATS

PROBABLY NO OTHER area generates as much confusion about healthy eating than do fats. Let's clear up the misinforma-tion so you have a solid, science-based plan for how and why to add healthy fats to your diet.

It is time to end the low fat = healthy eating myth.[85] That con-cept has not served us well. Food manufacturers simply removed fats and replaced them with sugars and refined grains, and the negative impact on our health has been frightening. According to the Harvard T.H. Chan School of Public Health, the percentage of fats in our diet, whether high or low, does not determine our risk of disease.[86] What matters is the type of fat in our diet. I want you to increase the amount of healthy fats in your diet and decrease, or even better, eliminate, unhealthy fats—saturated animal fats and trans fats. These increase your risk of disease. Unhealthy saturated fats typically come from animal sources and include red meat (which you can eat on occasion for protein and iron—but make sure it's grass-fed and organic), butter, cheese, and ice cream. You can spot these because they are solid at room temperature. Simply, avoid saturated animal fats, trans fats, hydrogenated vegetable oils, and processed foods.

> **DR. GREG'S 1% TIP: HEALTHY VERSUS UNHEALTHY FATS—HOW TO TELL?**
>
> Harmful fats are the saturated fats that come from animal sources (grain-fed meats, poultry, and full-fat dairy from grain fed cows) and the trans fats from hydrogenated vegetable oils. A good way to tell if your fat source is healthy is to see whether it is solid at room temperature. For example, butter is solid at room temperature (not healthy), whereas olive oil remains liquid (healthy). Healthy sources of fat include olive oil, safflower oil, peanut oil, salmon, trout, mackerel, sardines, and herring. Plant sources include flax, avocado, coconut, chia seeds, nuts, and seeds. If you want to dive into this topic, check out my podcast with Dr. Richard Bazinet from the University of Toronto.

PROCESSED FOODS TEND to contain trans fats such as hydrogenated vegetable oils. You should avoid trans or partially hydrogenated fats as much as possible. Trans fats are found in many baked goods, snacks such as chips and prepackaged popcorn, and fried foods.

We humans are not that good at eliminating things from our lives, but we are reasonably good at replacing them. I'd like you to consider replacing your high-saturated-fat foods and processed foods with healthy-fat alternatives. Healthy fats are found in fish, beans, nuts, seeds, coconut, avocados, and healthy oils.

The key to understanding the healthy-fat concept is to learn about two essential fatty acids: omega-3 and omega-6, called *essential* because they are the only two types of fat that our bodies can't make on their own. Since these fatty acids are essential to our good health, we need to consume them.

A healthy diet will have a ratio of about two omega-6 to one omega-3.[87] But our typical Western diet contains about 20 to 60 times more omega-6 than omega-3. The World Health Organization recommends a maximum ratio of 4:1. Omega-6 is found in most vegetable oils, grain-fed animal meats, and grain products (such as bread and cereal), which are food staples. Too much omega-6 in our diets causes excessive inflammation, which has been linked to heart disease and mental issues such as depression, ADHD, and dyslexia. Omega-3 fats have many health benefits, but most important is the concept of *balance*. We need a balanced intake of the omegas. The best sources of omega-3 are small fatty fish, grass-fed meats, nuts, and flaxseed. You can see that you're far more likely to consume more omega-6 than -3 if you consume the typical North American diet.

Here are ways to improve the balance between omega-3 and omega-6 fats:

- Use extra-virgin olive, walnut, coconut, and sustainably sourced palm oil. And when you cook with oil, never heat it past the smoking point, as the beneficial properties of the oil are ruined.
- Have a handful of raw nuts and seeds every day—focus on almonds, pecans, walnuts, flax, and chia.

- Eat small fatty fish (such as sardines and salmon) often and larger fish (such as tuna and swordfish) infrequently, as they contain higher levels of toxic heavy metals.
- Buy flax oil in dark bottles and keep it in the fridge (air, light, and heat cause it to break down). Use it in salads or other cold dishes or add it to cooked foods. You could also buy ground flaxseed to add to shakes, cereal, cooked grains, and stews.
- Eat grass-fed animals (grass is rich in omega-3) rather than grain-fed animals, and move to a more plant-based diet.
- Use cheese as a seasoning, not as a food. A small amount of old, flavourful cheese can be a nice addition to a salad or stir-fry. But cheese is not a healthy food, so limit your intake or avoid it completely.
- Serve healthy fats at the table. Use olive oil as a drizzle instead of butter, or guacamole instead of sour cream.
- Almonds are a good source of monounsaturated fatty acids and also contain an array of phenolic compounds and flavonoids, as well as vitamin E, riboflavin, magnesium, and manganese.[88] Studies show that almond consumption is linked to improved markers of oxidative stress and inflammation.[89] Almonds are an excellent addition to your diet if you're into sports or physical training. They are packed full of nutrients and provide potential performance-enhancing effects.
- Coconut oil has received a lot of attention as a potential health food in recent years. Much of the health-promoting talk relates to its composition of medium-chain fatty acids, which are digested differently from longer-chain fatty

acids. However, the main fatty acid in coconut oil, lauric acid, although considered medium to long chain, has a molecular weight that results in its behaving as a long chain. The evidence for faster breakdown and different transport of medium-chain fatty acids can't really be extrapolated to benefits in coconut oil.[90] Although it does not appear to raise bad cholesterol as much as butter, it is still a saturated fat and should be treated as such in your diet. It would be preferable to choose unsaturated fats over coconut oil for most cooking. Coconut oil is, however, preferable to butter if you need a small amount of oil to fry up some healthy pancakes, say. Vegans and vegetarians who eat very minimal saturated fat from animal products will also find coconut oil useful in healthy baking.

WORDS OF WISDOM: DR. RICHARD BAZINET ON HEALTHY FATS

I interviewed one of the world's leading researchers on healthy fats, Dr. Richard Bazinet, with the University of Toronto. He has brilliant insights on fats. You can listen to the complete interviews at http://drgregwells.com/community/dr-richard-bazinet-part-1 and http://drgregwells.com/community/dr-richard-bazinet-part-2.

It turns out that the brain is absolutely full of fat. It's full of omega-3s, very specific types of omega-3s. Most people think of fish as being brain food. That's true to some extent, but there's only so much fish in the world. People are really starting to think about ecology and nutrition, and fish gets really complicated. . . . We started to think about where else can we get omega-3s from. The answer was not animals. There is just almost no omega-3s in animals. Then I had a food writer, Mark Schatzker, call me up out of the blue. . . . He said he had some steaks [and] he wanted me to analyze the omega-3 content of them. I told him it's a waste of time. There is no omega-3s in steaks. He said, "Wait a second. These steaks have been fed grass their whole lives."

This is important. Many people listening to this right now might say, "Well, isn't that what cows eat?" In reality, most North American cows, anyway, they're fed grains. Grains is almost a euphemism for corn, which is full of omega-6s and has almost no omega-3s. That's why I answered that so confidently to Mark Schatzker. He had found some guys who were doing grass-fed steak. That completely changes [things], because grass is full of omega-3s. We analyzed these steaks. One way of looking at this is what you call the omega-6 to omega-3 ratio. There are a few ways to do that.

If you go into virtually any store right now and analyze a piece of steak or chicken or pork, it will have an omega-6 to omega-3 ratio of about 30 to 1. It varies. You might find 20 to 1; you might find 40 to 1. The stuff Mark Schatzker was giving me was 2 to 1 and 1 to 1, so it was quite different. We started to quantify this up and look at it and say a piece of steak is by no means a piece of salmon, but nutrition is not about these superfoods. It's about little steps and everything you do all day.

People eat a serving of beef a week. I've done the napkin calculations, and it can get you into an area where we think it might start to make a difference if you start consuming these foods. This is just your beef. You can also do this with your pork. You can do it with your chicken. Chicken is quite remarkable. It starts to look like some fish. It really can change. Then your eggs and it turns out your milk and your butter can all be changed quite a bit, depending on what you feed the animal.

I think this is exciting not just from a nutritional perspective but an ecological perspective. I don't have the expertise to really go too far on that, but there are a lot of people looking into these kinds of pasture-based farming systems as being ecologically friendly. Then thirdly, from an ethical perspective, and this is going to vary a lot by feeding systems, but on average I think these pasture-[based] farmers are doing an absolutely beautiful job with their animals. That's kind of where we got to, and the idea that we could change our food supply to include animal products that are not fish to give us some of these omega-3s [for] the brain is really quite remarkable.

DR. GREG'S 1% TIP: COOK WITH HEALTHY OILS

When you are cooking, pay attention to the oils you're using. Choose cold-pressed, extra-virgin oils more often, as they are less heat-processed and will have the best nutrient content. Most vegetable oils are very high in omega-6 fatty acids, which, although important, can swing you too far into a pro-inflammatory state. Choose olive, coconut, or avocado oil more often, and sunflower, corn, and soybean oil less often. It is also important to consider what you are doing with the oil. Fats that are very high in PUFAs (polyunsaturated fatty acids) are easily degraded with heat and are better off in salads rather than used for frying.

KEY #6: EAT HEALTHY CARBOHYDRATES

CARBOHYDRATES—"CARBS"—HAVE gotten a very bad rap lately. Let me try to clear up the confusion.

You might have noticed that with each food or diet trend, typically one component of food is demonized. First it was fat. We went on a low-fat kick. That didn't work, and eventually we learned that there are good fats and bad fats—as you just read in the discussion of Key #5. More recently there has been a trend toward low-carbohydrate diets, and once again, vilifying one nutrient and loading up on the other types has come with both successes and failures. What we've discovered is that, just like fats, there are good and bad carbohydrates. In general, complex carbohydrates that are high in fibre and are slow digesting (low glycemic index carbohydrates) can be quite healthful, whereas foods high in simple carbohydrates that are high glycemic can be problematic.

Healthy carbohydrates include quinoa, whole grains, vegetables (such as sweet potato), fruits (especially berries), beans, legumes, nuts, and seeds. Simple carbohydrates are often found in refined and processed foods like breakfast cereals, white bread, sports drinks, fruit juice, sugars, and syrups.

The rapid rise in sugar and fructose consumption in the 1980s mirrored a steep increase in obesity in the UK, Canada, and the United States. Trying to keep the obesity epidemic under control is incredibly challenging given that sugars are addictive and involve the same dopamine receptors in the brain that cause us to experience pleasure.[91] These are the same centres that are activated by cocaine, nicotine, and alcohol. Think about that the next time you have a sugar craving!

More recent data suggest that the types of foods we eat—especially foods that have a high glycemic index (e.g., white bread, white rice, cereals, juice, and pop)—can cause changes in our internal gut microflora (bacteria) that can lead to increased inflammation in our bodies. Diets high in simple sugars can also impact our immune systems. Problems that occur in the body when we eat too much sugar include a depression of the immune system, cancer, kidney damage, atherosclerosis, and oxidative stress.

When we get hungry or stressed, our bodies crave food that will provide us with the quickest supply of fuel: simple sugar and starches. It is no accident that we rarely hear people say they could "really go for a chicken breast right now." It's the starchy foods (bagels, crackers, cookies, chocolate, muffins, and so on) that make us drool when hungry. Overconsumption of starches and simple sugars results in fat being stored in our bodies, to be used as fuel at a later date. Our bellies empty sooner with starchy food, letting the craving cycle perpetuate. Setting up our morning with starchy sweets leads to a cascade of bad behaviour the rest of the day. Worse yet, these eating habits set the stage for exhaustion at the worst times. You may recall this point when trying to hide that yawn in the afternoon meeting or class.

Three things slow down the digestion of sugar: fat, fibre, and protein. This means that if we want to have balanced blood sugar, we need to slow down our digestion by making sure each meal has all of these elements.

Choose oatmeal (the kind that takes more than 3 minutes to cook!) with almond butter rather than cereal for breakfast. Choose plain full-fat yogurt with berries instead of the sweetened low-fat variety. Choose spaghetti squash with tuna pesto sauce instead of white pasta with tomato sauce.

KEY #7: EAT HEALTHY PROTEINS

BACK IN MY early days of consulting, a group I was working with was entering negotiations with another group of people in the same industry. The negotiations were important, and my team expected that the discussions would be confrontational and difficult.

I was pretty competitive at that point in my life, and so I was determined that my team would excel in this meeting. I wanted to set the stage for their brilliant performance, and I wanted to create a problematic scenario for the other group.

I asked that the meeting be scheduled between 1 p.m. and 4 p.m., because that's the time of day most people have their afternoon crash and their energy levels are the lowest. I asked my group to show up at noon, and I told them I'd have lunch ready.

For lunch, I gave them water to ensure they were hydrated, green tea to give them a small dose of caffeine, chicken salad to make sure they had lots of protein in their system, and avocado salad on the side, so that they had some quality fats in their bodies, for long-term energy lasting the entire afternoon. In a nutshell, I made sure they had mostly proteins, some fats, and a little carbohydrate.

I chose this combination because I wanted to increase the amount of the amino acid tyrosine in my team and keep its levels as high as possible during the meeting. Tyrosine is an essential precursor—a building block—to the neurotransmitters epinephrine, norepinephrine, and dopamine, which have stimulatory effects on the body and brain. Basically, they wake you up and help you concentrate. Neurotransmitters are small bundles of protein that work in the brain to carry signals from one nerve to another. This creates thoughts and memories and basically controls the way the brain is functioning. Higher levels of tyrosine help you feel good and improve your mood and can also improve concentration and mental performance. Sources of tyrosine include protein-rich foods such as meat, poultry, seafood, beans, tofu, and lentils. They should be consumed with a minimum of carbohydrates. Hence the chicken salad for lunch.

With my team primed for excellence, I welcomed the visiting group to our conference room, where I had prepared a buffet of croissants, muffins, bagels, coffee, tea, and soft drinks. It was a smorgasbord of simple carbohydrates and caffeine. The visitors were most appreciative and loaded up—most had skipped lunch to be at the meeting or had quickly eaten something at their desks.

By having them eat foods that were very high in simple carbohydrates and very low in protein, I ensured that their brain chemistry changed right before the negotiations were to begin. Eating those foods resulted in an increase in the amino acid tryptophan. Tryptophan has been shown to increase the production of serotonin, a neurotransmitter that helps relax the brain. Great stuff if you want to take a nap. Not so great if you need to concentrate for 3 hours.

As the meeting began, the members of the visiting group were jacked up on sugar and caffeine. They were aggressive and energetic. For about 45 minutes. And then they began to tire. They began to slump in their chairs. They became irritable and distracted. Two hours in, they were really struggling. The last hour was a train wreck for them. My team remained calm, cool, and consistent. We rocked the negotiations. My team felt great, had excellent energy the whole time, and were able to perform at their best—giving them an excellent advantage in the negotiations.

The point of this somewhat scary and pathetic story is that I essentially changed the chemistry of the bodies and brains of the people who came to negotiate with my group in such a way that they felt tired and couldn't concentrate. And I did that by feeding them the typical North American diet.

Now that you know about food and brain neurotransmitters, think about how crazy it is that we feed our workforce the way we do. Think about what is offered to students in schools. Even worse, consider what people are fed when they are sick and in the hospital. Or even just think about your own energy levels and ability to stay focused during the day. Can you see a relationship between your food intake and your energy, your performance, and ultimately your health?

You are not likely to choose every meal based on amino acid composition. That makes life just a little too complicated. But if you need to be alert—to perform at a work event or for an exam— go for a protein-rich meal low in simple carbohydrates. If you need to wind down and get to sleep at night, enjoy a higher-carbohydrate meal such as a bowl of yogurt sprinkled with a handful of raw and unsalted sunflower seeds. Use your food to help you perform better. The outcome will be that you'll be healthier too.

High-quality, nutrient-dense foods are the optimal fuel for our brains and bodies and help us deal with stress. In addition to our eating healthy carbohydrates and healthy fats, it's critical to eat healthy proteins, as they have such a powerful influence on our brain neurotransmitters. Protein provides amino acids that are the precursors for neurotransmitters. Eating high-quality protein during the day can give the neurons in your brain the building blocks they need to build the right neurotransmitters to power your concentration and mental performance.

It's a good idea to eat protein at every meal. That low-nutrient, high-carbohydrate breakfast of toast and orange juice will only lead to an energy crash. High-protein foods can help you maintain your attention and focus. Healthy proteins arrive in their most basic forms, not processed or battered. Healthy sources of protein include free-range organic eggs, beans, seeds, nuts, quinoa, chickpeas, cold-water fish, and lean organic meats.

DR. GREG'S 1% TIP: CHOOSE HIGH-QUALITY PROTEIN

1 cup of lentils provides 18 grams of protein; to get the full spectrum of amino acids, combine with rice or quinoa. Quinoa is complete on its own; rice has a complementary profile to lentils, meaning that if eaten together, you'll get a more complete protein source.

- Two hard-boiled eggs give you 12 grams of complete protein.
- 1 cup of cooked quinoa gives 9 grams of complete protein.
- Half a boneless, skinless chicken breast can provide you with more than 25 grams of protein. Aim to eat pasture-raised chicken, as it will provide you with a more favourable fatty acid profile.[92]
- 2 tbsp. of hemp seeds will provide you with 10 grams of protein. Add hemp seeds to your salads or to a morning smoothie.

Non-GMO tofu can provide 20 grams of protein per half cup and is also a rich vegetarian source of calcium. Although there is conflicting evidence on the estrogenic effects of soy, eating tofu a few times a week may be a great way for vegetarian and vegan athletes to add some quality protein to their diet. It is important to check the

> source of the tofu and to always buy organic. Soy is a top GMO food in North America, and although the effects of GMO are not fully known, buying organic will help reduce the pesticide chemicals you ingest.

BY EATING SMART, you can use nutrition to improve your health to reach your potential and live a world-class life.

National Geographic fellow Dan Buettner travelled around the world to study the lifestyles and environments of the people who live the longest. Demographers he was working with discovered seven places with a very high proportion of people who live to at least age 100.[93] These places were Sardinia in Italy, Ikaria in Greece, Nicoya Peninsula in Costa Rica, Loma Linda in California, and Okinawa in Japan. Once these locations were identified, a team of medical researchers, anthropologists, and epidemiologists travelled there to search for reasons people in these locations live longer than the norm. The teams identified nine common practices of the people living in these locations: (1) they are physically active continually throughout the day; (2) they have a purpose in life; (3) they take time each day to decompress and relax; (4) they stop eating at 80% full, and they eat small meals in the afternoon and evening; (5) they have one or two alcoholic drinks each day with friends; (6) they attend faith-based services once a week; (7) their families are close by, and they're married with children; (8) they have a close-knit social circle; and (9) they eat mostly plants, eating meat only about five times a month. Check out Buettner's TED Talk "How to Live to Be 100+," already viewed more than two million times, and his website, www.bluezones.com, for more information.

BIOHACKING CASE STUDY: THE GUT-BRAIN CONNECTION—THE MICROBIOME

THROUGHOUT THE HUMAN digestive tract live approximately 1×10^{13} to 1×10^{14} micro-organisms—that's more than 10 times the number of human cells we have and 150 times as many genes as our human genome.[94] These organisms can greatly impact all areas of our physiology.[95] Although these bacteria that we host are important for our digestion, they also help synthesize vitamins, impact our immune systems, and appear to play a large role with regard to our brain function. It appears, too, that we have a bidirectional gut–brain connection that provides communication using neural, hormonal, and immunological routes.[96]

Bacterial communities can vary greatly between people, and their composition is thought to be partially genetically determined.[97] Diet, however, can influence our microbiomes as well. Western diets that are becoming increasingly high in saturated fats and refined sugar appear to contribute to changes in the gut microbiota, which can affect the gastrointestinal tract, as well as the immune system.[98] Therefore, they likely have an impact on the brain too. Vegetarianism alters intestinal microbiota in humans because high amounts of fibre result in increased short-chain fatty acid production by microbes, which decreases intestinal pH. This prevents the growth of potentially pathogenic bacteria such as *E. coli* and other members of Enterobacteriaceae, which are potentially harmful or inflammatory.[99] One of the short-chain fatty acids produced by the digestion of fibre in the gut is butyrate. Butyrate is widely considered an important component in the communication between the gut and the brain. Although not yet demonstrated in humans, the diet of a mother while pregnant may influence the microbiota of her baby as well as her own.[100]

A growing body of evidence suggests that our intestinal microbiota play a role in the regulation of our behaviour and brain chemistry, particularly when it comes to mood and anxiety.[101] Studies have linked tryptophan concentration, the precursor to serotonin, to the microbiome. This may suggest a route through which the bacteria in our gut may influence serotonergic transmission in the central nervous system. Tryptophan, produced by bacteria in the gut, is able to cross into the brain, which is protected by what is known as the blood–brain barrier, a structure that keeps out many compounds, including serotonin. Once tryptophan crosses the blood–brain barrier, it can be used to produce serotonin, important in mood regulation. Drugs used to treat depression increase the concentration of serotonin in brain synapses, so with these healthy bacteria essentially having the same effect, there may be potential in developing probiotics as part of therapy to treat depression and anxiety.[102]

Probiotic bacteria have been defined as organisms that, when ingested in large enough amounts, can bring benefits to the host that ingested them. Research shows that consumption of good ("pro") bacteria ("biotics") improves our gut bacterial balance and in turn reduces local (intestinal) and systemic (whole-body) inflammation. These wonder-bugs are recognized for their part in treating and preventing conditions related to inflammation such as allergies, food sensitivities and intolerances, eczema, atopy, intestinal infections, diabetes, nutrient deficiencies, ulcers, and cancer. More research is needed to determine the optimal probiotic strains for each person or disorder.[103]

Fermented foods are a natural source of probiotic bacteria, and interestingly, most cultures have their own version of these foods. The key is to look for foods that have actually been naturally fermented (not just rapidly processed to taste like the real thing). Based on certain genetic characteristics and personal health history, you may respond best to fermented foods related to your ethnic background—for example, plain kefir (Eastern European), miso (Japanese), kimchi (Korean), or sauerkraut (German).

A *prebiotic* is a food that can promote the growth of these health-associated probiotics.[104] These are often non-digestible carbohydrate: fibre. Good sources of fibre are bananas, onions, garlic, and artichokes, as well as oats, barley, wheat, and rye. Fruits such as pears, apples, oranges, and plums also have a substantial amount of fibre that may be beneficial to gut bacteria.

An increasing amount of research is being done on the gut–brain connection in humans, and more information about specific bacterium strains will become available as this continues. Eating lots of fruits and vegetables in order to get enough fibre, while minimizing your intake of overly sweetened or processed foods, is a good way to take care of your gut bacteria and, in turn, your brain. If you're interested in supplementing with probiotics, consider asking a health care professional such as a doctor or naturopath for recommendations.

5
THINK CLEARLY

I learned this, at least, by my experiment: that if one
advances confidently in the direction of his dreams, and
endeavors to live the life which he has imagined, he will
meet with a success unexpected.

—Henry David Thoreau, *Walden: Or, Life in the Woods*

IN OCTOBER 2012, Felix Baumgartner stepped out of a small
capsule attached to a balloon that had climbed to an altitude of
127,852 feet—the edge of space. During the fall, Felix claimed
the title of the fastest man ever in freefall, having reached a
speed in excess of 1,300 km/hr. His heart rate ranged from 143
to 185 beats per minute (the same level as would be achieved in
a maximal-effort running race). He managed to maintain control
and to get out of a 13-second flat spin in which his body was
rotating at a rate of one full spin every second. It was without
question one of the most incredible human achievements and is
a perfect example of peak performance that required precise

preparation, elite execution, and clear thinking under pressure. But the mission almost failed because Felix was afraid of the suit he had to wear.

In the months leading up to the jump, Felix developed almost paralyzing claustrophobia. The suit was a sealed and pressurized space suit. It was not comfortable. Felix began to panic whenever he had to wear it. Before this particular jump, Felix had completed 2,500 others, including jumping off skyscrapers and out of airplanes. So he was no stranger to fear and managing his psychology.

To overcome this challenge, Felix enlisted the assistance of Dr. Michael Gervais, a sport psychologist and host of the fantastic Finding Mastery podcast (http://findingmastery.net). Dr. Gervais went to work with Felix to provide him with the tools and techniques he needed to execute his performance under tremendous pressure—in this case, while his life was on the line. He began by checking that Felix was in fact committed to the mission and not just using the suit as an excuse not to jump. The second step was to determine where Felix was focusing his thoughts and attention. He figured out that Felix was fixated on the suit and had lost his connection with the overall vision of the mission. He had lost the dream and was instead focused on the urgent issue of the day, not the important work that would lead to achievement.

Dr. Gervais and Felix began to work together to do a few key things. The first item they worked on was to reconnect Felix with the most powerful element of the mission, which was the dream to do something that no human had ever done before. Then they slowly began to desensitize Felix to the suit, getting him used to small parts of it one step at a time. For example, Felix would put on the boots, leaving them on for the day while doing other tasks. Slowly, Felix began to get used to the parts of the suit and was able, incrementally, to tolerate it. This mirrors the principle of the aggregate of 1% gains, which I talked about in the introduction. Dr. Gervais taught Felix how to control his breathing to calm himself, and how to speak to himself positively to stay focused. Finally, they worked on staying in the present so that Felix could manage his mind.

The message you can take from this is that everyone, even the most highly trained and experienced specialists, encounters mental challenges that affect their performance and health. However, by applying principles from sport psychology, positive psychology, and Eastern philosophies, we can learn to perform to our potential and to achieve better health at the same time. That's the foundation of what I call thinking clearly.

THE GLOBAL MENTAL HEALTH EPIDEMIC

"There is no health without mental health."
                                    —World Health Organization

THE NUMBER OF people affected by mental health challenges is staggering. Mental health disorders include depression, bipolar affective disorder, schizophrenia, anxiety disorders, dementia, Alzheimer's disease, intellectual disabilities, and developmental and behavioural disorders.[1] People with mental disorders experience 40 to 60% greater chances of disability and dying prematurely, often because physical health problems go untreated.[2]

One in five people will be affected by a mental health challenge during their lifetime.

To make things worse, mental health disorders are often "invisible," in that they're not obvious to an onlooker. So people often don't get the help and support they need. We stigmatize people with mental health challenges. We hide them away and don't talk about the issue. They are discriminated against, and there are even widespread human rights violations against people who experience mental disorders.

The way we are mismanaging the mental health epidemic is, sadly, just like how cancer was mismanaged in the 1950s and how the AIDS epidemic was mismanaged in the 1980s. We stigmatized people with these conditions, and we didn't treat the diseases effectively. In hindsight, we look back at the AIDS epidemic and wonder how on earth we could have treated people that way. And yet, that's exactly how people with mental health disorders are being treated right now by society as a whole.

We need to do better. We have a mental illness epidemic that is sweeping the world, and I hope you'll join me in turning the tide.

WHAT IS MENTAL HEALTH?

THE WORLD HEALTH Organization has defined mental health as "a state of well-being in which the individual realizes his or her own abilities, can cope with the normal stresses of life, can work productively, and is able to make contributions to his or her community."[3] It expands on mental health as it relates to children, stating that children should "have a positive sense of identity, an ability to manage their thoughts [and] emotions and to be able to build positive social relationships as well as having an aptitude for learning." I think those sound like good goals for adults as well.

Fortunately, there are many tools, tactics, strategies, and techniques that can be used to improve mental health. Those that I propose here are mostly focused on helping create better mental health, improve mental performance, and prevent mental illness. If, as a society, we each individually apply these ideas, we can have a huge impact and create a culture in which people experience much better mental health and where people with mental illnesses get comprehensive and holistic help. The ideas and concepts I am presenting cannot take the place of medical and psychiatric treatment. They are meant to be used as preventative and complementary therapies to improve mental and physical health and to help you unleash your potential.

The ripple effect of eating smarter, moving more, and sleeping soundly will all enhance your ability to think clearly and will improve your mental health. This is just the beginning. Thinking clearly is key to building your mental health and a happy, high-performance life. Practise these ideas, and share them with others. Together we can truly make a difference for ourselves and others so we can all live a world-class life where we can reach our potential, achieve our dreams, and be as healthy as we can be.

WORDS OF WISDOM:
DAN MILLMAN ON THE MIND–BODY CONNECTION

Dan Millman, former world champion gymnast, university coach, and author of *The Way of the Peaceful Warrior* and his latest book, *The Hidden School*, recently appeared on my podcast to share the following insights:

When we talk about the body, mind, and emotions, of course we're drawing an artificial distinction. We work as a unity in life, but we have these names and labels to help us understand ourselves for analysis, but it struck me that physical skills alone were not enough.

We've seen people who are physically skilled but who fall apart mentally in competition or under pressure or stress. That's when sports psychology was devised and psychologists tried to come up with techniques—methods like visualization, positive self-talk, and all that—to help athletes on the mental side of the game, and then the emotional side goes along with that.

How do we deal with self-doubt, fear, and other elements to help optimize our performance, not just in sport but in life? We know—we read all about it: athletes who are getting in trouble with the law, having relationships break up. Being physically skilled is being physically skilled, and it's an achievement. It's something to honour. It represents practice over time, but how finely do we need to sculpt our bodies to be happy? That's when I started looking at what makes up the whole human being.

What do we mean by "personal development"? Personal growth, spiritual growth, if you will. It does involve a holistic attitude, and the ancient warriors—in the Budo tradition, the martial arts of Asia and Japan and China and so on. In that tradition, the samurai, for example, recognized that physical skill alone was not enough in a duel to the death with razor-sharp swords. The mind had to be focused and [as] sharp as the sword. The emotions had to be opened, and even existentially one had to be willing to give up one's life.

Those who faced death every morning and died in their mind were the most successful warriors. Those who clung to their life ended up losing it. It led me to a path that I call "the way—or path—of the peaceful warrior," in terms of this holistic emphasis that we're here as a whole human being and life. It's not as if there's some Marine boot-camp program everyone has to go through to become this chiselled body/mind/spirit athlete.

It's that recognizing daily life is a kind of classroom. Planet Earth might be seen as a school. We all notice lessons repeat themselves until we learn them, and if we don't learn easier lessons, they get more dramatic. In a way, life is a perfect school, just doing what we do with awareness. That's all I can do, is remind people of what they already know on deeper levels but we tend to forget.

DR. GREG'S 1% TIP: FOLLOW FIVE HAPPINESS STRATEGIES TO BOOST YOUR LIFE PERFORMANCE

You probably know that stress undermines your performance in just about every aspect of your life. When stressed, you don't sleep well, your concentration suffers, your patience bucket shrinks to the size of a teacup, and your ability to generate strategies and solutions plummets.

So one way to reduce stress and live better is to be happier. Seems obvious, right? Who doesn't want to be happier—and lower stress, increase well-being, and boost daily energy?

But the question is, how?

Maybe you're thinking that the best way to be happier is to get a promotion in your job or make more money or move into a grander house—so you'll just work harder to be happier. It turns out this won't work. A Princeton study published in 2010 found that an annual household income of $75,000 (about $83,000 in today's dollars) is the happiness tipping point.[4] After that, people are no happier. So we can't attach much of our happiness to dollars earned or the status of our neighbourhood.

So, how *can* you become legitimately happier, thereby reducing stress, sleeping better, focusing more sharply, maintaining the patience of a saint, and generating creative solutions to life's challenges? Researchers suggest that happiness varies considerably between people, and about 50% of that variability appears to be because of genetics. You have inherited, to some degree, your potential for happiness.

But let's consider the other 50%. About 40% of happiness variability is because of your own thoughts, actions, and behaviours, and only 10% is because of external circumstances.

So let's focus on that 40% that we can definitely affect. This is an area you can change and develop. Here are some approaches to life that researchers have shown increase happiness and decrease stress levels.

1. PRACTISE DAILY GRATITUDE

IN MY WORK with the national swim team, we spent a lot of time on the road at training camps and competitions. These situations were stressful at times. A key habit we developed in daily meetings was to have each team member say what

someone else had done to help them that day. Expressing gratitude helped bring the team together and make everyone happier.
Science now backs up this practice. Practising daily gratitude for
anything helps you recognize the good parts of life and appreciate them even more.

2. SPEND TIME ON RELATIONSHIPS

HAPPY PEOPLE TEND to have deep relationships with others.
So invest time each week on building deeper relationships with
your family and friends. Make a phone call to catch up with
someone, go to the park with your kids, take your spouse out for
dinner, or do a workout with a friend. Leaving work behind to
build personal relationships will even have a positive impact on
your work performance.

3. BUY EXPERIENCES, NOT POSSESSIONS

RESEARCH SHOWS THAT spending our hard-earned money
on experiences can increase our long-term happiness. Recently,
I spent $150 on surf lessons. I loved the experience and will
remember it fondly for many years. Replace retail therapy with
more fun experiences.

4. VOLUNTEER YOUR TIME OR MONEY

CONTRIBUTING YOUR TIME or resources to help people has
been shown to improve happiness. Find a cause you care about
and get involved. You will be amazed how little time and money it
takes to make a difference that you can really feel good about.

5. ENGAGE DEEPLY WITH LIFE

WE LIVE IN the age of distraction, constantly bombarded by emails, text messages, and phone calls. This disrupts our ability to engage with our activities and experiences. Put your phone away at dinnertime and while working out. My daughter quoted a line from the movie *Shrek* once when we were in the park and I was distractedly responding to an email: "Your job is not my problem!" This priceless moment reminded me to be mindful and present when with her. Research tells us that distractions distract us from our own happiness.

If you practise these techniques, you will amplify your happiness, increase your energy, decrease your stress, and boost your performance in all aspects of life. Give them a try!

THINK CLEARLY TO ACHIEVE BETTER HEALTH

"I've had many troubles in life, most of which never happened." —Mark Twain

MENTAL HEALTH IS the grand challenge of our time. In much the same way as the world is not set up for us to sleep or eat well, our environments are having a negative effect on our mental health. Chronic stress is problematic. Our constantly connected devices, while helpful and enabling, can be damaging to our health unless we learn how to use them to our advantage.

Building habits and applying specific strategies to improve your mental health will help you get and stay on top of your game—whether that is being a CEO, athlete, student, parent, or some other.

A new area of psychological science has emerged in recent years, that of positive psychology. Traditionally, psychology focuses on identifying and treating mental illness—which is critical. However, a focus on illness has resulted in an incomplete picture of mental health. Scientists and practitioners are now exploring the promotion of well-being, happiness, pleasure, positive relationships, and accomplishment. This is the new field of positive psychology. Needless to say, I'm a big fan.

Positive psychology does not propose that life should always be happy and perfect. Ups and downs are inevitable and are essential for an interesting and challenging life. But this new field has identified tools to help us navigate the challenges, improve our mental health, and perform to our potential.

Let's first look at the links between mental health and health challenges, before exploring the keys to building mental health and performance. Many of the concepts I introduce here are based on traditional psychology and sport psychology, as well as Eastern philosophies and the emerging field of positive psychology.

MENTAL HEALTH AND CANCER

ONE OF THE more interesting discoveries in recent years is that the immune system is involved with the control of cancer. Cancer has proven to be a terribly difficult disease to treat, probably because to some extent *cancer* is a word used to broadly describe many very different diseases that share similar characteristics. For example, lung cancer is actually a very different disease from pancreatic cancer, prostate cancer, and so on.

The immune system and the various cells that make up the system's response to infection also serve to combat cancer in the human body. Immune-system cells can target and destroy tumour cells or other types of cancer cells, especially certain kinds of lymphomas. However, suppression of the immune system owing to stress or other factors can increase the incidence of cancer.

After World War 2, researchers monitored the incidence of cancer in a group of 6,284 Jewish Israelis who had lost an adult son during the war. There were higher rates of cancer among the bereaved parents than among non-bereaved members of the population. In this case, it appears that the chronic stress response suppressed the immune system and created an opportunity for cancer cells to grow and propagate.

The concept that the brain can control the immune system, and that the immune system can have an impact on cancer progression, is a powerful one.[5] Although the thought that stress can weaken our immune-system response and increase our chances of having cancer progress uncontrollably in our bodies is frightening, there is an exciting side to that discovery—that our responses to events in our lives are, to a large extent, controllable. We can practise meditation, mindfulness, deep breathing, and muscular meditation, all of which relax the sympathetic nervous system (the "fight or flight" system) and activate the parasympathetic nervous system (the "rest and digest" system). Spending time in nature, and with friends and family, can have the same effect (assuming you like your friends and family). Research has shown that women who have breast cancer and who have active social support networks have a much better chance of survival and lower rates of recurrence.[6]

The physiological explanation is that when we are stressed, the sympathetic nervous system is activated. This helps prepare us for physical activity—a beneficial response from an evolutionary perspective, but a harmful one in today's world, where we can't run away from our stressors. Think about what would happen if you got stressed out during a moment at work and you suddenly sprinted away from your desk or out of a meeting. It would be an epic YouTube moment, but it might not be so great for your career, or for your health.

Activation of the sympathetic system may lower the ability of immune-system cells to unleash their full anti-cancer-cell potential.[7] And that may open up the possibility of tumour growth. More research is needed to better understand this relationship, but, again, the message is clear. Controlling your stress levels will help improve your mental health and ultimately decrease your risk of many chronic diseases, including cancer.

> **DR. GREG'S 1% TIP: STRESS-BUSTER FOOD: DARK CHOCOLATE**
> Chocolate with 70% cocoa or more contains all kinds of goodness: fibre, iron, magnesium, copper, manganese, good fats, flavonoids, and polyphenols. Polyphenols have been shown to improve vascular reactivity—or the ability of your blood vessels to change their diameter so that more oxygen and nutrient-carrying blood can flow through them. Improved vascular reactivity can increase blood flow and oxygen to the brain, thereby increasing mental performance and alertness. For a delicious and healthy treat, eat a little bit (less than an ounce) of dark chocolate a day.

MENTAL HEALTH AND INFLAMMATION

MENTAL HEALTH IS closely tied to inflammation in the body. Earlier I described the inflammatory process and how inflammation is linked to most chronic diseases, including cancer, cardiovascular disease, and obesity. Well, the link is not just between inflammation and physical health but between inflammation and mental health as well.

Research by Dr. Janice Kiecolt-Glaser and her colleagues has shown that depression and inflammation fuel one another.[8] This relationship is bidirectional: basically, depression amplifies the inflammatory response, and inflammation can lead to increased risk of depression. Dr. Kiecolt-Glaser, the director of the Ohio State Institute for Behavioral Medicine Research, describes a vicious circle where inflammation and depression can result in severe mental and physical health challenges.

She describes how stressors and illnesses (such as childhood adversity and obesity) can lead to increased levels of inflammation in the body. The increased inflammation causes pain or poor sleep. This then causes lower levels of physical activity, which exaggerates and worsens the inflammation and can lead to depression and related symptoms. The final link she outlines is depression, poor diet, inactivity, and inflammation then altering the gut microbiome and damaging the intestines, leading to negative physical and mental outcomes.

This is the perfect example of the ripple effect gone bad. Fortunately, the bidirectional links between mental health, exercise, nutrition, and sleep all provide opportunities for powerful interventions that can prevent and in many cases reverse both physical disease and mental illnesses.

One such intervention that can help reduce anxiety and depression is mindfulness. Mindfulness has been described as purposeful and non-judgmental awareness of the present moment. Imagine stopping to smell a flower outside. You are completely engaged in that moment—the beauty of the flower, the smell, the sounds of the birds around you. Nothing else is on your mind, and you are purely enjoying the moment. Mindfulness practice has been shown to be powerfully beneficial in treating anxiety and depression.[9] In a recent meta-analysis study published in the journal *Medicine*, researchers show that mindfulness training has a significant positive impact on anxiety and depression levels in cancer patients.

DR. GREG'S 1% TIP: USE MUSIC AS MEDICINE

Listening to music has beneficial effects on anxiety, pain, mood, and overall quality of life. So add music you enjoy to your life as often as possible. The music I listen to depends on the occasion. For instance, I typically listen to concerts or full albums by my favourite artists when doing creative work; calming playlists on my commute home from the office; fast-tempo, high-energy songs while training; and acoustic performances during meals with my family. Create the soundtrack for your life and reap the rewards.

MENTAL HEALTH AND OBESITY

THE OBESITY EPIDEMIC is perhaps the greatest threat to worldwide health. Most people realize that obesity causes physical health problems and disease. There is now a growing and frightening realization that obesity also causes mental illness.[10] People with mental illnesses are two to three times more likely to be obese, and conversely people with obesity have a 30 to 70% chance of having a mental illness. Obesity is linked to mood disorders, anxiety, personality disorders, attention deficit hyperactivity disorder (ADHD), depression, and schizophrenia.

The exact mechanisms linking obesity to mental illness and vice versa are not clear, but they may include global inflammation, alterations in the gut microbiome, and the physiological damage caused by simple sugars, saturated animal fats, and hydrogenated vegetable oils.

The association between mental health and obesity is extremely complicated; however, I wanted to raise the issue and bring awareness to the challenge. What we can take away from this information is that obesity and mental health are related bidirectionally and that if we can create better mental and physical health, we can improve our odds of overcoming the obesity epidemic and helping millions of people live healthier, happier lives.

Research has shown that aerobic fitness is related to depressive symptoms in teenagers.[11] This means that building their aerobic fitness can help improve the physiology and physical health of those with obesity, even if the patients don't lose any weight. The emerging links between aerobic exercise and depressive symptoms[12] provide some hope that activities such as walking, cycling, hiking, and swimming can potentially help alleviate depressive symptoms in people of all ages.

THINK CLEARLY TO PERFORM BETTER

BEFORE THE LONDON Olympics, I attended a training camp with some of the paddling athletes I work with. During the training, I asked them to work through what I call a descending set. Basically, you start slow and easy and build your effort through faster and faster speeds, even faster than race pace. It's a tough workout, but I love it because it lets me see where fatigue sets in and how athletes respond to the buildup of lactic acid, carbon dioxide, and other chemicals in their muscles and blood. The training eventually causes a battle between mind and body. It is in that battle that you can see the true psychology and physiology of the athlete.

Between taking blood samples, I took photographs of the athletes as their workouts got harder, tougher, and more painful. When I looked at the photos later that night, I saw striking differences between two athletes who were training side by side. One athlete's face was completely relaxed, the hands gently cradling the paddle. The other athlete's face was a mask of tension, and his hands gripped the paddle—hard. The first exuded energy and relaxation. The second showed stress and tension. Both were performing at the same level and going exactly the same speed. But their approach to the performance was completely different. Think effortless energy versus anxiety and tension. Think "fast" versus "hard."

At the Olympics Games, mere weeks after I took those photos, the relaxed high-performer won a silver medal. The tense athlete finished seventh.

When athletes face physical and mental challenges as they go faster, they either get tense and tight or they relax. This ability to relax into the speed is the key to performing at a world-class level while improving health at the same time.

Elite athletes can achieve world-class performances with minimal stress and tension despite being faced with overwhelming challenges. Sadly, most people go through life applying lots of tension and effort to difficult tasks—just like the second athlete. We mistakenly think that working "harder" is the key to success.

Tension makes us feel as if we're working hard, but it leads to distress, decreased circulation, bad moods, fatigue, and poorer performance. This approach is killing us—70% of the deaths on all continents of the world except Africa are caused by stress-related illnesses.

We can do things differently. Highly successful people increase their energy output to go "faster or better" but not "harder." Adopting the high-energy, low-tension approach to life will enable you to perform better and reach your potential. We need to apply energy in a focused way to the task while staying as relaxed and tension-free as possible. This is true regardless of whether you're training for a triathlon, practising a music piece, studying for exams, or trying to complete a work project. By living differently—that is, according to the principles outlined in this chapter—we can get healthier and perform better at whatever we're most passionate about, which will help us reach our potential by leveraging the effect on the brain of sleeping soundly, eating smarter, and moving more, so that we can think and perform at a completely different level. This is how we can unlock our health and potential.

DR. GREG'S 1% TIP: IDENTIFY AND USE YOUR STRENGTHS

In the face of setbacks, we often focus on why we were not able to accomplish that task or get that job/award/raise/ etc. By shifting our attention to our strengths, we can gain great confidence in our abilities, despite setbacks, and we can often see where we should be directing our energies. Ask yourself questions such as the following: Are you a leader? Are you creative? Do you like learning new things? Are you good at working in a team? Are you good at getting loads of work done when alone? You can take an online test on Martin Seligman's website (www.authentichappiness.org) to explore your personal strengths.

THINK CLEARLY TO SLEEP SOUNDLY

SLEEPING BETTER IS a profound challenge in today's always connected world. Earlier I described how defending your last hour can help set the stage for sleeping soundly and recovering and regenerating better. Meditation is proving to be another powerful tool for improving our mental health and helping us sleep better. The body of research on meditation is small—I could find only 273 studies when I searched for "meditation" and "sleep" (together) in PubMed, the US National Institutes of Health's archive of biomedical literature, but there is growing interest in the benefits of meditation, and so I'm sure the science will expand.

Early findings show that practising cyclic meditation improves subsequent sleep.[13] Cyclic meditation involves alternating yoga postures and supine resting. Those participants who practised this technique experienced more slow-wave sleep and fewer awakenings than on nights when they did not practise. They also reported being more refreshed, and feeling better, in the morning. Other researchers suggest that the improvements observed after meditation are a result of better "global regulation in behavioural states," which includes better immune-system function, better regulation of hormones, and more activation of the autonomic nervous system (the nervous system that promotes recovery and regeneration).[14]

Mindfulness meditation has also been studied and appears to be effective for adults who had previously experienced sleep disturbances.[15] It was reported to be more effective than simply providing the participants with sleep hygiene education. Meditation not only works to improve sleep in people with minor sleep disturbances but also appears to be very effective for people with cognitive decline like dementia or Alzheimer's disease.[16] Research findings show that practising a simple meditation program for 6 months improves sleep, quality of life, mood, well-being, and stress in patients with cognitive decline.

Ultimately, this research shows that if you are interested in sleeping soundly and improving your mental and physical health, meditation is a powerful tool for you to explore.

MUSCULAR MEDITATION

THIS CHAPTER IS all about the tools and techniques you can use to break the stress cycle, improve your mental health, and ultimately reach your potential. To highlight the power of the mind–body connection, I want to introduce a technique called *muscular meditation*. The brain and body are linked, and we can achieve better mental health by doing things that improve our physical health. When we do activities that work on both at the same time, the results can be potent.

Muscular meditation is any activity in which you move in a repetitive, rhythmic pattern—walking, swimming, cycling, jogging, rowing, and paddling are examples. Basically, any type of exercise where your muscles are contracting in a consistent pattern over a period. This form of movement helps put the brain in a state where it can relax and the mind can wander. If you do this regularly, it can reduce stress significantly, as well as decrease symptoms of depression and anxiety.[17]

Here are keys to muscular meditation:

1. Give yourself at least 15 minutes. You want to be able to go for a walk, jog, bike ride, or whatever without worrying about time. Give yourself a break and the time you need to move until your mind slows down and relaxes. The first time you try this, you might notice that your mind actually becomes more active. That's okay. After a few sessions, you'll be able to relax your mind while moving your body.

2. Go easy. You don't want to be exercising so hard that it's uncomfortable. This type of exercise should be light. A good way to tell if you're exercising at the right intensity is if you're breathing more than when you're sitting down— just enough so that you can hear air moving in and out of your nose and mouth, but not so much that a conversation would be difficult.

3. Use music, not TV. Music is okay as long as it puts you in a relaxed state. I'd recommend one album or playlist that helps you relax. Don't put it on shuffle: you could be listening to a calming classical piece and in a great place mentally, then be jolted by the opening chords of AC/DC. Watching TV on a treadmill or bike in the gym also defeats the purpose. Just put on the headphones and allow yourself to move and let your mind wander.

4. Use nature. Research shows that being in nature settings improves health and reduces stress and related stress symptoms.[18] If you can go for a walk in a park or somewhere where you can see trees, or even better, water, you'll

reap the benefits. One of my favourite stress-reducing postwork activities is heading out onto the lake on my paddleboard. After 15 minutes of being on the water, I feel awesome and I can come back home and really engage with my family.

There are options beyond walking, swimming, and cycling when it comes to muscular meditation. For thousands of years, practices have been developed in India, China, and Japan that improve both mental and physical health. For our purposes of exploring ways to optimize our stress levels through physical movement, let's focus on yoga, tai chi, and a simple progressive relaxation technique.

Yoga involves moving through various postures while breathing smoothly and deeply. It is excellent for reducing stress levels and improving mental health (lowering depression and anxiety). It can also ease insomnia. On a more metabolic level, yoga has been shown to lower systemic inflammation in patients with obesity and cardiovascular disease. Even more promising is that the physiological and psychological benefits of practising yoga appear in as little as 10 days.

Tai chi is another option. It's a martial art that became popular as a defensive fighting technique but has evolved over the years as primarily a method for relieving stress and anxiety. Tai chi involves a series of movements performed in a slow, focused manner while deep breathing. It's a gentle way to relieve stress.

> **DR. GREG'S 1% TIP: TAI CHI**
>
> According to the Mayo Clinic, benefits of tai chi include the following:
>
> - Decreased stress, anxiety, and blood pressure
> - Increased aerobic capacity, energy, and stamina
> - Increased flexibility, balance, and agility
> - Increased muscle strength and definition
> - Enhanced quality of sleep
> - Enhanced immune-system function

YOU CAN FIND tai chi classes in most communities. Ask some questions to get a sense of the qualifications of the instructor, as there is no certification for tai chi instruction in Canada. It is particularly beneficial to practise tai chi at the same time of day and to be consistent. You'll be amazed at how quickly your skills develop and your stress is relieved.

The third option is *progressive relaxation*. This is a personal favourite. I've done it during long meetings, on planes, and in bed if I'm having trouble sleeping. I also practised this when I was a competitive swimmer, in the days leading into competitions, to help speed recovery and eliminate nervousness and tension. If you want to try the technique, you'll find instructional videos online, including one from the University of New Hampshire. You'll also find detailed instructions in chapter 2.

The body–mind link is powerful. Moving your body in these ways really will improve your mental health and your resilience in the face of challenges.

DR. GREG'S 1% TIP: EXERCISE = ENDORPHINS

Exercise releases endorphins, which cause deep feelings of well-being and sometimes even euphoria—also known as the runner's high. Exercise daily to improve happiness. Amplify this experience by working out with a friend.

MEDITATE TO CREATE

I RECENTLY PARTICIPATED in a thought leadership exercise at a school in Toronto. The school was interested in developing a strategic plan for how the leaders and faculty could help students prepare for the future, which is more uncertain than ever.

I was asked to provide my thoughts on what skills and characteristics the graduate of the future would need to be successful. Repeatedly, others also participating in this exercise highlighted the need for graduates to be agile in their thinking and to be creative—these were considered the skills that would enable them to overcome the challenges they inevitably would face in their careers.

Practising mindfulness and meditation has been shown both in applied practice and in the research to improve attentional control, problem solving, concentration, and creativity. [19] New imaging techniques—including functional magnetic resonance imaging, which shows brain activation, and diffusion tensor imaging, which shows the neural networks in the brain—are demonstrating that mindfulness and meditation can improve brain function and increase neural connectivity in specific parts of the brain. Consider meditation as strength training for the brain. Just as you would lift weights to build and strengthen your muscles, you can use meditation to build and strengthen your brain and then, in addition, to control and sharpen your mind. [20]

Most of the elite performers I have had the privilege of working with over the last few years have a meditation practice. I have just started one—I'm about 6 months into my journey of consistent meditation. The practice has helped me decrease stress, increase calmness, speed recovery, and think more clearly. I really notice the difference between the days when I meditate in the morning and those when I miss my practice. If you want to try out meditation, I suggest the downloadable Headspace app.

THE SEVEN KEYS TO THINKING CLEARLY

BY THINKING CLEARLY, you will be able to function at a higher level in everything you do. The challenge is that because it's the brain and the mind you're working with, you have to practise and be consistent. The research shows that if you can do just that, you will end up changing the structure of your brain, and ultimately it will be easier to concentrate, problem-solve, live in the moment, and reach your potential. Here are my seven keys to thinking clearly.

KEY #1: USE STRESS TO YOUR ADVANTAGE

IT IS WISE to recognize the presence of stress in your life and to act sensibly on this knowledge. It is all about learning how to use stress to help you perform better in the moment and to minimize its negative effects.

Does it sound odd to suggest that there are advantages to stress? Isn't it just damaging and to be avoided at all costs? Interestingly, no. Stress is a lot like food. Not having any at all is bad for us, and too much can make us sick. There are actually two types of stress. Good stress (eustress) and bad stress (distress).

We generally associate the word *stress* with distress, but stress can be positive too (like starting a new job or working on a really cool project). We need to control our stress levels, as much as we can, and help our bodies and minds recover between moments of distress in our lives. But if we're going to learn how to control our stress levels and use stress to our advantage, it's critical that we understand how and why our bodies respond to stress. Let's face it. Even short bursts of stressful situations can be uncomfortable. As a result, we all have a stress response that evolved as a survival strategy.

Our brains can perceive a situation as a threat. We respond to threats in the environment (a sabre-toothed tiger coming toward us, or someone competing with us for food) by increasing our ability to perform physically and mentally (run faster or fight better). We activate a cascade of events that involve the brain, the spinal cord, and a number of endocrine glands that release hormones. That's the stress response.

The activation of the nervous system and the effect of hormones improve our brain function and the strength and power of our muscles. The upside is that we are built to improve our performance. The problem is that running and fighting are not acceptable responses when your team leader announces a new project with a tight deadline.

Our eyes and ears send information to the amygdala, the emotion centre in the brain that classifies objects or events as a threat (e.g., deadlines) or not (e.g., a beautiful flower). If the situation is determined to be a threat, the amygdala sends a distress signal to another structure in the brain called the hypothalamus (which regulates our circadian rhythms, among other things, as you may recall from chapter 2).

The hypothalamus is like a command centre. It activates the

autonomic nervous system (ANS), which controls breathing, heart rate, blood pressure, the liver, the digestive tract, and the lungs. If the hypothalamus receives a distress signal, heart rate and blood pressure go up, breathing increases, the liver dumps sugar into the blood, and the digestive tract shuts down (hence the dry mouth you might experience when scared or nervous).

Perceived threats from the environment create distress signals that activate the adrenal glands, which sit right over the kidneys. The adrenal glands then dump hormones like epinephrine (also known as adrenaline) and cortisol into the blood. Adrenaline and cortisol increase the activity of various organs like the heart and the lungs, as well as the muscles. Can you remember a time when you were startled, and then a few seconds later, your heart started pounding in your chest? When that happened, you were feeling the effects of adrenaline on your heart muscle.

The benefit of hormones like adrenaline and cortisol is that they increase our capacity to function at a high level, both mentally and physically. This is a good thing in short bursts. But it's a bad thing if we keep the gas pedal pressed to the floor for long periods. Because if those hormones remain in our systems over time, or they are constantly being dumped into our bloodstream day after day, they can cause problems.

This increased activation is known as the *sympathetic response*. The opposite *parasympathetic response* is relaxation and calm, when the heart and breathing slow, the liver stores energy, and the digestive tract works to digest food. Think of these two responses like the gas pedal and brake on the car. The sympathetic system gives us bursts of energy so we can deal with the environment, and the parasympathetic system helps us rest and calm down after the danger has passed. Being aware of the balance between your sympathetic (gas pedal) response and the parasympathetic (brake) response is the key to managing your stress.

It's really hard to live a high-performance life when high stress is a daily reality. Chronic stress damages your body, threatens your mental health, puts strain on relationships, and takes the joy out of life. Why is it so bad? Because you have no time to recover from unrelenting stress. Short bursts of stress (called acute stress) are essential for helping us perform at a higher level. But elevated stress over long periods (chronic stress) can make us sick.

According to research conducted at the Harvard Medical School, prolonged stress contributes to high blood pressure, promotes the formation of artery-clogging deposits, and causes brain changes that may contribute to anxiety, depression, and addiction. When epinephrine (adrenaline) damages your blood vessels, making them stiff, the resulting elevated blood pressure increases your risk for heart attack and stroke. And constant increased cortisol levels result in depleted energy and an increase in your appetite, which can lead to weight gain and obesity.

So how can we reduce the ongoing flow of damaging stress hormones—and even find peace? The key is to break up stressful times with periods of rest, recovery, and regeneration. The good news is that anyone can learn techniques that can counter the damage of the stress response. Make sure that each day you take some time to break the stress cycle and activate your parasympathetic system to rest, recover, and regenerate. Doing this not only helps you perform better in the moment but also recharges your body and brain to stay healthy over the long term.

Here are proven techniques that can help you recover from chronic stress.

1. MOVE YOUR BODY

RHYTHMIC, REPEATED MOTION is particularly soothing to the mind and body. A long walk, cycling, swimming, or running will all work, but any kind of movement will relieve tension, improve circulation, and clear your mind.

2. GET INTO NATURE

HEAD OUTSIDE TO the garden, the park, or the woods to lower your blood pressure, strengthen your immune system, reduce tension and depression, and boost your mood. It's stunning how good it is for your health to be in nature. Leave the cellphone and earbuds at home.

3. PRACTISE YOGA OR TAI CHI

LIKE NATURE THERAPY, yoga and tai chi decrease stress and anxiety, increase energy, and boost the immune system. They also give you more stamina—needed in stressful times—and improve the quality of your sleep.

4. HAVE PERSPECTIVE

DON'T BE SO quick to conclude that you "can't handle" a stressful situation. This is truly a mind-over-matter opportunity. Believing that you are strong and resourceful actually makes you stronger and more resourceful. Don't give in to negative self-talk about not having what it takes to manage life.

5. CHANGE THE NATURE OF YOUR RESPONSE

RESEARCH INDICATES THAT taking an active, problem-solving approach to life's challenges relieves stress and can transform it into something positive. If you withdraw, deny the problem, or spend all your time venting, you'll feel helpless. Instead, be determined to make a change, put effort into it, and plan for better results.

DR. GREG'S 1% TIP: PERFORM SLOW, DEEP BREATHING

Here's a powerful tool you can implement right now that will make a huge difference in your life: start applying the power of deep breathing each day.

Start small by taking three deep breaths each time you sit down at your desk—in the morning, after breaks, after lunch, and so on. At the same time, practise progressive relaxation:

- Sit comfortably.
- Drop and relax your shoulders and arms.
- Relax your face, legs, and core.

Follow this simple routine of breathing deeply and relaxing many times a day. (You'll find more detailed instructions in chapter 2.) It will help you become more patient, calm, and relaxed. Deep-breathing exercises have been part of yoga practices for thousands of years, but recent research at Harvard's Massachusetts General Hospital documents the positive impact deep breathing has on the body's ability to deal with stress.[21]

KEY #2: GET IN A STATE OF FLOW

A STATE OF flow is a magical zone where you can perform at your absolute best, yet you're in control and the performance almost seems easy. Have you ever been completely focused and absorbed in a task, and then an hour later, you emerge from "the flow" and realize you have just done some of the best thinking you've ever done? Or a day when you were working or studying and understood everything easily—and the words you wrote just flowed out smoothly onto the page? Or gone for a run and settled into a smooth rhythm in which your mind quieted down and you flowed through the steps, when running became easy and you were able to perform at a level you never knew you were capable of until that moment?

Just about everyone can identify with moments like this. Unfortunately, for most of us, these moments are rare and seem random. But when we explore the science of human performance, you'll see that the flow state—"the zone," also known as the ideal performance zone—is something you can achieve on demand, and it is a state you can control.

American psychologists Robert Yerkes and John Dodson first described the ideal performance zone in 1908.[22] Basically, their Yerkes–Dodson Law describes the activation–performance relationship. When our activation is low, or we don't care, we're not motivated, or we're tired and fatigued, and we don't perform very well. Similarly, when we are too activated, like when we're nervous, agitated, anxious, stressed, or tense, we do not perform well. But somewhere between these two activation states (either too activated or not activated enough) lies the ideal performance state, the state in which we are energized, motivated, focused, happy, and able to perform at our best.

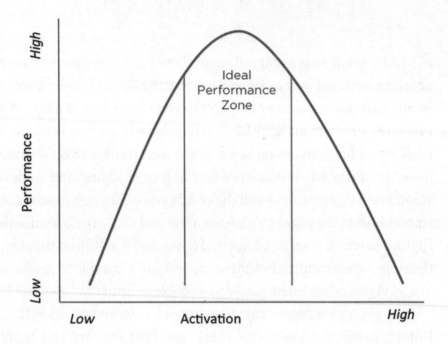

The physiology behind how you feel at each of these extremes is interesting. The fatigue and lack of motivation result in a poor performance. At the extreme high end of activation, you have too much of the stress hormone cortisol and too much adrenaline. As a result, your performance and health suffer. You need to get your internal body chemistry sorted out so you can perform both mentally and physically. Doing so will make you healthier as well: you'll have a lower chance of developing the diseases associated with chronically high cortisol, and you'll be less burned out and fatigued.

The way you get to your optimal performance zone may differ depending on the task you're doing. For example, when I'm playing with my daughter, I need to be slow and calm, almost meditative. Before public speaking, I need to get really psyched up, so I activate my body just like I used to before a swim race, and I try to become a bit nervous so that I have great energy to start the talk. For television appearances, I need to have energy and clarity of thought and total focus. If I'm thinking about anything other than the topic of the day, the appearance does not go well. Focusing on the task at hand is the key.

We can build a different performance zone for each part of our lives. The wonderful thing is that we can control our performance zones by applying simple tools and techniques, and in doing so improve our performance and health.

So, how can you learn to re-create your flow state on demand, anytime you want, rather than just having it "happen"? By knowing what your zone is—which may take some time and a little work to figure out. Try this: Think about the last time you were doing a really great job at work, or you wrote an exam and did brilliantly, or you were at the gym and had a great practice. That fantastic performance didn't just happen. Rather, you put everything together. And you can do it again—if you remember what you did in those moments.

Think about the last time you performed really well at something. Make a note of that moment—write it down—then ask yourself a few questions. What were you doing before that moment? What were your actions? Were you stretching? Did you have a good breakfast? Figure out what you were doing. Write it down. Now you need to figure out what you were thinking: What mindset did you have? Did you say affirmations? Did you listen to a podcast on the way to work? Did you tell yourself what you were going to do? Remember what you were thinking. Write it down. The final step is to remember what you were feeling. What were your emotions? Were you angry? Excited? Motivated? Happy? Write it down.

What you'll end up with is the roadmap for the process elite athletes go through when they're preparing for an event. The best public speakers use this process as well. That's why athletes and public figures typically have routines that they're almost religious about keeping. They know that if they do certain things, they will give themselves the best chance of performing at their best.

Shortly before the London Olympics, diver Alexandre Despatie was training in Spain when he hit his head on the board, leading to a concussion and a 10-centimetre gash in his forehead that required surgery. With the Games only a few weeks away, the injury was shocking.

Alex followed his doctor's return-to-sport protocol closely and resumed training 10 days after the accident. And by the time the Games started, he was ready to compete, which meant he'd have to perform the dive that had led to his injury. If you put yourself in Alex's shoes (or bare feet on the diving board), you can just imagine the emotion he must have been feeling of performing that dive in front of thousands of people in the aquatics centre and millions of viewers. How would he feel? Tense? Nervous? Scared? Anxious?

He was none of these. I know, because I was there at the pool that day to see him use a deliberate technique to prepare for the dive. He stood under the board, going through the motions of the dive—right down to the facial expression—acting as if there were no fear or tension in his body. And by acting the part, he was able to get his thoughts and feelings to go along. I call it act, think, feel.

The basic physiology is simple: if you move your body in a particular way—say, by consciously smiling by contracting your facial muscles—you tell your body to release hormones that change the way you think and feel. The challenge we all face is that this is not the typical sequence. Usually, negative emotions like fear, nervousness, upset, or anger come first and create negative thoughts that lead to particular actions—that is, feel, think, act. But like everything else, we can create a healthier and effective way of living if we put our knowledge of physiology to use.

The key to this skill is to make the shift from feel, think, act to act, think, feel when you are under pressure or feeling stressed. So the next time you're anxious, nervous, or tense, try to shift your body positioning to one of confidence, and note the difference that creates in terms of your thoughts and emotions.

Regardless of how you're feeling, always adopt a posture of confidence and control. Breathe deeply and relax. Unclench your hands. Change your thoughts and emotions through action. You'll be amazed by what you can achieve!

Once you have figured out the three components of getting into a flow state—actions, thoughts, and feelings—you can replicate them. You just need to re-create those conditions. Experiment with this and you will be able to create your ideal performance zone on demand.

> ### DR. GREG'S 1% TIP: SEEK OUT FLOW EXPERIENCES
> Being in the zone or in a state of flow each day is powerful for your mental health and your mental performance. It can lead to being more creative, accomplishing more effortlessly, building a sense of control, and becoming happier and healthier. Key ways to get into the state of flow are to remove all distractions, breathe smoothly and deeply, perform only one task, and concentrate.

KEY #3: BE MINDFUL

MINDFULNESS, OR KEEPING your awareness in the here and now, is important for mental health and elite performance. The key is to stay in the moment in the face of distraction, no matter how great it may be.

Controlling your awareness and mind is integral for success in any discipline, be it music, sports, drama, or business. Yet we live in the age of distraction. Email, social media, text messages, and YouTube all compete for our attention, not to mention the job we are supposed to be doing. The problem is that distraction and multi-tasking go against how our brains work. No matter how much we want to take the drug that Bradley Cooper's character uses to access 100% of his brain in the movie *Limitless*, the reality is that our brains can focus on only one thing at a time.

The nerves that make up the brain have very little stored energy. When we think, problem-solve, or create memories, the brain needs oxygen, glucose, and nutrients to work. This fuel is provided by blood flow to whatever part of the brain is working on the specific task. But blood flow to the brain is limited and can be delivered to only a few small areas at once. If we activate different parts of our brains by trying to think about the past, future, or what does not exist in our reality, we end up shifting the blood flow between locations, never giving the brain what it needs to get a single job done properly.

If you practise mindfulness, you will

- strengthen your ability to stay in the present moment,
- develop your capacity to focus,

- increase the flow of information between mind and body, and
- enter into and stay in your performance zone with more ease.

So as you improve how you manage your mental space, try being mindful by increasing your awareness of what is happening in and around you. Merely register the data from your senses or thoughts with detachment and objectivity as pure facts—watching and observing without labelling, judging, interpreting, or analyzing.

Take a few minutes to do nothing but collect data through your senses. What are you touching, and how does it feel (cold, warm, hot, smooth, rough, soft, hard)? What can you see in terms of shape, colour, texture, distance, closeness? What sounds are close by and farther away, and can you identify them all? What smells are in the air (cologne, coffee, someone's lunch)? What taste do you have in your mouth (sweet, sour, metallic, bitter)? Practise for a few moments each day and you will develop your ability to stay present, develop focus, connect to your body, and stay in your flow state.

This technique involves being 100% present in the moment, with all your attention directed at one thing only. I can do this when I listen to a great piece of music. And at an art gallery: when faced with a masterpiece, I really can't think about anything else. In a conversation with a friend or family member, try being absolutely focused on what they're saying, not allowing your mind to wander and not worrying about how you're going to respond. Just listen and try to understand what they're saying. One of the deepest human needs is to be listened to—so you'll be amazed by the power of listening carefully to others.

And sharpening your focus and living in the moment are great ways to dissipate stress. So much of our stress comes from thinking about the past or the future. When we stay in the present, we often realize that things are pretty good.

DR. GREG'S 1% TIP: BUILD GREAT MEMORIES

Or, as my colleague Robin Sharma says, create perfect moments. Take mental photographs of special moments in your life. Recently, I had an incredible moment when I learned how to stand up on a surfboard on a wave in Australia (before being pummelled and reminded that Nature is the boss). You can rely on the memory images of happy and excited moments for years to come in times of stress.

KEY #4: CULTIVATE MORE ENERGY, LESS TENSION

NOW THAT YOU have an idea about what your performance zones are and what your flow states feel like, let's look at how you can stay in a state of flow when things get tough. And they will. The biggest threat to your being in the zone is that something will happen that increases your stress or anxiety. That will force you from the nice, relaxed high-energy, high-performance state you were in to a state where tension creeps in, and as a result, your performance decreases, your effort increases, and your health suffers. Once again, we can look to world-class performers for both inspiration and concrete examples of how to handle pressure and stress to get back in the performance zone.

There was a moment at the Vancouver Olympics that captured the hearts of people all over the world. Figure skater
Joannie Rochette was heading out onto the ice for the women's
competition. But this was not a typical situation. Joannie's mom
had died just days before the Olympics began. Joannie chose to
compete anyway.

When she went out to skate her program, the crowd went
crazy in support. Millions around the world were glued to their
TVs. Joannie became emotional. She lost control. She became
tense, nervous, and upset. Joannie was way out of her zone. And
she had mere seconds to get back to where she needed to be.

To her credit, she didn't force the performance. She stopped,
turned around, and went back to her coach. Then she drank some
water; took a few slow, deep breaths; and calmed down. She used
a very specific technique—relaxation breathing—to calm her body
and therefore her mind, which allowed her to move back into her
high-performance zone from her high-tension, high-anxiety state.

There is a physiological rationale for why doing this is so effective. Breathing and tension are closely related from a physiological perspective. The centres of the brain that control breathing
are closely linked to the areas of the brain that control stress. If
we can calm the electrical activity in the breathing centre, we
have a good chance of also calming the stress-control centres in
the brain. This is why yoga is such a powerful stress-relieving
activity, and why meditation often begins by focusing on the
breath. The beneficial effects on our physiology are profound.

Felix Baumgartner, whom I mention at the beginning of this
chapter, learned this critical tool from Dr. Gervais in preparation
for his jump. They call it "combat breathing," where Felix would
do deep, controlled breathing to help calm himself when he

became anxious or stressed. I use this technique all the time now to help calm down when things get tough, like when I hear bad news during my workday at the hospital, or when I've had a bad day and I'm about to walk into my house to play with my kids.

You too can do deep breathing anytime, to help you get back into your ideal performance zone. Here's how:

1. Get into good posture. Good posture simply means aligning your spine as you would if you were standing tall. You can do this lying down, sitting in a chair, or standing.
2. Relax your muscles. Do a body scan: search for tension and then take a slow, deep breath and "let go" of the tension as you exhale. It might take a few breaths to get certain areas—your shoulders or forehead, say—to release and relax.
3. Once you feel generally relaxed, take a few controlled breaths. Inhale for 4 seconds, hold for 2 seconds, then exhale for 6 seconds. Make sure your exhale is longer than the inhale. If you need to psyche up or increase your energy, take a longer inhale and exhale more quickly.

Deep breathing is a great tool for relaxing the body and letting the past go so that you can stay mentally and physically healthy in the face of stressful circumstances.

To take advantage of this technique, use it when you're stressed or anxious. It doesn't make much difference if you relax deeply when everything is going well and you're not under pressure. What matters is that you can calm down and bring yourself back into your performance zone when it matters the most—like when you're getting ready to deliver a big presentation at work, or going out on stage to play a piece of music, or getting ready to write an exam, or arriving home after a long and stressful day at work. Just give yourself a moment to breathe and get back in your performance zone.

> ### DR. GREG'S 1% TIP: RELEASE YOUR TENSION
>
> Have you ever felt so relaxed you thought you might melt right through the chair? Or run an extra mile without any effort? Or laughed off every nuisance that would normally be a deep source of irritation?
>
> Sometimes life feels so good, you want to take it out to dinner, drive it home, and tuck it into bed with a kiss on the forehead. Why? Because relaxation is a great pleasure. It also helps us move and think better.
>
> Muscle tension consumes energy inefficiently and decreases circulation, leading to physical aches and pains. If you can achieve a relaxed state, you can get relief from aches and pains and also improve digestion, cardiovascular function, and sleep—all of which will improve your mental functioning.
>
> If you tense your muscles for long periods, you will begin to feel the effects of that body tension in your mind. Your patience goes down. You are less lighthearted. You become mentally fatigued. Clenched fists have the same effect, by triggering the body to start generating anger and upset.
>
> The mind–body link runs both ways, so releasing tension from the body frees the mind from strain and pressure and is a critical physical and mental skill to learn. For example, practising tension release to stop yourself from bracing—a habit of lifting your shoulders and clenching your muscles—can lead to relaxation and

improved mental performance by increasing circulation and energy. To accomplish this, begin by becoming aware of muscle tightness and body position. Do so by asking yourself several questions:

1. Can I drop my shoulders?
2. Can I relax my hands? Stomach? Legs? Forehead?
3. Can I sit in a more comfortable position?
4. Can I relax my core and deepen my breathing?

When you find an area of tension, breathe in deeply and then slowly exhale as you relax and release the tension and free your body and mind of limitations.

The key to executing this technique is being aware of your body. You have to recognize when you're tense— and take 10 to 15 seconds to relax and breathe slowly as you release tension from your body and mind. Once you get good at it, you'll be able to do it more and more quickly, until it will become almost automatic.

PRACTISE RELAXATION AND tension-release techniques for a few minutes each day. It's incredible how these small strategies can help you release tension from the day, calm your mind, and set you up for sleep.

KEY #5: FOCUS RELENTLESSLY

IF I HAD to pick one skill or factor that consistently determines whether someone will be successful during the Olympics, it would be concentration—essentially, the ability to stay in the zone. Athletes who are able to stay on task despite pressure and distractions are able to perform to their potential. Those who are engaged with things that are not relevant to their preparation and performance are the ones who make mistakes or don't perform to expectations. Often they're confused, because they tried so hard in the event yet didn't execute under pressure. The skills and techniques that athletes use to get into the zone and stay there are not complicated, and we can all use them anytime to improve our performance and control our stress levels. The outcome of this improved performance is also improved mental and physical health. For example, we know that if you exercise before an exam, you will improve your academic results, and we know that exercise helps with depression.

When we focus on what's important in the face of distractions and pressures, we can achieve incredible things. Baseball pitchers ignore the crowd and focus on delivering the pitch. Skiers focus on technique when they're about to perform. Musicians get into the music they are playing and forget about the crowd. Actors become the characters they are playing, and the cameras become just objects in the environment. Agents of change like Nelson Mandela, Mahatma Gandhi, and Mother Teresa focus on their beliefs in the face of extreme difficulties, which enables them to act in alignment with their dreams—ultimately changing the world.

Focus is equally powerful in business. Steve Jobs was a legendary leader who was able to build Apple Computer Company into one of the most successful businesses in the world. At one point in his career, he was fired from Apple, returning later to resurrect the company. At his first board meeting back, he did something that highlights the power of focus in business. At that time, Apple was making many different configurations of computers, printers, monitors, and other products. None were very good, nor were they selling well. The stock price had fallen to dangerous lows. When Jobs entered the boardroom, he walked over to a whiteboard, picked up a marker, and drew a grid. He said that from that point on, Apple would make four products only. In each of the four quadrants of the grid, he wrote the name of one product. Apple, he said, would make a personal and a business version of a laptop and a desktop computer. Everything else had to go.

Ultimately, by focusing on just four products, Apple was able to establish a culture of excellence, where the focus was on designing great products. This laid the foundation for the creation of the iPod, which revolutionized the music industry, then the iPhone, which revolutionized the mobile phone industry. Without focus, these achievements would not have been possible. Focus allowed Apple to get into and stay in its performance zone.

For you, this means you can think about your dreams and get excited and energized to follow them. You can control your energy to get into the performance state that you need to be in to move toward your goals. And then you can focus on what you're doing that gives you the chance to achieve your dreams, goals, and objectives, thus crafting the life you have the potential to live.

Sadly, our world is just not set up for deep focus and concentration. We are constantly distracted, and many people try to multi-task. Physiologically, we are not built for multi-tasking. Our brains work best when we focus on one thing at a time. Imagine what would happen if a baseball pitcher paused for a moment to look into the crowd and wave to his mom right before trying to deliver a pitch in the bottom of the ninth with the bases loaded and the World Series on the line. It would never happen because the pitcher knows that getting distracted would rapidly lead to a grand slam home run and living in infamy. Yet we try to multi-task all the time. When I ask people who attend my presentations if they can carve out 1 hour each day to focus completely with no distractions on their most important work, I often get panicked stares. Yet world-class performers in all disciplines make this a key part of their daily routines. Jeff Weiner, CEO of LinkedIn, was known to set aside 2 to 3 hours each day to reflect, think, and focus on the strategic direction of his company. If the CEO of one of the largest social media networks in the world today can do it, I think we can probably do it as well.

Consider the game of baseball when it comes to single-tasking and focus. There are few moments that completely capture my attention as when an elite pitcher and clutch hitter square off with a game on the line. The pitcher's eyes focus on the target, blocking out the crowd, the TV cameras, and the crushing idea that this is a career-defining moment. The hitter breathes deeply to stay calm and relaxed while trying to remain on edge so he can deliver explosive power and energy at the precise instant. Both athletes are living entirely in the moment without thinking about the past or the future (recalling Key #3: Be Mindful). If either athlete became distracted during that battle, it would be over. It's that way for us as well in our daily lives, but we don't notice it because the stakes are lower and we're not on TV, with thousands of people watching us.

If we focus, we can do more in less time, which makes better use of our energy. To improve mental focus, try single-tasking. Single-tasking demands that we pick the most important task to work on first and perform that task as exclusively as possible. I try to work in 90-minute blocks, followed by 30 minutes of recovery. I can then get in four or five great blocks of high-performance work each day while keeping my energy levels up.

All you need to do is remember the focus of a hitter getting ready to smack the ball out of the park, remove all your distractions, and commit to concentrating for a period, and you too can achieve that level of laser-like attention control. Ultimately, you'll perform better and improve your health as well, since you'll be recovering and regenerating all day long.

DR. GREG'S 1% TIP: BLOCK TIME FOR SINGLE-TASKING

Each day this week, schedule time in your calendar for focusing exclusively on one task. This task should be something that is very important to you.

Doing several things at once might make it seem as if you are working hard, but it's an illusion. Your body and mind are not designed to work that way. Switching from task to task reduces your proficiency. Why? Because of how blood flows in our brains.

The nerves that make up the brain have very little stored energy. When we think, problem-solve, or create memories, the brain needs oxygen, glucose, and nutrients to function. This "fuel" is provided by blood flow to whatever part of the brain is working on the specific task. But blood flow to the brain is limited, and if we activate different parts of our brains by trying to multi-task, the blood flow to any particular area is reduced, never giving the brain what it needs to get a single job done properly. It's like a firefighter trying to put out multiple fires at once by spraying water from a hose quickly across several burning houses, rather than extinguishing one blaze and then moving on to the next.

New research from the UK shows that when workers are distracted by phone calls, emails, and text messages, they suffer a greater loss of IQ than a person smoking marijuana! Dr. Glenn Wilson, a psychiatrist at King's College, London University, conducted clinical trials where he monitored the IQ of workers throughout the day. He found that multi-tasking could decrease IQ by an average of 10 points (15 for men and 5 for women). This is equivalent to missing a whole night's sleep!

The concept behind single-tasking is that you start with the most important task—*not* the most urgent one—and work on it exclusively until it is either complete or you are out of time. Then you move on to whatever is next. Urgent tasks often distract us from the important work we need to be doing that will make a positive difference in our and others' lives. By managing how you spend your mental energy, you help ensure that you excel at whatever you do. I recommend avoiding email first thing in the morning so that you don't get derailed by something urgent but not important. I also suggest checking messages at two or three specific times of the day and doing nothing but messages for that period.

The myth that multi-tasking results in productivity is a deeply embedded one in our society, and you might find it difficult at first to change the way you work. Just keep at it, and you will be putting the science to work for you.

KEY #6: USE POWER WORDS AND SELF-TALK

YOU CAN USE specific tools to help you focus and stay in your performance zone. Skier Alexandre Bilodeau used a technique that sport psychologists call "cue words" at the 2010 Vancouver Olympics to help him win a gold medal. The pressure of the moment was huge. (You can watch it online by searching "Alexandre Bilodeau," "gold medal," "men's moguls.")

As he stood at the top of the moguls run looking down at the course, the potential for distraction was massive. Photographers and video cameras lined both sides of the course. At the bottom of the run were 10,000 cheering fans.

To stay completely focused on the only things that mattered to him at that time, Alexandre repeated two words to himself over and over: "forward" and "soft." He wanted his knees to go forward over the bumps, and he wanted to be soft and relaxed in the air. These were pre-arranged cue words that he used to stay focused on the most important elements he needed to execute to stay in the zone and win gold.

Breaking down your performance into small, manageable components and then simplifying those components so much that you can describe them in one word is a powerful way to make sure you focus on the elements of your life that matter to you, especially when you are faced with life's challenges.

When I rode my bike across Africa in 2003, I had time on my hands at night. We had no Internet access, and I spent evenings in my tent to avoid the malaria-carrying mosquitoes that emerged around dusk. So I spent my time reading—several biographies that profoundly influenced me, including those of Mandela, Gandhi, and Mother Teresa. Each of them had simplified their beliefs, even their lives, to a single word that guided their decision making and actions. Then they acted consistently with this word, despite their lives being threatened, being placed in jail, or working in the worst conditions possible for humanity, respectively. Gandhi's word was "truth." By sticking to this word, he liberated India from British rule. Mandela's word was "equality." Because of his commitment to the principles captured by this word, he spent 25 years in jail and eventually broke the will of the South African government and forced the abandonment of apartheid. Mother Teresa's word was "love." It didn't matter how sick or how poor someone was, she loved them. She would help them. She would care for them.

We need to plan, be specific, and take action if we are to create a high-performance life for ourselves. Making changes is hard under the best of circumstances and can be near impossible when we are busy, tired, distracted, stressed, and short on time. This is where self-talk comes in.

Self-talk is a core mental skill that I encourage everyone to use as often as possible. It's incredibly effective. Imagine standing in the blocks right before the final of the 100-metre dash at the Olympics. There are 80,000 people in the stadium watching you and several billion checking you out on TV. What would you be saying to yourself? Olympic runners will be saying things like "Okay, let's GO!" or "Fast, fast, fast!" or "You've done the training, now it's time to RACE." You won't have many athletes in the blocks saying, "I'm tired" or "Man, I have a lot to do today" or "Wow, I feel old." What you think is what you are. And you can have only one thought in your head at any given time. Make it a positive one. And make sure you start your day with one.

Positive self-talk can change, for the better, the way your brain and body work. Research from Carnegie Mellon University shows that self-affirmations can help protect against the damaging effects of stress and can improve academic performance and problem-solving ability in underperforming students.[23] Positive self-talk triggers the right hormones to be released from organs throughout your body. Researchers have also shown that using positive affirmations consistently enhances how well we can learn and improve after making mistakes.[24]

World-renowned motivational speaker Wayne Dyer regularly says that "your intentions create your reality." He is referring to the incredible human capacity to imagine the future and then take action to bring that vision to life. His assertion is supported by extensive research on how our brains work. For example, intentions have the power to eliminate negative thoughts that can get in the way of action. By arriving in a situation with a plan of action for how you will handle it, you reduce the likelihood that you will make a poor decision in the heat of the moment. Intentions also help us avoid "confirmation bias," where we interpret situations subjectively and, as a result, act according to an impulse rather than in alignment with our goals.

The elite athletes I work with are brilliant at this. They start each day with a clearly defined sense of what they are hoping to accomplish and what their training sessions are for. This gives them a sense of purpose and motivation that optimizes their development. You can do the same thing—but only if you set your intentions for improvement at the start of the day. Going into the day with a vague sense of what you hope to accomplish will only lead to your getting into bed at night and thinking, "I meant to do it."

The advice I give people is to express clear and specific

actions they will take each day to get them closer to the self they hope to achieve. These intentions can be simple: "I am going to listen more in the meeting today so I really understand what the client is saying." "I am going to go for a walk at lunch to get the blood flowing instead of having another cup of coffee." "I am going to get someone to read over the report before I send it out to make sure it is as good as possible."

By identifying and setting your intentions and expressing them clearly, you set the stage for a healthy, high-performance life.

DR. GREG'S 1% TIP: ESTABLISH YOUR POWER WORD

Follow these steps to come up with your own power word:

1. Identify your dream or goal performance.
   Example: I'd like to qualify for the Boston Marathon.
2. List a skill, technique, or strategy that is critical to your execution of this dream or goal performance.
   Example: Improve running technique, build fitness, develop strength.
3. List the key elements of that skill, technique, or strategy that will result in a successful performance.
   Example: The ability to run for long distances without losing my technique.
4. What one word or short phrase summarizes the response you should have? That is your power word.
   Example: "Hold form."

NOW THAT YOU have found your power word, it is important to remember to use it!

Example: I need to remind myself of this on the second half of my long Sunday-morning runs.

KEY #7: MEDITATE

EARLIER IN THE chapter, I describe how meditation can help improve sleep and creativity. Meditation, when done consistently, can change your brain for the better. Recent research at Harvard University shows that meditating a few times per week for as little as 8 weeks can actually increase the grey matter in the parts of the brain responsible for emotional regulation and learning. I've found through my own experience that meditation is essential for learning how to manage and sharpen my mind. It is an essential practice for anyone looking to live a world-class life.

New research has demonstrated that regular meditation helps change the responses of a region of the brain called the amygdala to environmental events.[25] Overall, these changes result in better emotional control both during the meditation and in the hours that follow, meaning that meditation has residual effects on mood and emotion that last after the meditation session ends.

Other research shows that meditation improves mood, stress, and hormone levels and can reduce anxiety, pain, and depression. It is an incredible tool that will make a huge difference in your life. As hip hop mogul Russell Simmons says, "If you don't have time to meditate for 30 minutes, you need to meditate for 3 hours."

Meditation can be done anytime, anywhere. Eventually, if you practise, the relaxation response and mind clarity become almost automatic. Start by doing it 1 minute a day. First do a body scan where you find areas that are tight or tense, and then do slow, deep breathing as you relax those areas. Focus your mind and energy on each section of the body, from head to toe. As you direct your focus to each body part, notice any tension and use your breathing to relax that area and let the tension go. Focus on your breathing, and let your thoughts come and go without judgment. You can learn this technique through a guided meditation practice or through an app like Headspace. Make this a habit and you might even be able to change the way your brain controls emotions and learning.

There are several forms of meditation. Concentration meditation, heart-centred meditation, mindfulness meditation, transcendental meditation, tai chi (moving meditation), qigong, and walking meditation are all great options. Explore each of these techniques and see what works best for you.

THINKING CLEARLY IS how we can take our better physical health and energy and translate that into a better life on a daily basis and to actualize excellence. It is the true potential of the mind–body connection. In the same way that daily exercise builds a healthy, high-performance body and improves our health and many aspects of our brains and psychology, daily mental health practices like those discussed in this chapter will enable you to learn, focus, be creative, and be positive and happy so that you can unleash your beautiful ideas on the world.

THE SEVEN PATHWAYS:
USING THE RIPPLE EFFECT TO LIVE
A WORLD-CLASS LIFE

If you love what you do and are willing to do what it takes,
it's within your reach.   —Steve Wozniak

EACH OF US is capable of exceptional things. Your exceptional
may not result in swimming the fastest lap. Your extraordinary
may not make the history books or dazzle a crowd. Your remarkable may not even excite your friends or your dog! But to you,
it's everything. It's living better, achieving more, feeling good,
having energy, staying healthy, and believing in yourself. It's
offering your best at work, at home, and on the court/track/
trail/bike/mat.

And now you know how to build a foundation upon which you
can construct a world-class life. You know how to sleep soundly,
move more, and eat smarter, which all directly relate to keeping
you physiologically healthy and performing at your best physically. They also relate to the brain and mind.

Keep in mind that the words *world-class* and *exceptional* can mean many things. For my Olympic athletes, it's being the best in the world at a sport. For a musician, it might mean playing a beautiful piece of music well. For a businessperson, it might mean coming up with a new solution for a client or delivering a great presentation. It might mean being a good friend and listening patiently to someone who is struggling with life. It might mean being able to let go of distractions and to be fully present with your children in a park. If you are battling cancer, it might mean walking up and down a hallway after a chemotherapy treatment. As a wonderful little girl at SickKids hospital said to me once, "You can't let cancer ruin your day." She was thinking clearly despite being faced with an incomprehensible challenge.

Building the ripple effect principles into your life will help you be healthier and perform better at your life's passion project. These powerful ideas can unlock your potential and enable you to pursue your dreams. You're a unique person with unique challenges and in a unique situation. What follows are some high-level ideas about how certain people can implement these ideas to build a world-class life. Remember that this is a journey, that you need to work on only one principle at a time, and that this process may take years. Just be consistent and patient.

This chapter explores how seven avatars—the CEO, the athlete, the student, the parent, the performer, the transformer, and the health advocate—might use the principles discussed in this book. For each avatar, you'll find an overview and a highlight of which keys from chapters 2 through 5 to focus on. Following this is a "day in the life" that shows you how to implement the principles on a day-to-day basis; use this as a template, customizing it to your advantage, and seek help in organizing your nutrition and workouts if necessary.

You may identify with more than one avatar, and that's fine. These are just examples to get you thinking and pointed in the right direction. Each of us is starting at a different point. For some people, the journey might be minor tweaking to an already healthy routine; for others, it might be a complete lifestyle overhaul.

Above all, have fun exploring how to apply the ideas in this book to make your life better and to bring the wonderful people around you along for an incredible journey. As always, feel free to share your journey with me on Twitter or Instagram (@drgregwells) or on my Facebook page (www.facebook.com/gregwellsphd)—I would love to hear from you.

THE CEO

AS A LEADER in business, you're pushing the limits on a daily basis, and your time is your most valuable commodity. The key to success is to discover a way to consistently perform at a very high level while gradually building in health disciplines you can follow during the day.

Organizing yourself to stay on track while travelling is another challenge (see the discussion on jet lag, pp. 62–68). Choosing the right hotels and finding restaurants that serve good, healthy food and a place to train while on the road are essential.

You also want to spend true quality time with your family, despite your obligations. When you're home, you need to really be home—in your mind as well as your body.

Finally, you will need to program in strategic recovery and regeneration. Regular and consistent work-cycling and vacations are critical if you are to stay focused and productive, but most importantly if you are to be creative and to problem-solve.

Fortunately, the world has changed, and a healthy CEO is now expected. If you make healthy decisions and take action to improve your health in the workplace, people will notice. By taking action and letting others see you get healthy, fit, and hyperproductive, you will enable them to do the same with their lives. It will change your corporate culture for the better. If you are a business leader and want help implementing these principles, contact us at www.thewellsgroup.co.

MOST IMPORTANT KEYS FOR THE CEO

Sleep Soundly

Key #2:	Defend your last hour
Key #3:	Keep your sleep cave dark
Key #4:	Be cool

Move More

Key #1:	Build your fitness
Key #2:	Build your strength
Key #7:	Use it or lose it

Eat Smarter

Key #1:	Hydrate
Key #3:	Consume more nutrients, fewer calories
Key #4:	Eat anti-inflammatory foods

Think Clearly

Key #2:	Get in a state of flow
Key #4:	Cultivate more energy, less tension
Key #5:	Focus relentlessly
Key #7:	Meditate

A DAY IN THE LIFE OF THE CEO

05:00	Wake, water, power snack
05:30	Morning movement practice and training session
06:15	Meditation and integration
06:30	Cold shower
07:00	Super brain-powering smoothie (see p. 161), caffeine
07:30	At work; use the first 90 minutes for solitary consideration/strategizing

09:00	2 x 75- to 90-minute work blocks; power snack at 10:30
12:00	Healthy lunch and 10-minute walk
13:00	2 x 45- to 60-minute work blocks; power snack at 14:30
15:30	30-minute recharge (stretching, meditation, and the second-wind workout—a short blast of exercise that re-energizes your brain in the afternoon) and green tea
16:00	1 x 90-minute work block
18:30	Dinner and family time
21:00	Sleep routine: tea, daily gratitude, meditation, reading fiction, and hot or cold bath
22:00	Sleep

THE ATHLETE

THE PATH FOR the athlete is all about being at the top of your game physically and mentally. You need to perform at your best, then recover and regenerate. The healthier you are, the better you will perform.

Sleep is the foundation for success, so focus on setting up your bedroom to be conducive to sleep, and on being consistent. Most importantly, create a good routine in the hour before you fall asleep. Athletes need at least 7.5 hours and often 9. Naps are your friend.

Athletes also face the challenge of developing their physical capacities while mastering skills and technique. The fitter and stronger you are, the easier it will be to learn these skills and to execute them under stress and strain.

Nutrition is the foundation of human performance, and so it is important that you move beyond the high-calorie and high-sugar diets common among athletes. Learn to eat for maximum nutrition and health, and your performance will follow.

Finally, if you can practise mental skills and get as strong mentally as you are physically, nothing will keep you from reaching your potential. The bonus is that the mental skills and techniques that you learn will help you in all areas of your life.

MOST IMPORTANT KEYS FOR THE ATHLETE

Sleep Soundly

Key #2:	Defend your last hour
Key #5:	Sleep 7 to 8 hours each night
Key #6:	Nap guilt-free

Move More

Key #1:	Build your fitness
Key #2:	Build your strength
Key #3:	Build your speed
Key #4:	Build your mobility
Key #6:	Be a 24-hour athlete

Eat Smarter

Key #1:	Hydrate
Key #4:	Eat anti-inflammatory foods
Key #5:	Eat healthy fats
Key #6:	Eat healthy carbohydrates
Key #7:	Eat healthy proteins

Think Clearly

Key #2:	Get in a state of flow
Key #4:	Cultivate more energy, less tension
Key #5:	Focus relentlessly
Key #6:	Use power words and self-talk

A DAY IN THE LIFE OF THE ATHLETE

05:30	Wake, water, preworkout snack
06:00	Morning movement practice and training session
07:30	Meditation and integration
08:00	Power breakfast
08:30	School or work
10:30	Power snack or smoothie
12:00	Healthy recovery lunch (example: greens, wild fish, wild rice, water)
12:30	Nap
14:00	Power snack
14:30	School or work
16:00	Afternoon movement practice and training session
17:30	Recovery and regeneration (massage, therapy, stretching)
18:30	Dinner
20:30	Sleep routine: tea, daily gratitude, and hot or cold bath
21:30	Sleep

THE STUDENT

ACADEMIC ACHIEVEMENT CAN be extremely challenging. Students have to put in hours to learn the material and participate in extracurricular activities, not to mention spending quality time with their friends. As a student, it is far too easy to burn the candle at both ends and to get burned out and exhausted. That exhaustion leads to overuse of caffeine and cravings for junk food. You can do better.

Students can do well at academics, get healthy, and have a great social life. It starts with making sure that you sleep consistently. Be regular during the week, and aim to get to bed as early as you can, and sleep in and take naps on weekends. Put some effort into making your bedroom dark and cool, and minimize the use of your mobile devices at night.

Nutrition is the foundation for your academic performance and your life. If you're young, you can get away with some poor choices without it affecting you as much as it affects your parents, but ultimately your brain and body will thank you for feeding them high-quality foods that will enable them to work at their best. Not to mention grow and become stronger.

Regular exercise is essential for your physical health, but even more importantly for your mental health. Find something that you love doing and schedule it in. Walking, yoga, lifting weights, playing basketball—it's all good. Find a friend or partner to do your workouts with, for motivation.

Finally, as someone who is studying hard and pushing their brains to the limit, your mental health is a priority. Sadly, far too many students have mental health challenges, and tragedies abound. Take care to give yourself some recovery and regeneration daily, weekly, monthly, and yearly. Take a break from your devices. Get into nature. Let your mind take a break and get healthy.

MOST IMPORTANT KEYS FOR THE STUDENT

Sleep Soundly
- Key #2:   Defend your last hour
- Key #5:   Sleep 7 to 8 hours each night
- Key #6:   Nap guilt-free

Move More
- Key #1:   Build your fitness
- Key #5:   Move in nature

Eat Smarter
- Key #1:   Hydrate
- Key #3:   Consume more nutrients, fewer calories
- Key #5:   Eat healthy fats
- Key #7:   Eat healthy proteins

Think Clearly
- Key #1:   Use stress to your advantage
- Key #2:   Get in a state of flow
- Key #5:   Focus relentlessly

A DAY IN THE LIFE OF THE STUDENT

07:00	Wake, water
07:30	Power breakfast with omega-3s
08:30	School
10:00	Power snack or high-protein smoothie; hydrate
10:30	School
12:00	Healthy lunch
12:30	Movement (walk, stretch, work out)
13:00	School
14:30	High-protein power snack; hydrate
16:00	Afternoon movement practice and workout (run, ride, lift, or stretch)
17:30	Studying and homework
18:30	Dinner
19:00	Social time/homework
21:30	Sleep routine: tea, daily gratitude, and hot or cold bath
22:00	Sleep

THE PARENT

AS A PARENT, you may have the triple responsibilities of being a parent, maintaining a relationship with your spouse or partner, and managing a career at the same time. You may also have to help with taking care of your aging parents. This can be a very stressful time of your life. Many parents end up putting everyone else ahead of themselves. But unless you are healthy and happy yourself, you can't be your best for the people around you who are counting on you. Put your health first and everyone will benefit.

Sleeping has probably taken a big hit with children or teenagers in the house. Prioritize sleep for your whole family, and remember that sleep is a skill that can be learned and trained. Consistency is key, and you might need to deal with short-term challenges to set the routines for the family before everyone settles into the new pattern. Trust me, it's worth it.

Nutrition is something you can control, though it does take time. Batch food preparation and cooking as much as possible. Make extra food at dinner, for lunches the next day. Keep cut vegetables on hand in sealed containers. Fresh fruit always makes for easy and fast snacks. You can even batch-cook foods such as proteins. My colleague Dr. John Berardi recommends batch-cooking chicken breasts, veggie burgers, and lean steaks on Sundays and Wednesdays so you have cooked protein on hand for a few days, to add to stir-fries and salads. Remember that if it is in the house, you or someone you love will eat it. So the more healthy food and the less junk food you keep in the house, the healthier you and your family will be.

Getting workouts in while taking care of your family, working, and managing your home life can be difficult. The benefits of exercise begin with as little as 15 minutes per day. The key is to find little blocks of time when you can get active. Take a 10-minute walk during a break at work. When you go to the park with your kids, don't just sit on the bench watching them play—play with them; run around with them. Schedule a yoga class once a week. Plan active adventures on the weekends.

Undoubtedly, parenting is one of the toughest challenges we take on in our lives. Your mental health is vital. Take breaks. Get into nature regularly. Take time to yourself each day to recover, regenerate, and recharge, even if it is only for 15 minutes to sit by yourself and meditate, or 30 minutes at the end of the day for a quiet bath with no interruptions.

MOST IMPORTANT KEYS FOR THE PARENT

Sleep Soundly
- Key #1:   Save your caffeine for the morning
- Key #2:   Defend your last hour
- Key #3:   Keep your sleep cave dark

Move More

Pick one of Keys #1 to #4 (see chapter 3) to focus on; build fitness through running, or strength through CrossFit, or mobility through yoga
- Key #5:   Move in nature
- Key #7:   Use it or lose it

Eat Smarter
- Key #1:   Hydrate
- Key #2:   Eat mostly plants
- Key #3:   Consume more nutrients, fewer calories

Think Clearly
- Key #1:   Use stress to your advantage
- Key #3:   Be mindful
- Key #7:   Meditate

A DAY IN THE LIFE OF THE PARENT

06:00	Wake, water
06:30	30- to 45-minute movement practice
07:30	Power breakfast with omega-3s
08:00	Travel/family time
09:00	Work or home management
10:30	Power snack or high-protein smoothie; hydrate
12:00	Healthy lunch
12:30	Movement (walk, stretch, work out)
13:00	Work or home management
14:30	High-protein power snack; hydrate
16:00	Afternoon movement practice and workout or travel/family time
17:30	Meal prep
18:00	Dinner
19:00	Family and personal time
21:30	Sleep routine: tea, daily gratitude, and hot or cold bath
22:00	Sleep

THE PERFORMER

AS SOMEONE WHO is focused on developing your music or acting skills, say, and delivering brilliant performances, your priorities are to practise at an elite level as often as possible and to learn new skills as quickly and efficiently as possible. You have big dreams, and your lifestyle will determine your success.

Sleep is of the utmost importance, as sleeping is when you consolidate all the learning you did during the day. This is when new neural pathways are built that help you permanently encode your new skills and build new memories that you can draw upon in the future for practices and performances. Prioritize your sleep and you will give yourself a great chance of maximizing your potential.

Nutrition is fuel for you and your brain. To learn effectively and have the consistent energy to present and perform is of critical importance for you. Eating healthy foods will provide you with the nutrients you need to practise, learn, memorize, and perform at your best.

Movement practice can be used to sculpt your body and activate your mind. Actors and dancers need to be able to deliver a physical performance, and musicians need to have physical energy and health to unleash the brilliance of their music. Regular exercise will enable you to do your artistry at a completely new level.

The performer is the ultimate practitioner of the mind–body connection. Mental skills and mental health are the foundation of your life as an artist. World-class health will enable you to activate your brilliant creativity and artistry, and achieving flow is how the great performers connect to and transform audiences.

MOST IMPORTANT KEYS FOR THE PERFORMER

Sleep Soundly

Key #1:	Save your caffeine for the morning (substitute "practice" for "morning")
Key #5:	Sleep 7 to 8 hours each night
Key #6:	Nap guilt-free

Move More

Key #6:	Be a 24-hour athlete

Eat Smarter

Key #1:	Hydrate
Key #3:	Consume more nutrients, fewer calories
Key #5:	Eat healthy fats
Key #7:	Eat healthy proteins

Think Clearly

Key #2:	Get in a state of flow
Key #4:	Cultivate more energy, less tension
Key #5:	Focus relentlessly
Key #7:	Meditate

A DAY IN THE LIFE OF THE PERFORMER

08:30	Wake, water, light breakfast
09:00	Morning movement practice (walking, stretching)
09:30	Meditation and integration
10:00	Practice/research/rehearsal
11:30	Power snack or smoothie
12:00	Practice/research/rehearsal
13:30	Healthy lunch
14:00	Nap
15:30	Power snack or smoothie
16:00	Practice/research/rehearsal
17:30	Mental preparation (meditation, visualization)
18:30	Small meal
20:00	Performance
23:30	Sleep routine: tea, daily gratitude, and hot or cold bath
00:30	Sleep

THE TRANSFORMER (LIFE CHANGE)

WELCOME TO YOUR new life. If you identify with the need to transform your body, mind, and life, you are likely also emerging from a crisis point. Crisis means both danger and opportunity. The danger is continuing to do things the old way; the opportunity lies in crafting a new life for yourself.

To have the energy you need to build your new life, sleeping is key. Make sleep the foundation of your daily power and you will be able to make the changes you need to make.

Hydrate so you improve your health, cleanse your body, and energize your mind. Eat healthy foods so you have the energy you need to pursue your new passion project. Eliminate junk food so you feel great about yourself.

Move daily. Create a movement practice that you build into your life. Spend time in nature to rediscover your creativity and mental health.

Dedicate yourself to cleaning up your mental life. Eliminate distractions, and protect time each day to think, problem-solve, and plan. Allow your mind time to get clear and for your brain to recover and regenerate.

The ripple effect principles will open up new opportunities and a new life for you.

MOST IMPORTANT KEYS FOR THE TRANSFORMER

Sleep Soundly

Key #2:	Defend your last hour
Key #5:	Sleep 7 to 8 hours each night
Key #7:	Wake up naturally

Move More

Key #1:	Build your fitness
Key #5:	Move in nature
Key #7:	Use it or lose it

Eat Smarter

Key #2:	Eat mostly plants
Key #3:	Consume more nutrients, fewer calories
Key #4:	Eat anti-inflammatory foods

Think Clearly

Key #2:	Get in a state of flow
Key #3:	Be mindful
Key #7:	Meditate

A DAY IN THE LIFE OF THE TRANSFORMER

07:00	Wake, water
07:30	Power breakfast with omega-3s
08:30	Movement practice
10:00	Power snack or high-protein smoothie; hydrate
10:30	Work on passion project/personal development
12:00	Healthy lunch
12:30	Movement (walk, stretch, work out)
13:00	Work on passion project/personal development
14:30	High-protein power snack; hydrate
16:00	Afternoon movement practice and workout (run, ride, lift, or stretch)
17:30	Social time
18:30	Dinner
19:00	Daily gratitude and journalling
21:30	Sleep routine: tea, daily gratitude, and hot or cold bath
22:00	Sleep

THE HEALTH ADVOCATE

YOU ARE ALL in on being as healthy as you can be. Sleep, nutrition, and exercise are priorities in your life. Your family is on board (for the most part), and you have good routines and disciplines. For you, reading this book and applying the principles will be about refining your approach and working on the nuanced details that will make the difference for you and get you that last 5% gain you've been looking for.

You are uniquely positioned to take advantage of the ripple effect and can work on perfecting your sleep, refining your nutrition, and pushing your fitness to a new level. Mental health and mental skills will add depth to your life and supercharge your health and performance.

Consider getting professional coaching to ensure you are maximizing your talents and tactics. A skilled coach will be able to find the little things you can do better. A great personal trainer, or knowledgeable naturopathic doctor or dietitian, or insightful meditation teacher can make all the difference when you have a good foundation and are looking to improve the finer details.

At this point in your life, you have probably done a lot of work to build your routines, your health, and your performance to a wonderful level. Now is the time to enjoy your investment. Use your health and performance abilities to unleash your potential on the world and to inspire others around you to make the best of their lives also.

MOST IMPORTANT KEYS FOR THE HEALTH ADVOCATE

Sleep Soundly

Key #2:	Defend your last hour
Key #3:	Keep your sleep cave dark
Key #5:	Sleep 7 to 8 hours each night

Move More

Key #1:	Build your fitness
Key #2:	Build your strength
Key #3:	Build your speed
Key #4:	Build your mobility

Eat Smarter

Key #2:	Eat mostly plants
Key #4:	Eat anti-inflammatory foods
Key #5:	Eat healthy fats
Key #6:	Eat healthy carbohydrates
Key #7:	Eat healthy proteins

Think Clearly

Key #2:	Get in a state of flow
Key #3:	Be mindful
Key #7:	Meditate

A DAY IN THE LIFE OF THE HEALTH ADVOCATE

05:30	Wake, water, preworkout snack
06:00	Morning movement practice and training session
07:30	Meditation and integration
08:00	Power breakfast
08:30	Work on passion project
10:30	Power snack or smoothie
12:00	Healthy recovery lunch
13:00	Work on passion project
14:30	Power snack
16:00	Afternoon movement practice and training session
17:30	Recovery and regeneration (massage, therapy, stretching)
18:30	Dinner
19:00	Social and family time
21:00	Sleep routine: tea, daily gratitude, and hot or cold bath
22:00	Sleep

ACKNOWLEDGEMENTS

THANK YOU TO my family. I have missed you so much and thank you for sacrificing time with me to allow me to write this book. Without you I wouldn't be able to pursue my dreams.

My parents have given me everything. Without them there is no way I'd be where I am today. Thank you.

To my extended family—Sarah, Brent, Declan, Sadie-Grace, Margaret, David, Thompson, Terry, and Chris—thank you for your love and constant support.

I am so fortunate to have gained so much knowledge and experience from my friends and colleagues at SickKids hospital, the University of Toronto, and Toronto General Hospital as well as from the athletes and coaches I've worked with. I stand on the shoulders of giants.

In this book, I share stories of athletes, clients, and patients whom I have had the opportunity to spend time with. You are the inspiration that drives everything in my professional life. Thank you for trusting me and for giving me the chance to work with you.

A special thank you to Robin Sharma for having me as part of his faculty for the Titan Summit for the last 3 years. Having to take the stage at this event with iconic world leaders has pushed me to reach for and grasp heights I never would have thought possible.

I have the best editor in the business. Thanks to Brad Wilson for helping me find the vision and giving me the opportunity to publish a second book with you and HarperCollins.

NOTES

INTRODUCTION

1. Science Daily. "Global 'sleeplessness epidemic' affects an estimated 150 million in developing world." 2012. http://www.sciencedaily.com/releases/2012/08/120801093617.htm.
2. World Health Organization. "Noncommunicable diseases." Fact sheet 355 (January 2015). http://www.who.int/mediacentre/factsheets/fs355/en.
3. Centers for Disease Control and Prevention. "Overweight and obesity." 2016. http://www.cdc.gov/obesity/data/adult.html.
4. World Health Organization. "Global strategy on diet, physical activity and health." 2004. http://www.who.int/dietphysicalactivity/strategy/eb11344/strategy_english_web.pdf.
5. Government of Canada. "The human face of mental health and mental illness in Canada 2006." 2006. http://www.phac-aspc.gc.ca/publicat/human-humain06/pdf/human_face_e.pdf.

CHAPTER 2: SLEEP SOUNDLY

1. Jones, Stan. "Records detail long hours worked by crew of Exxon Valdez." www.adn.com (September 11, 1989). https://www.adn.com/exxon-valdez-oil-spill/article/records-detail-long-hours-worked-crew-exxon-valdez/1989/09/11.
2. Mitler, M. M., M. A. Carskadon, C. A. Czeisler, W. C. Dement, D. F. Dinges, and R. C. Graeber. "Catastrophes, sleep, and public policy: consensus report." *Sleep* 11, no. 1 (February 1988): 100–109. PMCID: PMC2517096 NIHMSID: NIHMS58740.

3.　　NASA. "Report of the Presidential Commission on the Space Shuttle Challenger accident: human factor analysis." February 1986. http://history.nasa.gov/rogersrep/v2appg.htm.

4.　　Stranges, S., W. Tigbe, F. X. Gómez-Olivé, M. Thorogood, and N.-B. Kandala. "Sleep problems: an emerging global epidemic? Findings from IN DEPTH WHO-SAGE study among more than 40,000 older adults from 8 countries across Africa and Asia." *Sleep* 35, no. 2 (February 1, 2012): 287–302. doi:10.5665/sleep.2012.

5.　　*Nature.* "Waking up to the importance of sleep." *Nature* 437, no. 7063 (October 27, 2005): 1207. http://www.nature.com/nature/journal/v437/n7063/pdf/4371207a.pdf.

6.　　Grandner, M. A., L. Hale, M. Moore, and N. P. Patel. "Mortality associated with short sleep duration: the evidence, the possible mechanisms, and the future." *Sleep Medicine Reviews* (June 2010): doi:10.1016/j.smrv.2009.07.006. Epub November 25, 2009.

7.　　Fullagar, H. H., S. Skorski, R. Duffield, D. Hammes, A. J. Coutts, and T. Meyer. "Sleep and athletic performance: the effects of sleep loss on exercise performance, and physiological and cognitive responses to exercise." *Sports Medicine (Auckland, NZ)* 45, no. 2 (February 2015): doi:10.1007/s40279-014-0260-0.

8.　　Thompson, C. L., and L. Li. "Association of sleep duration and breast cancer OncotypeDX recurrence score." *Breast Cancer Research and Treatment* 134, no. 3 (July 2012): 1291–1295. doi:10.1007/s10549-012-2144-z.

9.　　University Hospitals Case Medical Center. "Lack of sleep found to be a new risk factor for colon cancer." *Cancer* (February 8, 2011). http://www.eurekalert.org/pub_releases/2011-02/uhcm-los020811.php.

10.　 Brown, G. M. "Light, melatonin and the sleep–wake cycle." *Journal of Psychiatry and Neuroscience* 19, no. 5 (November 1994): 345–353. http://www.ncbi.nlm.nih.gov/pmc/articles/PMC1188623.

11.　 Blask, D. E. "Melatonin, sleep disturbance and cancer risk." *Sleep Medicine Reviews* 13, no. 4 (August 2009): 257–264. doi:http://dx.doi.org/10.1016/j.smrv.2008.07.007.

12.　 Ruiz-Núñez, B., L. Pruimboom, D. A. J. Dijck-Brouwer, and F. A. J. Muskiet. "Lifestyle and nutritional imbalances associated with Western diseases: causes and consequences of chronic systemic low-grade inflammation in an evolutionary context." *Journal of Nutritional Biochemistry* 24, no. 7 (July 2013): 1183–1201. doi:http://dx.doi.org/10.1016/j.jnutbio.2013.02.009.

13.　 Irwin, M. R., R. Olmstead, and J. E. Carroll. "Sleep disturbance, sleep duration, and inflammation: a systematic review and meta-analysis of cohort studies and experimental sleep deprivation." *Biological Psychiatry* 80, no. 1 (July 2016): 40–52. http://www.ncbi.nlm.nih.gov/pubmed/26140821.

14. Patel, S. R., X. Zhu, A. Storfer-Isser, R. Mehra, N. S. Jenny, R. Tracy, and S. Redline. "Sleep duration and biomarkers of inflammation." *Sleep* 32, no. 2 (March 2009): 200–204. https://www.researchgate.net/profile/Reena_ Mehra2/publication/24036428_Sleep_duration_and_biomarkers_of_ inflammation_Sleep_32_200-204/links/5630d1ad08ae8eb6f27394ba.pdf.

15. Ayas, N. T., D. P. White, J. E. Manson, M. J. Stampfer, F. E. Speizer, A. Malhotra, and F. B. Hu. "A prospective study of sleep duration and coronary heart disease in women." *Archives of Internal Medicine* 163, no. 2 (January 27, 2003): 205– 209. http://www.ncbi.nlm.nih.gov/pubmed/12546611.

16. Cappuccio, F. P., D. Cooper, L. D'Elia, P. Strazzullo, and M. A. Miller. "Sleep duration predicts cardiovascular outcomes: a systematic review and meta-analysis of prospective studies." *European Heart Journal* 32, no 12. (June 2011): 1484–1492. doi:10.1093/eurheartj/ehr007.

17. Broussard, J. L., D. A. Ehrmann, E. Van Cauter, E. Tasali, and M. J. Brady. "Impaired insulin signaling in human adipocytes after experimental sleep restriction: a randomized, crossover study." *Annals of Internal Medicine* 157, no. 8 (October 16, 2012): 549–557. doi:10.7326/0003-4819-157-8-201210160-00005.

18. University of Chicago Medical Center. "Even your fat cells need sleep, according to new research." *Annals of Internal Medicine* (October 10, 2012): Article ID: 594692. http://www.newswise.com/articles/even-your-fat-cells-need-sleep-according-to-new-research.

19. Donga, E., M. van Dijk, J. G. van Dijk, N. R. Biermasz, G. J. Lammers, K. W. van Kralingen, E. P. Corssmit, and J. A. Romijn. "A single night of partial sleep deprivation induces insulin resistance in multiple metabolic pathways in healthy subjects." *Journal of Clinical Endocrinology and Metabolism* 95, no. 6 (June 2010): 2963–2968. doi:10.1210/jc.2009-2430. Epub April 6, 2010.

20. Harvard Medical School. "Sleep and mental health." Harvard Health Publications (July 2009). http://www.health.harvard.edu/newsletter_ article/Sleep-and-mental-health.

21. Xie, L., H. Kang, Q. Xu, M. J. Chen, Y. Liao, M. Thiyagarajan, J. O'Donnell, D. J. Christensen, C. Nicholson, J. J. Iliff, et al. "Sleep drives metabolite clearance from the adult brain." *Science* 342, no. 6156 (October 18, 2013): 373–377. doi:10.1126/science.1241224.

22. Iliff, J. J., M. Wang, Y. Liao, B. A. Plogg, W. Peng, G. A. Gundersen, H. Benveniste, G. E. Vates, R. Deane, S. A. Goldman, et al. "A paravascular pathway facilitates CSF flow through the brain parenchyma and the clearance of interstitial solutes, including amyloid β." *Science Translational Medicine* 4, no. 147 (August 15, 2012): 147ra111. doi:10.1126/scitranslmed.3003748.

23. Res, P. T., B. Groen, B. Pennings, M. Beelen, G. A. Wallis, A. P. Gijsen, J. M. Senden, and L. J. Van Loon. "Protein ingestion before sleep improves postexercise

overnight recovery." *Medicine and Science in Sports and Exercise* 44, no. 8 (August 2012): 1560–1569. doi:10.1249/MSS.0b013e31824cc363.

24. Mah, C. D., K. E. Mah, E. J. Kezirian, and W. C. Dement. "The effects of sleep extension on the athletic performance of collegiate basketball players." *Sleep* 34, no. 7 (July 1, 2011): 943–950. doi:10.5665/SLEEP.1132.

25. Schwartz, J., and R. D. Simon Jr. "Sleep extension improves serving accuracy: a study with college varsity tennis players." *Physiology and Behavior* 155 (November 1, 2015): 541–544. doi:10.1016/j.physbeh.2015.08.035. Epub September 1, 2015.

25.b Nédélec, M., S. Halson, A. E. Abaidia, S. Ahmaidi, and G. Dupont. "Stress, sleep and recovery in elite soccer: a critical review of the literature." *Sports Medicine (Auckland, NZ)* 45, no. 10 (October 2015): 1387–1400. doi:10.1007/s40279-015-0358-z.

25.c Yarnell, A. M., and P. Deuster. "Sleep as a strategy for optimizing performance." *Journal of Special Medicine* 16, no. 10 (Spring 2016): 81–85. http://www.ncbi.nlm.nih.gov/pubmed/27045502.

26. Van Helder, T., and M. W. Randomski. "Sleep deprivation and the effect on exercise performance." *Sports Medicine* 7, no. 4 (1989): 235–247.

27. Kain, D. "Let me sleep on it: creative problem solving enhanced by REM sleep." UC San Diego News Center (June 9, 2009).

28. Killgore, W. D. "Effects of sleep deprivation on cognition." *Progress in Brain Research* 185 (2010): 105–129. doi:10.1016/B978-0-444-53702-7.00007-5.

28.b Chan, A. L. "New study provides physical evidence of the sleep–learning link." *Healthy Living* (June 10, 2014). http://www.huffingtonpost.com/2014/06/10/sleep-learning-memory-dendritic-spines_n_5460623.html?ncid=txtlnkusaolp00000595.

28.c Gallagher, J. "Sleep's memory role discovered." *BBC News Health* (June 6, 2014): Twitter. http://www.bbc.com/news/health-27695144#?utm_source=twitterfeed&utm_medium=twitter.

29. Euston, D. R., and H. W. Steenland. "Memories: getting wired during sleep." *Science* 344, no. 6188 (June 6, 2014): 1087–1088. doi:10.1126/science.1255649.

30. Yang, G., C. S. W. Lai, J. Cichon, L. Ma, W. Li, and W. B. Gan. "Sleep promotes branch-specific formation of dendritic spines after learning." *Science* 344, no. 6188 (June 6, 2014): 1173–1178. doi:10.1126/science.1249098.

31. Fenn, K. M., and D. Z. Hambrick. "Individual differences in working memory capacity predict sleep-dependent memory consolidation." *Journal of Experimental Psychology: General*. PDF advance online publication (September 12, 2011): doi:10.1037/a0025268.

32. Hysing, M., S. Pallesen, K. M. Stormark, R. Jakobsen, A. J. Lundervold, and B. Sivertsen. "Sleep and use of electronic devices in adolescence: results from a large population-based study." *BMJ Open* 5, no. e006748 (2015): doi:10.1136/bmjopen-2014-006748.

33. Wood, B., M. S. Rea, B. Plitnick, and M. G. Figueiro. "Light level and duration of exposure determine the impact of self-luminous tablets on melatonin suppression." *Applied Ergonomics* 44, no. 2 (March 2013): 237–240. doi:10.1016/j.apergo.2012.07.008. Epub 2012.

34. Blau, R. "The light therapeutic." *Intelligent Life: What Light Does to Our Health* (May 2014).

35. Onen, S. H., F. Onen, D. Bailly, and P. Parquet. "Prevention and treatment of sleep disorders through regulation of sleeping habits." *Presse Medicale (Paris, France: 1983)* 23, no. 10 (March 12, 1994): 485–489. http://www.ncbi.nlm.nih.gov/pubmed/8022726.

36. Y. Chen and F. S. Celi. "Temperature-acclimated brown adipose tissue modulates insulin sensitivity in humans." *Diabetes* 63, no. 11 (November 2014): 3686–3698. doi:10.2337/db14-0513. Epub June 22, 2014.

37. Grandner, M. A., L. Hale, M. Moore, and N. P. Patel. "Mortality associated with short sleep duration: the evidence, the possible mechanisms, and the future." *Sleep Medicine Reviews* (June 2010). doi:10.1016/j.smrv.2009.07.006. Epub November 25, 2009.

38. Simon, H. B., ed. "On call: caught napping." Harvard Health Publications (September 2008). http://www.health.harvard.edu/newsletter_article/on-call-caught-napping.

38.b Mednick, S. C., P. A. Sean, A. Drummond, C. Arman, and G. M. Boynton. "Perceptual deterioration is reflected in the neural response: MRI study between nappers and non-nappers." *Perception* 37, no. 7 (2008): 1086–1097. http://www.ncbi.nlm.nih.gov/pmc/articles/PMC2716730.

39. Anwar, Y. "An afternoon nap markedly boosts the brain's learning capacity." *UC Berkeley News* (February 22, 2010). http://newscenter.berkeley.edu/2010/02/22/naps_boost_learning_capacity.

40. Tietzel, A. J., and L. D. Lack. "The recuperative value of brief and ultra-brief naps on alertness and cognitive performance." *Journal of Sleep Research* 11, no. 3 (September 2002): 213–218. http://www.ncbi.nlm.nih.gov/pubmed/12220317.

CHAPTER 3: MOVE MORE

1. World Health Organization. "Global strategy on diet, physical activity and health." 2004. http://www.who.int/dietphysicalactivity/strategy/eb11344/strategy_english_web.pdf.

2.   World Health Organization. "Physical activity." Fact sheet 385 (June 2016). http://www.who.int/mediacentre/factsheets/fs385/en.

3.   World Health Organization. "Physical activity." Fact sheet 385 (June 2016). http://www.who.int/mediacentre/factsheets/fs385/en.

4.   *JNCI*. "Sedentary behavior increases the risk of certain cancers." *Journal of the National Cancer Institute* (June 2014). http://jnci.oxfordjournals.org/content/106/7/dju206.full.

5.   Ford, E. S., and C. J. Caspersen. "Sedentary behaviour and cardiovascular disease: a review of prospective studies." *International Journal of Epidemiology* 41, no. 5 (October 2012): 1338–1353. doi:10.1093/ije/dys078. Epub May 26, 2012.

6.   Zhang, D., X. Shen, and X. Qi. "Resting heart rate and all-cause and cardiovascular mortality in the general population: a meta-analysis." *Canadian Medical Association Journal* 188, no. 3 (February 16, 2016): E53–63. doi:10.1503/cmaj.150535. Epub November 23, 2015.

7.   West, S. L., A. Gassas, T. Schechter, R. M. Egeler, P. C. Nathan, and G. D. Wells. "Exercise intolerance and the impact of physical activity in children treated with hematopoietic stem cell transplantation." *Pediatric Exercise Science* 26, no. 3 (August 2014): 358–364. doi:10.1123/pes.2013-0156. Epub April 10, 2014.

8.   Knobf, M. T., and K. Winters-Stone. "Exercise and cancer." *Annual Review of Nursing Research* 31 (2013): 327–365. doi:10.1891/0739-6686.31.327.

9.   On breast cancer see:

9.b   Travier, N., M. J. Velthuis, C. N. Steins Bisschop, B. van den Buijs, E. M. Monninkhof, F. Backx, M. Los, F. Erdkamp, H. J. Bloemendal, C. Rodenhuis, et al. "Effects of an 18-week exercise programme started early during breast cancer treatment: a randomised controlled trial." *BMC Medicine* 13, no. 121 (June 8, 2015). doi:10.1186/s12916-015-0362-z.

On prostate cancer see:

9.c   Bourke, L., D. Smith, L. Steed, R. Hooper, A. Carter, J. Catto, P. C. Albertsen, B. Tombalf, H. A. Payneg, and D. J. Rosario. "Exercise for men with prostate cancer: A systematic review and meta-analysis." *European Urology* 69, no. 4 (April 2016): 693–703. doi:10.1016/j.eururo.2015.10.047. Epub November 26, 2015.

On lung cancer see:

9.d   Andersen, A. H., A. Vinther, L. L. Poulsen, and A. Mellemgaard. "Do patients with lung cancer benefit from physical exercise?" *Acta Oncologica (Stockholm, Sweden)* 50, no. 2 (February 2011): 307–313. doi:10.3109/0284186X.2010.529461.

On colon cancer see:

9.e   Van Vulpen, J. K., M. J. Velthuis, C. N. Steins Bisschop, N. Travier, B. J. Van Den Buijs, F. J. Backx, M. Los, F. L. Erdkamp, H. J. Bloemendal, M. Koopman, et al. "Effects of an exercise program in colon cancer patients undergoing chemotherapy." *Medicine and Science in Sports and Exercise* 48, no. 5 (May 2016): 767–775. doi:10.1249/MSS.0000000000000855.

On other types of cancer see:

9.f   Moore, S. C., I. Lee, E. Weiderpass, P. T. Campbell, J. N. Sampson, C. M. Kitahara, S. K. Keadle, H. Arem, A. Berrington de Gonzalez, et al. "Association of leisure-time physical activity with risk of 26 types of cancer in 1.44 million adults." *JAMA Internal Medicine* 176, no. 6 (June 2016): 816–825. doi:10.1001/jamainternmed.2016.1548.

9.g   Loprinzi, P. D., and H. Lee. "Rationale for promoting physical activity among cancer survivors: literature review and epidemiologic examination." *Oncology Nursing Forum* 41, no. 2 (March 1, 2014): 117–125. doi:10.1188/14.ONF.117-125.

9.h   Arem, H., S. C. Moore, Y. Park, R. Ballard-Barbash, A. Hollenbeck, M. Leitzmann, and C. E. Matthews. "Physical activity and cancer-specific mortality in the NIH-AARP Diet and Health Study cohort." *International Journal of Cancer* 135, no. 2 (July 15, 2014): 423–431. doi:10.1002/ijc.28659. Epub December 18, 2013.

10.   Kruijsen-Jaarsma, M., D. Révész, M. B. Bierings, L. M. Buffart, and T. Takken. "Effects of exercise on immune function in patients with cancer: a systematic review." *Exercise Immunology Review* 19 (2013): 120–143. http://www.ncbi.nlm.nih.gov/pubmed/23977724.

11.   Mills, C. D., L. L. Lenz, and R. A. Harris. "A breakthrough: macrophage-directed cancer immunotherapy." *Cancer Research* 76, no. 3 (February 1, 2016): 513–516. doi:10.1158/0008-5472.CAN-15-1737. Epub January 15, 2016.

12.   Pedersen, L., M. Idorn, G. H. Olofsson, B. Lauenborg, I. Nookaew, R. H. Hansen, H. H. Johannesen, J. C. Becker, K. S. Pedersen, C. Dethlefsen, et al. "Voluntary running suppresses tumor growth through epinephrine- and IL-6-dependent NK cell mobilization and redistribution." *Cell Metabolism* 23, no. 3 (March 8, 2016): 554–562. http://dx.doi.org/10.1016/j.cmet.2016.01.011.

13.   McFarlin, B. K., K. C. Carpenter, T. Davidson, and M. A. McFarlin. "Baker's yeast beta glucan supplementation increases salivary IgA and decreases cold/flu symptomatic days after intense exercise." *Journal of Dietary Supplements* 10, no. 3 (September 2013): 171–183. doi:10.3109/19390211.2013.820248. Epub August 9, 2013.

14.   Wells, G. D., D. L. Wilkes, J. E. Schneiderman, T. Rayner, M. Elmi, H. Selvadurai, S. D. Dell, M. D Noseworthy, F. Ratjen, I. Tein, et al. "Skeletal muscle metabolism in cystic fibrosis and primary ciliary dyskinesia." *Pediatric Research* 69, no. 1 (January 2011): 40–45. doi:10.1203/PDR.0b013e3181fff35f.

15. Trapp, D., W. Knez, and W. Sinclair. "Could a vegetarian diet reduce exercise-induced oxidative stress? A review of the literature." *Journal of Sport Sciences* 29, no. 12 (October 2010): 1261–1268. doi:10.1080/02640414.2010.507676.

16. Kazuki, H., D. Ippeita, K. Yasushi, S. Kazuya, B. Kyeongho, O. Genta, K. Morimasa, and S. Hideaki. "The association between aerobic fitness and cognitive function in older men mediated by frontal lateralization." *NeuroImage* 125 (January 15, 2016): 291–300. http://www.sciencedirect.com/science/article/pii/S1053811915008848.

17. Mundstock, E., H. Zatti, F. M. Louzada, S. G. Oliveira, F. T. Guma, M. M. Paris, A. B. Rueda, D. G. Machado, R. T. Stein, M. H. Jones, et al. "Effects of physical activity in telomere length: systematic review and meta-analysis." *Aging Research Reviews* 22 (July 2015): 72–80. doi:10.1016/j.arr.2015.02.004. Epub May 5, 2015.

18. Vidoni, E. D., D. K. Johnson, J. K. Morris, A. Van Sciver, C. S. Greer, S. A. Billinger, J. E. Donnelly, and J. M. Burns. "Dose-response of aerobic exercise on cognition: a community-based, pilot randomized controlled trial." *PLOS ONE* 10, no. 7 (July 9, 2015): e0131647. doi:http://dx.doi.org/10.1371/journal.pone.0131647.

19. Jeon, C. Y., R. P. Lokken, F. B. Hu, and R. M. Van Dam. "Physical activity of moderate intensity and risk of type 2 diabetes: a systematic review." *Diabetes Care* 30, no. 3 (March 2007): 744–752. http://care.diabetesjournals.org/content/diacare/30/3/744.full.pdf.

20. Welly, R. J., T. W. Liu, T. M. Zidon, J. L. Rowles, Y. M. Park, T. N. Smith, K. S. Swanson, J. Padilla, and V. J. Vieira-Potter. "Comparison of diet versus exercise on metabolic function and gut microbiota in obese rats." *Medicine and Science in Sports and Exercise* 48, no. 9 (September 2016): 1688–1698. doi:10.1249/MSS.0000000000000964.

21. Canadian Mental Health Association. "Fast facts about mental illness." 2016. http://www.cmha.ca/media/fast-facts-about-mental-illness.

22. Zhai, L., Y. Zhang, and D. Zhang. "Sedentary behaviour and the risk of depression: a meta-analysis." *British Journal of Sports Medicine* 49, no. 10 (2015): 705–709. doi:10.1136/bjsports-2014-093613.

23. Kvam, S., C. L. Kleppe, I. H. Nordhus, and A. Hovland. "Exercise as a treatment for depression: a meta-analysis." *Journal of Affective Disorders* 202 (September 15, 2016): 67–86. doi:10.1016/j.jad.2016.03.063. Epub May 20, 2016.

23.b Cooney, G. M., K. Dwan, C. A. Greig, D. A. Lawlor, J. Rimer, F. R. Waugh, M. McMurdo, and G. E. Mead. "Exercise for depression." *Cochrane Database of Systematic Reviews* 9 (September 12, 2013): CD004366. doi:10.1002/14651858.CD004366.pub6.

24. Gartlehner, G., B. N. Gaynes, H. R. Amick, G. Asher, L. C. Morgan, E. Coker-Schwimmer, C. Forneris, E. Boland, L. J. Lux, S. Gaylord, et al. "Non-pharmacological versus pharmacological treatments for adult patients with

major depressive disorder." *Comparative Effectiveness Review* no. 161 (December 2015). AHRQ Publication No. 15(16)-EHC031-EF. Rockville, MD: Agency for Healthcare Research and Quality.

25. Edenfield, T. M., and S. A. Saeed. "An update on mindfulness meditation as a self-help treatment for anxiety and depression." *Psychology Research and Behavior Management* 5 (2012): 131–141. doi:10.2147/PRBM.S34937.

26. Costa, A., and T. Barnhofer. "Turning towards or turning away: a comparison of mindfulness meditation and guided imagery relaxation in patients with acute depression." *Behavioral and Cognitive Psychotherapy* 44, no. 4 (July 2016): 410–419. doi:10.1017/S1352465815000387.

27. Alderman, B. L., R. L. Olson, C. J. Brush, and T. J. Shors. "MAP training: combining meditation and aerobic exercise reduces depression and rumination while enhancing synchronized brain activity." *Translational Psychiatry* 6 (February 2, 2016): e726. doi:10.1038/tp.2015.225.

28. Shors, T. J., R. L. Olson, M E. Bates, E. A. Selby, and B. L. Alderman. "Mental and physical (MAP) training: a neurogenesis-inspired intervention that enhances health in humans." *Neurobiology of Learning and Memory* 115 (November 2014): 3–9. doi:10.1016/j.nlm.2014.08.012. Epub September 9, 2014.

29. Yang, P. Y., K. H. Ho, H. C. Chen, and M. Y. Chien. "Exercise training improves sleep quality in middle-aged and older adults with sleep problems: a systematic review." *Journal of Physiotherapy* 58, no. 3 (2012): 157–163. doi:10.1016/S1836-9553(12)70106-6.

30. O'Connor, P. J., and S. D. Youngstedt. "Influence of exercise on human sleep." *Exercise and Sport Sciences Reviews* 23 (1995): 105–134. http://europepmc.org/abstract/MED/7556348.

31. Oaten, M., and K. Cheng. "Longitudinal gains in self-regulation from regular physical exercise." *British Journal of Health Psychology* 11, Pt. 4 (2006): 717–733. doi:10.1348/135910706X96481.

32. Oppezzo, M., and D. L. Schwartz. "Give your ideas some legs: the positive effect of walking on creative thinking." *Journal of Experimental Psychology: Learning, Memory, and Cognition* 40, no. 4 (2014): 1142–1152. 0278-7393/14. http://dx.doi.org/10.1037/a0036577.

33. Chaddock, L., K. I. Erickson, R. S. Prakash, M. Van Patter, M. W. Voss, M. B. Pontifex, L. B. Raine, C. H. Hillman, and A. R. Kramer. "Basal ganglia volume is associated with aerobic fitness in preadolescent children." *Developmental Neuroscience* 32, no. 3 (August 2010): 249–256. doi:10.1159/000316648. Epub August 6, 2010.

34. Aberg, M. A. I., N. L. Pedersen, K. Torén, M. Svartengren, B. Bäckstrand, T. Johnsson, C. M. Cooper-Kuhn, N. D. Aberg, M. Nilsson, and H. G. Kuhn. Edited by F. H. Gage. "Cardiovascular fitness is associated with cognition in young

adulthood." *Proceedings of the National Academy of Sciences of the United States of America* 106, no. 49 (2009): 20906–20911. doi:10.1073/pnas.0905307106.

35. Booth, J. N., S. D. Leary, C. Joinson, A. R. Ness, P. D. Tomporowski, J. M. Boyle, and J. J. Reilly. "Associations between objectively measured physical activity and academic attainment in adolescents from a UK cohort." *British Journal of Sports Medicine* 48, no. 3 (February 2014): 265–270. doi:10.1136/bjsports-2013-092334. Epub October 22, 2013.

36. Gothe, N., M. B. Pontifex, C. Hillman, and E. McAuley. "The acute effects of yoga on executive function." *Journal of Physical Activity and Health* 10, no. 4 (May 2013): 488–495. http://www.ncbi.nlm.nih.gov/pubmed/22820158.

37. Zhou, B., R. K. Conlee, R. Jensen, G. W. Fellingham, J. D. George, and A. G. Fisher. "Stroke volume does not plateau during graded exercise in elite male distance runners." *Medicine and Science in Sports and Exercise* 33, no. 11 (November 2001): 1849–1854. http://www.ncbi.nlm.nih.gov/pubmed/11689734.

38. Nokia, M. S., S. Lensu, J. P. Ahtiainen, P. P. Johansson, L. G. Koch, S. L. Britton, and H. Kainulainen. "Physical exercise increases adult hippocampal neurogenesis in male rats provided it is aerobic and sustained." *Journal of Physiology* 594, no. 7 (April 1, 2016): 1855–1873. doi:10.1113/JP271552.

39. Hartig, T., M. Mang, and G. W. Evans. "Restorative effects of natural environment experience." *Environment and Behavior* 23 (1991): 3–26. doi:10.1177/0013916593256004.

40. White, M. P., A. Smith, K. Humphries, S. Pahl, D. Snelling, and M. H. Depledge. "The importance of water for preference, affect and restorative ratings of natural and built scenes." *Journal of Environmental Psychology* 30, no. 2 (December 2010): 482–493. http://www.ecehh.org/research-projects/water-restorativeness.

41. Pretty, J., J. Peacock, M. Sellens, and M. Griffin. "The mental and physical health outcomes of green exercise." *International Journal of Environmental Health Research* 15, no. 5 (October 2015): 319–337. doi:10.1080/09603120500155963.

41.b Peacock, J., R. Hine, and J. Pretty. "The mental health benefits of green exercise activities and green care." *Mind Week Report* (February 2007). https://www.piuvivi.com/docs/the-mental-health-benefits-of-green-exercise-activities-and-green-care.pdf.

41.c Barton, J., R. Hine, and J. Pretty. "The health benefits of walking in green-spaces of high natural and heritage value." *Journal of Integrative Environment Sciences* 6, no. 4 (2009): 1–18. doi:10.1080/19438150903378425.

42. Park, B. J., Y. Tsunetsugu, T. Kasetani, T. Kagawa, and Y. Miyazaki. "The physiological effects of Shinrin-yoku (taking in the forest atmosphere or forest bathing): evidence from field experiments in 24 forests across Japan." *Environmental Health and Preventive Medicine* 15, no. 1 (January 2010): 18–26. doi:10.1007/s12199-009-0086-9. Epub January 2010.

43. Bird, Dr. W. J. "Natural fit: can green space and biodiversity increase levels of physical activity?" *Royal Society for the Protection of Birds* (October 2004). PDF.

44. Li, Q., K. Morimoto, A. Nakadai, H. Inagaki, M. Katsumata, T. Shimizu, Y. Hirata, H. Suzuki, Y. Miyazaki, T. Kagawa, et al. "Forest bathing enhances human natural killer activity and expression of anti-cancer proteins." *International Journal of Immunopathology and Pharmacology* 20, no. 2 (April–June 2007): 3–8. http://www.ncbi.nlm.nih.gov/pubmed/17903349.

45. Jayakody, K., S. Gunadasa, and C. Hosker. "Exercise for anxiety disorders: systematic review." *British Journal of Sports Medicine* 48, no. 3 (February 2014): 187–196. doi:10.1136/bjsports-2012-091287. Epub January 7, 2013.

45.b Chu, A. H., D. Koh, F. M. Moy, and F. Müller-Riemenschneider. "Do workplace physical activity interventions improve mental health outcomes?" *Occupational Medicine (Oxford: England)* 64, no. 4 (June 2014): 235–245. doi:10.1093/occmed/kqu045.

46. Tarazona-Díaz, M. P., F. Alacid, M. Carrasco, I. Martínez, and E. Aguayo. "Watermelon juice: potential functional drink for sore muscle relief in athletes." *Journal of Agricultural and Food Chemistry* 61, no. 31 (August 7, 2013): 7522–7528. doi:10.1021/jf400964r. Epub July 29, 2013.

47. Schneiderman, J. E., D. L. Wilkes, E. G. Atenafu, T. Nguyen, G. D. Wells, N. Alarie, E. Tullis, L. C. Lands, A. L. Coates, M. Corey, et al. "Longitudinal relationship between physical activity and lung health in patients with cystic fibrosis." *European Respiratory Journal* 43, no. 3 (March 2014): 817–823. doi:10.1183/09031936.00055513.

CHAPTER 4: EAT SMARTER

1. Wells, G. D., M. D. Noseworthy, J. Hamilton, M. Tarnopolski, and I. Tein. "Skeletal muscle metabolic dysfunction in obesity and metabolic syndrome." *Canadian Journal of Neurological Sciences* 35, no. 1 (March 2008): 31–40. http://www.ncbi.nlm.nih.gov/pubmed/18380275.

2. Panickar, K. S. "Effects of dietary polyphenols on neuroregulatory factors and pathways that mediate food intake and energy regulation in obesity." *Molecular Nutrition and Food Research* 57, no. 1 (January 2013): 34–47. doi:10.1002/mnfr.201200431. Epub November 2, 2012. https://www.ncbi.nlm.nih.gov/pubmed/23125162.

3. Samoylenko A., J. A. Hossain, D. Mennerich, S. Kellokumpu, J. K. Hiltunen, and T. Kietzmann. "Nutritional countermeasures targeting reactive oxygen species in cancer: from mechanisms to biomarkers and clinical evidence." *Antioxidants and Redox Signaling* 19, no. 17 (December 10, 2013): 2157–2196. doi: 10.1089/ars.2012.4662.

3.b Lelièvre, S. A., and C. M. Weaver. "Global nutrition research: nutrition and breast cancer prevention as a model." *Nutrition Reviews* on behalf of

International Life Sciences Institute 71, no. 11 (November 2013): 742–752. http://dx.doi.org/10.1111/nure.12075.

3.c   Pericleous, M., R. E. Rossi, D. Mandair, T. Whyand, and M. E. Caplin. "Nutrition and pancreatic cancer." *Anticancer Research* 34, no. 1 (January 2014): 9–21. http://www.ncbi.nlm.nih.gov/pubmed/24403441.

3.d   Tong, L. X., and L. C. Young. "Nutrition: the future of melanoma prevention?" *Journal of American Academy of Dermatology* 71, no. 1 (July 2014): 151–160. doi:10.1016/j.jaad.2014.01.910. Epub March 20, 2014.

4.   Filaire, E., C. Dupuis, G. Galvaing, S. Aubreton, H. Laurent, R. Richard, and M. Filaire. "Lung cancer: what are the links with oxidative stress, physical activity and nutrition." *Lung Cancer (Amsterdam: Netherlands)* 82, no. 3 (December 2013): 383–389. https://www.ncbi.nlm.nih.gov/pubmed/24161719.

5.   Tasevska, N., R. Sinha, V. Kipnis, A. F. Subar, M. F. Leitzmann, A. R. Hollenbeck, N. E. Caporaso, A. Schatzkin, and A. J. Cross. "A prospective study of meat, cooking methods, meat mutagens, heme iron, and lung cancer risks." *American Journal of Clinical Nutrition* 89 (2009): 1884–1894.

6.   Hu, J., C. La Vecchia, M. de Groh, E. Negri, H. Morrison, L. Mery, and Canadian Cancer Registries Epidemiology Research Group. "Dietary trans fatty acids and cancer risk." *European Journal of Cancer Prevention* 20 (2011): 530–538.

6.b   Chajès, V., A. Thiébaut, M. Rotival, E. Gauthier, V. Maillard, M. C. Boutron-Ruault, V. Joulin, G. M. Lenoir, and F. Clavel-Chapelon. "Serum phospholipid trans-monounsaturated fatty acids are associated with increased risk of breast cancer in women." *American Journal of Epidemiology* 167 (2008): 1312–1320.

7.   Choi, Y., E. Giovannucci, and J. E. Lee. "Glycaemic index and glycaemic load in relation to risk of diabetes-related cancers: a meta-analysis." *British Journal of Nutrition* 108 (2012): 1934–1947.

8.   Chajès, V., and I. Romieu. "Nutrition and breast cancer." *Maturitas* 77, no. 1 (January 2014): 7–11.

9.   Pericleous, M., R. E. Rossi, D. Mandair, T. Whyand, and M. E. Caplin. "Nutrition and pancreatic cancer." *Anticancer Research* 34, no. 1 (January 2014): 9–21. http://www.ncbi.nlm.nih.gov/pubmed/24403441.

10.   Tong, L. X., and L. C. Young. "Nutrition: the future of melanoma prevention?" *Journal of American Academy of Dermatology* 71, no. 1 (July 2014): 151–160. doi:10.1016/j.jaad.2014.01.910. Epub March 20, 2014.

11.   Norat, T., S. Bingham, P. Ferrari, N. Slimani, M. Jenab, M. Mazuir, K. Overvad, A. Olsen, A. Tjønneland, F. Clavel, et al. "Meat, fish, and colorectal cancer risk: the European Prospective Investigation into cancer and nutrition." *Journal of the National Cancer Institute* 97, no. 12 (June 2005): 906–916. http://www.ncbi.nlm.nih.gov/pubmed/15956652.

12. Vargas, A. J., and P. A. Thompson. "Diet and nutrient factors in colorectal cancer risk." *Nutrition in Clinical Practice* 27, no. 5 (October 2012): 613–623. doi:10.1177/0884533612454885. Epub August 14, 2012.

13. Ayers, E., and J. Verghese. "Locomotion, cognition and influences of nutrition in ageing." *Proceedings of the Nutrition Society* 73, no. 2 (May 2014): 302–308. doi:10.1017/S0029665113003716. Epub November 1, 2013.

13.b Gorelick, P. B. "Role of inflammation in cognitive impairment: results of observational epidemiological studies and clinical trials." *Annals of the New York Academy of Sciences* 1207 (October 2010): 155–162. doi:10.1111/j.1749-6632.2010.05726.x.

14. Yaffe, K., A. Kanaya, K. Lindquist, E. M. Simonsick, T. Harris, R. I. Shorr, F. A. Tylavsky, and A. B. Newman. "The metabolic syndrome, inflammation, and risk of cognitive decline." *Journal of the American Medical Association* 292, no. 18 (November 10, 2004): 2237–2242. doi:10.1001/jama.292.18.2237.

15. Cordain, L., S. Boyd Eaton, A. Sebastien, N. Mann, S. Lindeberg, B. A. Watkins, J. H. O'Keefe, and J. Brand-Miller. "Origins and evolution of the Western diet: health implications for the 21st century." *American Journal of Clinical Nutrition* 81, no. 2 (February 2005): 341–354.

15.b Beilharz, J. E., J. Maniam, and M. J. Morris. "Short exposure to a diet rich in both fat and sugar or sugar alone impairs place, but not object recognition memory in rats." *Brain, Behavior, and Immunity* (December 3, 2013): pii: S0889-1591(13)00575-8. doi:10.1016/j.bbi.2013.11.016. Epub December 3, 2013.

16. Ruiz-Núñez, B., L. Pruimboom, D. A. J. Dijck-Brouwer, and F. A. J. Muskiet. "Lifestyle and nutritional imbalances associated with Western diseases: causes and consequences of chronic systemic low-grade inflammation in an evolutionary context." *Journal of Nutritional Biochemistry* 24, no. 7 (July 2013): 1183–1201. doi:http://dx.doi.org/10.1016/j.jnutbio.2013.02.009.

17. Hibbeln, J. R., L. R. Nieminen, T. L. Blasbalg, J. A. Riggs, and W. E. Lands. "Healthy intakes of n-3 and n-6 fatty acids: estimations considering worldwide diversity." *American Journal of Clinical Nutrition* 83 (2006): (Suppl) 1483S–1493S.

18. Labrousse, V. F., A. Nadjar, C. Joffre, L. Costes, A. Aubert, S. Grégoire, L. Bretillon, and S. Layé. "Short-term long chain omega3 diet protects from neuroinflammatory processes and memory impairment in aged mice." *PLOS ONE* 7, no. 5 (2012): e36861. doi:10.1371/journal.pone.0036861. Epub May 25, 2012.

18.b Dong, S., Q. Zeng, E. S. Mitchell, J. Xiu, Y. Duan, C. Li, J. K. Tiwari, Y. Hu, X. Cao, and Z. Zhao. "Curcumin enhances neurogenesis and cognition in aged rats: implications for transcriptional interactions related to growth and synaptic plasticity." *PLOS ONE* 7, no. 2 (2012): e31211. doi:10.1371/journal.pone.0031211. Epub February 16, 2012.

18.c   Grundy, T., C. Toben, E. J. Jaehne, F. Corrigan, and B. T. Baune. "Long-term omega-3 supplementation modulates behavior, hippocampal fatty acid concentration, neuronal progenitor proliferation and central TNF-α expression in 7 month old unchallenged mice." *Frontiers in Cellular Neuroscience* 8 (November 21, 2014): 399. doi:10.3389/fncel.2014.00399. eCollection 2014.

19.   Bauer, J., G. Biolo, T. Cederholm, M. Cesari, A. J. Cruz-Jentoft, J. E. Morley, S. Phillips, C. Sieber, P. Stehle, D. Teta, et al. "Evidence-based recommendations for optimal dietary protein intake in older people: a position paper from the PROT-AGE Study Group." *Journal of the American Medical Directors Association* 14, no. 8 (August 2013): 542–559. doi:10.1016/j.jamda.2013.05.021. Epub July 16, 2013.

19.b   Stonehouse, W., C. A. Conlon, J. Podd, S. R. Hill, A. M. Minihane, C. Haskell, and D. Kennedy. "DHA supplementation improved both memory and reaction time in healthy young adults: a randomized controlled trial." *American Journal of Clinical Nutrition* 97, no. 5 (May 2013): 1134–1143. doi:10.3945/ajcn.112.053371. Epub March 20, 2013.

19.c   Fontani, G., F. Corradeschi, A. Felici, F. Alfatti, S. Migliorini, and L. Lodi. "Cognitive and physiological effects of omega-3 polyunsaturated fatty acid supplementation in healthy subjects." *European Journal of Clinical Investigation* 35, no. 11 (November 2005): 691–699. doi:10.1111/j.1365-2362.2005.01570.x

19.d   Nilsson, G. E., D. L. Dixson, P. Domenici, M. I. McCormick, C. Sorensen, S.-A. Watson, and P. L. Munday. "Near-future carbon dioxide levels alter fish behaviour by interfering with neurotransmitter function." *Nature Climate Change* 2 (2012): 201–204. doi:10.1038/nclimate1352.

19.e   Yurko-Mauro, K., D. McCarthy, D. Rom, E. B. Nelson, A. S. Ryan, A. Blackwell, N. Salem Jr., M. Stedman, and MIDAS Investigators. "Beneficial effects of docosahexaenoic acid on cognition in age-related cognitive decline." *Alzheimers & Dementia: Journal of the Alzheimer's Association* 6, no. 6 (November 2010): 456–464. doi:10.1016/j.jalz.2010.01.013.

19.f   Chilton, W., F. Z. Marques, J. West, G. Kannourakis, S. P. Berzins, B. J. O'Brien, and F. J. Charchar. "Acute exercise leads to regulation of telomere-associated genes and microRNA expression in immune cells." *PLOS ONE* 9, no. 4 (2014): e92088. doi:10.1371/journal.pone.0092088.

20.   Galland, L. "Diet and inflammation." *Nutrition in Clinical Practice: Official Publication of the American Society for Parenteral and Enteral Nutrition* 25, no. 6 (December 2010): 634–640. doi:10.1177/0884533610385703.

20.b   Martínez-Lapiscina, E. H., P. Clavero, E. Toledo, R. Estruch, J. Salas-Salvadó, B. San Julián, A. Sanchez-Tainta, E. Ros, C. Valls-Pedret, and M. Á Martinez-Gonzalez. "Mediterranean diet improves cognition: the PREDIMED-NAVARRA randomised trial." *Journal of Neurology, Neurosurgery, and Psychiatry* (2012). Revised March 8, 2013. 304792v1.

21.   Milbury, P. E., C. Y. Chen, G. G. Dolnikowski, and J. B. Blumberg. "Determination of flavonoids and phenolics and their distribution in almonds." *Journal of Agricultural Food Chemistry* 54 (2006): 5027–5033.

21.b   Yi, M., J. Fu, L. Zhou, H. Gao, C. Fan, J. Shao, B. Xu, Q. Wang, J. Li, G. Huang, et al. "The effect of almond consumption on elements of endurance exercise performance in trained athletes." *Journal of the International Society of Sports Nutrition* 11 (May 11, 2014): 18.

22.   Chen, C. Y., and J. B. Blumberg. "In vitro activity of almond skin polyphenols for scavenging free radicals and inducing quinone reductase." *Journal of Agricultural Food Chemistry* 56 (2008): 4427–4434.

22.b   Rajaram, S., K. M. Connell, and J. Sabaté. "Effect of almond-enriched high-monounsaturated fat diet on selected markers of inflammation: a randomised, controlled, crossover study." *British Journal of Nutrition* 103 (2010): 907–912.

22.c   Mandalari, G., C. Bisignano, T. Genovese, E. Mazzon, M. S. Wickham, I. Paterniti, and S. Cuzzocrea. "Natural almond skin reduced oxidative stress and inflammation in an experimental model of inflammatory bowel disease." *International Immunopharmacology* 11 (2011): 915–924.

23.   Laitinen, M. H., T. Ngandu, S. Rovio, E. L. Helkala, U. Uusitalo, M. Viitanen, A. Nissinen, J. Tuomilehto, H. Soininen, and M. Kivipelto. "Fat intake at midlife and risk of dementia and Alzheimer's disease: a population-based study." *Dementia and Geriatric Cognitive Disorders* 22, no. 1 (2006): 99–107. Epub May 19, 2006.

23.b   Vercambre, M. N., F. Grodstein, and J. H. Kang. "Dietary fat intake in relation to cognitive change in high-risk women with cardiovascular disease or vascular factors." *European Journal of Clinical Nutrition* 64, no. 10 (October 2010): 1134–1140. doi:10.1038/ejcn.2010.113. Epub July 21, 2010.

23.c   Berti, V., J. Murray, M. Davies, N. Spector, W. H. Tsui, Y. Li, S. Williams, E. Pirraglia, S. Vallabhajosula, P. McHugh, et al. "Nutrient patterns and brain biomarkers of Alzheimer's disease in cognitively normal individuals." *Journal of Nutrition Health and Aging* 19, no. 4 (2015): 413–423. doi:10.1007/s12603-014-0534-0.

23.d   Dyall, S. C. "Long-chain omega-3 fatty acids and the brain: a review of the independent and shared effects of EPA, DPA and DHA." *Frontiers in Aging Neuroscience* 7, no. 52 (2015). Published online April 21, 2015. doi:10.3389/fnagi.2015.00052.

24.   Gillette-Guyonnet, S., M. Secher, and B. Vellas. "Nutrition and neurodegeneration: epidemiological evidence and challenges for future research." *British Journal of Clinical Pharmacology* 75 (2013): 738–755. doi:10.1111/bcp.12058.

24.b   Sydenham, E., A. D. Dangour, and W. S. Lim. "Omega 3 fatty acid for the prevention of cognitive decline and dementia." *Cochrane Database of Systematic Review* 6 (June 13, 2012): CD005379. doi:10.1002/14651858. CD005379.pub3.

24.c   Calderon, F., H. Y. Kim. "Docosahexaenoic acid promotes neurite growth in hippocampal neurons." *Journal of Neurochemistry* 90, no. 4 (August 2004): 979–988. doi:10.1111/j.1471-4159.2004.02520.x

25.   O'Connor, A. "Coca-Cola funds scientists who shift blame for obesity away from bad diets." *Well* (August 9, 2015). http://well.blogs.nytimes.com/2015/08/09/coca-cola-funds-scientists-who-shift-blame-for-obesity-away-from-bad-diets.

26.   Brasilia: Ministry of Health of Brazil. Translated by Carlos Augusto Monteiro. "Dietary guidelines for the Brazilian population." *Ministry of Health of Brazil* 2nd edition (2014). http://www.foodpolitics.com/wp-content/uploads/Brazilian-Dietary-Guidelines-2014.pdf.

27.   Lennerz, B., D. C. Alsop, L. M. Holsen, E. Stern, R. Rojas, C. B. Ebbeling, J. M. Goldstein, and D. S. Ludwig. "Effects of dietary glycemic index on brain regions related to reward and craving in men." *American Journal of Clinical Nutrition* (June 26, 2013). doi:10.3945/ajcn.113.064113.

28.   Nabavi, B., A. J. Mitchell, and D. Nutt. "A lifetime prevalence of comorbidity between bipolar affective disorder and anxiety disorders: a meta-analysis of 52 interview-based studies of psychiatric population." *EBioMedicine* 2, no. 10 (September 8, 2015): 1405–1419. doi:10.1016/j.ebiom.2015.09.006. eCollection 2015.

29.   Gramza, A., R. Wójciak, J. Korczak, M. Hęś, J. Wiśniewska, and Z. Krejpcio. "Influence of the Fe and Cu presence in tea extracts on antioxidant activity." *Electronic Journal of Polish Agricultural Universities* 8, no. 4 (2005): 30.

30.   Grosso G., A. Micek, S. Castellano, A. Pajak, and F. Galvano. "Coffee, tea, caffeine and risk of depression: a systematic review and dose-response meta-analysis of observational studies." *Molecular Nutrition & Food Research* 60, no. 1 (January 2016): 223–34. doi: 10.1002/mnfr.201500620.

31.   Pase, M. P., A. B. Scholey, A. Pipingas, M. Kras, K. Nolidin, A. Gibbs, K. Wesnes, and C. Stough. "Cocoa polyphenols enhance positive mood states but not cognitive performance: a randomized, placebo-controlled trial." *Journal of*

Psychopharmacology (Oxford, England) 27, no 5 (May 2013): 451–458. doi:10.1177/0269881112473791. Epub January 29, 2013.

32. Liperoti, R., G. Onder, F. Landi, K. L. Lapane, V. Mor, R. Bernabei, and G. Gambassi. "All-cause mortality associated with atypical and conventional antipsychotics among nursing home residents with dementia: a retrospective cohort study." *Journal of Clinical Psychiatry* 70, no. 10 (October 2009): 1340–1347. doi:10.4088/JCP.08m04597yel.

33. Sánchez-Villegas, A., P. Henríquez, M. Bes-Rastrollo, and J. Doreste. "Mediterranean diet and depression." *Public Health Nutrition* 9, no. 8A (December 2006): 1104–1109. doi:10.1017/S1368980007668578.

33.b Tiemeier, H., H. R. van Tujil, A. Hofman, A. J. Kiliaan, and M. M. B. Breteler. "Plasma fatty acid composition and depression are associated in the elderly: the Rotterdam Study." *American Journal Clinical Nutrition* 78, no. 1 (July 2003): 40–46. http://ajcn.nutrition.org/content/78/1/40.full#abstract-1.

34. Mikkelsen K., L. Stojanovska, and V. Apostolopoulos. "The effects of vitamin B in depression." *Current Medicinal Chemistry* 23, no. 38 (2016): 4317–4337.

35. Bottiglieri, T. "Folate, vitamin B12, and neuropsychiatric disorders." *Nutrition Reviews* 54, no. 12 (December 1996): 382–390.

36. Selhub, J., L. C. Bagley, J. Miller, and I. H. Rosenberg. "B vitamins, homocysteine, and neurocognitive function in the elderly." *American Journal of Clinical Nutrition* 71, no. 2 (February 2000): 614S–620S. https://www.ncbi.nlm.nih.gov/pubmed/10681269.

37. Davison, K. M., and B. J. Kaplan. "Nutrient intakes are correlated with overall psychiatric functioning in adults with mood disorders." *Canadian Journal of Psychiatry* 57, no. 2 (February 2012): 85–92.

38. Haas, T. "The latest science on nutrition that protects your mind." *MedCan* (July 5, 2016). http://medcan.com/medcan-insights/expert-perspectives/radar-brain-food-scale.

39. Halson, S. L. "Sleep in elite athletes and nutritional interventions to enhance sleep." *Sports Medicine (Auckland, NZ)* 44, Suppl. 1 (May 2014): S13–23. doi:10.1007/s40279-014-0147-0.

40. Jalilolghadr, S., A. Afaghi, H. O'Connor, and C. M. Chow. "Effect of low and high glycaemic index drink on sleep pattern in children." *Journal of the Pakistan Medical Association* 61, no. 6 (June 2011): 533–536.

40.b Lindseth, G., P. Lindseth, and M. Thompson. "Nutritional effects on sleep." *Western Journal of Nursing Research* 35, no. 4 (April 2013): 497–513. doi:10.1177/0193945911416379. Epub August 4, 2011.

41. Fernstrom, J. D., and R. J. Wurtman. "Brain serotonin content: physiological dependence on plasma tryptophan levels." *Science* 173 (July 9, 1971): 149–152.

41.b   Silber, B. Y., and J. A. Schmitt. "Effects of tryptophan loading on human cognition, mood, and sleep." *Neuroscience and Biobehavioral Reviews* 34, no. 3 (March 2010): 387–407. doi:10.1016/j.neubiorev.2009.08.005. Epub August 26, 2009.

42.   Afaghi, A., H. O'Connor, and C. M. Chow. "High-glycemic-index carbohydrate meals shorten sleep onset." *American Journal of Clinical Nutrition* 85, no. 2 (February 2007).

43.   Howatson, G., P. G. Bell, J. Tallent, B. Middleton, M. P. McHugh, and J. Ellis. "Effect of tart cherry juice (Prunus cerasus) on melatonin levels and enhanced sleep quality." *European Journal of Nutrition* 51, no. 8 (December 2012): 909–916. doi:10.1007/s00394-011-0263-7. Epub October 30, 2011.

43.b   Ferracioli-Oda, E., A. Qawasmi, and M. H. Bloch. "Meta-analysis: melatonin for the treatment of primary sleep disorders." *PLOS ONE* 8, no. 5 (May 17, 2013): e63773. doi:10.1371/journal.pone.0063773. Print 2013.

43.c   Bent, S., A. Padula, D. Moore, M. Patterson, and W. Mehling. "Valerian for sleep: a systematic review and meta-analysis." *American Journal of Medicine* 119, no. 12 (December 2006): 1005–1012. doi:10.1016/j.amjmed.2006.02.026.

44.   Popkin, B. M., and C. Hawkes. "Sweetening of the global diet, particularly beverages: patterns, trends, and policy responses." *The Lancet: Diabetes & Endocrinology* 4, no. 2 (2015): 174–186.

45.   Huskisson, E., S. Maggini, and M. Ruf. "The role of vitamins and minerals in energy metabolism and well-being." *Journal of International Medicine Research* 35, no. 3 (May–June 2007): 277–289.

46.   Huskisson, E., S. Maggini, and M. Ruf. "The role of vitamins and minerals in energy metabolism and well-being." *Journal of International Medicine Research* 35, no. 3 (May–June 2007): 277–289.

47.   Mattson, M. P., W. Duan, S. L. Chan, A. Cheng, N. Haughey, D. S. Gary, Z. Guo, J. Lee, and K. Furukawa. "Neuroprotective and neurorestorative signal transduction mechanisms in brain aging: modification by genes, diet and behavior." *Neurobiology of Aging* 23, no. 5 (September–October 2002): 695–705.

47.b   Prins, R. G., J. Panter, E. Heinen, S. J. Griffin, and D. B. Ogilvie. "Causal pathways linking environmental change with health behaviour change: Natural experimental study of new transport infrastructure and cycling to work." *Preventive Medicine* 87 (June 2016): 175–182.

47.c   Seshadri, S., A. Beiser, J. Selhub, P. F. Jacques, I. H. Rosenberg, R. B. D'Agostino, P. W. Wilson, and P. A. Wolf. "Plasma homocysteine as a risk factor for dementia and Alzheimer's disease." *New England Journal of Medicine* 346, no. 7 (February 14, 2002): 476–483. doi:10.1056/NEJMoa011613.

48. Ravaglia, G., P. Forti, F. Maioli, A. Muscari, L. Sacchetti, G. Arnone, V. Nativio, T. Talerico, and E. Mariani. "Homocysteine and cognitive function in healthy elderly community dwellers in Italy." *American Journal of Clinical Nutrition* 77, no. 3 (March 2003): 668–673. PMID: 12600859. https://www.ncbi.nlm.nih.gov/pubmed/12600859.

49. Hoyland, A., L. Dye, and C. L. Lawton. "A systematic review of the effect of breakfast on the cognitive performance of children and adolescents." *Nutrition Research Reviews* 22, no. 2 (December 2009): 220–243. doi:10.1017/S0954422409990175. Epub December 2009.

50. Shukitt-Hale, B., F. C. Lau, A. N. Carey, R. L. Galli, E. L. Spangler, D. K. Ingram, and J. A. Joseph. "Blueberry polyphenols attenuate kainic acid-induced decrements in cognition and alter inflammatory gene expression in rat hippocampus." *Nutritional Neuroscience* 11, no. 4 (August 2008): 172–182. doi:10.1179/147683008X301487.

51. *AMJA.* "Polyphenols: food sources and bioavailability." *American Journal of Clinical Nutrition* 79, no. 5 (May 1, 2004): 727–747.

52. Commenges, D., V. Scotet, S. Renaud, D. Jacqmin-Gadda, P. Barberger-Gateau, and J. F. Dartigues. "Intake of flavonoids and risk of dementia." *European Journal of Epidemiology* 16, no. 4 (April 2000): 357–363.

52.b Letenneur, L., C. Proust-Lima, A. Le Gouge, J. F. Dartigues, and P. Barberger-Gateau. "Flavonoid intake and cognitive decline over a 10-year period." *American Journal of Epidemiology* 165, no. 12 (June 15, 2007): 1364–1371.

53. Sokolov, A. N., M. A. Pavlova, S. Klosterhalfen, and P. Enck. "Chocolate and the brain: neurobiological impact of cocoa flavanols on cognition and behavior." *Neuroscience Biobehavioral Review* 37, no. 10. Pt. 2 (December 2013): 2445–2453. doi:10.1016/j.neubiorev.2013.06.013. Epub June 26, 2013.

54. Gonzalez-Gallego, J., S. Sanchez-Campos, and M. J Tuñón. "Anti-inflammatory properties of dietary flavonoids." *Nutricion hospitalaria: organo oficial de la Sociedad Espanola de Nutricion Parenteral y Enteral* 22, no. 3 (February 2007): 287–293. ISSN 0212-1611. https://www.researchgate.net/publication/6226174_Anti-Inflammatory_properties_of_fietary_flavonoids.

55. Joseph, J. A., B. Shukitt-Hale, N. A. Denisova, D. Bielinski, A. Martin, J. J. McEwen, and P. C. Bickford. "Reversals of age-related declines in neuronal signal transduction, cognitive, and motor behavioral deficits with blueberry, spinach, or strawberry dietary supplementation." *Journal of Neuroscience* 19, no. 18 (1999): 8114–8121.

55.b Joseph, J. A., B. Shukitt-Hale, N. A. Denisova, R. L. Prior, G. Cao, A. Martin, G. Taglialatela, and P. C. Bickford. "Long-term dietary strawberry, spinach, or vitamin E supplementation retards the onset of age-related neuronal signal-transduction and cognitive behavioral deficits." *Journal of Neuroscience* 18, no. 19 (1998): 8047–8055. https://www.ncbi.nlm.nih.gov/pubmed/9742171.

56. Kempton, M. J., U. Ettinger, R. Foster, S. C. R. Williams, G. A. Calvert, A. Hampshire, F. Zelaya, R. L. O'Gorman, T. McMorris, A. M. Owen, et al. "Dehydration affects brain structure and function in healthy adolescents." *Human Brain Mapping* 32 (March 24, 2010): 71–79. doi:10.1002/hbm.20999.

57. Gomez-Pinilla, F. "The combined effects of exercise and foods in preventing neurological and cognitive disorders." *Preventive Medicine* 52, Suppl 1 (June 2011): S75–80. doi:10.1016/j.ypmed.2011.01.023. Epub January 31, 2011.

58. Kempton, M. J., U. Ettinger, R. Foster, S. C. R. Williams, G. A. Calvert, A. Hampshire, F. Zelaya, R. L. O'Gorman, T. McMorris, A. M. Owen, et al. "Dehydration affects brain structure and function in healthy adolescents." *Human Brain Mapping* 32 (March 24, 2010): 71–79. doi:10.1002/hbm.20999.

59. Adan, A. "Cognitive performance and dehydration." *Journal of American College of Nutrition* 31, no. 2 (April 2012): 71–78. http://www.ncbi.nlm.nih.gov/pubmed/22855911.

60. Wang, X., Y. Ouyang, J. Liu, M. Zhu, G. Zhao, W. Bao, and F. B Hu. "Fruit and vegetable consumption and mortality from all causes, cardiovascular disease, and cancer: systematic review and dose-response meta-analysis of prospective cohort studies." *British Medical Journal* 349 (July 29, 2014): g4490. doi:http://dx.doi.org/10.1136/bmj.g4490.

61. Oude, G. L. M., W. M. Verschuren, D. Kromhout, M. C. Ocké, and J. M. Geleijnse. "Colours of fruit and vegetables and 10-year incidence of CHD." *British Journal of Nutrition* 106, no. 10 (November 2011): 1562–1569. doi:10.1017/S0007114511001942. Epub June 8, 2011.

62. Bao, Y., J. Han, F. B. Hu, E. L. Giovannucci, M. J. Stampfer, W. C. Willett, and C. S. Fuchs. "Association of nut consumption with total and cause-specific mortality." *New England Journal of Medicine* 369 (2013): 2001–2011. doi:10.1056/NEJMoa1307352.

63. Benzie, I. F., and S. W. Choi. "Antioxidants in food: content, measurement, significance, action, cautions, caveats, and research needs." *Advances in Food and Nutrition Research* 71 (2014): 1–53. doi:10.1016/B978-0-12-800270-4.00001-8.

64. Boeing, H., A. Bechthold, A. Bub, S. Ellinger, D. Haller, A. Kroke, E. Leschik-Bonnet, M. J. Müller, H. Oberritter, M. Schulze, P. Stehle, et al. "Critical review: vegetables and fruit in the prevention of chronic diseases." *European Journal of Nutrition* 51, no. 6 (September 2012): 637–663. doi:10.1007/s00394-012-0380-y. Epub June 9, 2012.

64.b Craig, W. J. "Nutrition concerns and health effects of vegetarian diets." *Nutrition in Clinical Practice* 25, no. 6 (December 2010): 613–630. doi:10.1177/0884533610385707.

65. Sultan, M. T., M. S. Buttxs, M. M. N. Qayyum, and H. A. R. Suleria. "Immunity: plants as effective mediators." *Critical Reviews in Food Science and Nutrition* (May 14, 2013): 1298–1308. http://www.tandfonline.com/doi/abs/10.1080/10408398.2011.633249.

66. Cradock, A. L., E. L. Kenney, A. McHugh, L. Conley, R. S. Mozaffarian, J. F. Reiner, and S. Gortmaker. "Evaluating the impact of the healthy beverage executive order for city agencies in Boston, Massachusetts." *Preventing Chronic Disease* 12 (2015): 2011–2013. doi:http://dx.doi.org/10.5888/pcd12.140549.

67. Gleeson, M. "Immunological aspects of sport nutrition." *Immunology and Cell Biology* 94, no. 2 (February 2016): 117–123. doi: 10.1038/icb.2015.109.

68. Ghosh, D., and A. Scheepens. "Vascular action of polyphenols." *Molecular Nutrition & Food Research* 53, no. 3 (March 2009): 322–331. doi: 10.1002/mnfr.200800182.

69. Caracciolo, B., W. Xu, S. Collins, and L. Fratiglioni. "Cognitive decline, dietary factors and gut-brain interactions." *Mechanisms of Ageing and Development* (March/April 2014): 136–137, 59–69. doi: 10.1016/j.mad.2013.11.011.

70. Gleeson, M. "Immunological aspects of sport nutrition." *Immunology and Cell Biology* 94, no. 2 (February 2016): 117–123. doi: 10.1038/icb.2015.109.

71. Totsch, S. K., M. E. Waite, and R. E. Sorge. "Dietary influence on pain via the immune system." *Progress in Molecular Biology and Translational Science* 131 (2015): 435–469. doi: 10.1016/bs.pmbts.2014.11.013.

72. Rendeiro, C., J. S. Rhodes, and J. P. E. Spencer. "The mechanisms of action of flavonoids in the brain: direct versus indirect effects." *Neurochemistry International* 89 (October 2015): 126–139. doi: 10.1016/j.neuint.2015.08.002.

73. Totsch, S. K., M. E. Waite, and R. E. Sorge. "Dietary influence on pain via the immune system." *Progress in Molecular Biology and Translational Science* 131 (2015): 435–469. doi: 10.1016/bs.pmbts.2014.11.013.

74. Krikorian R., M. D. Shidler, T. A. Nash, W. Kalt, M. R. Vinqvist-Tymchuk, B. Shukitt-Hale, and J. A. Joseph. "Blueberry supplementation improves memory in older adults." *Journal of Agriculture and Food Chemistry* 58, no. 7 (April 14, 2010): 3996–4000. doi: 10.1021/jf9029332.

75. Kalt W., Y. Liu, J. E. McDonald, M. R. Vinqvist-Tymchuk, and S. A. Fillmore. "Anthocyanin metabolites are abundant and persistent in human urine." *Journal of Agricultural and Food Chemistry* 62 (2014): 3926–3934. doi: 10.1021/jf500107j.

76. Martin, R. C. G., H. S. Aiyer, D. Malik, and Y. Li. "Effect on pro-inflammatory and antioxidant genes and bioavailable distribution of whole tumeric vs. curcumin: similar root but different effects." *Food and Chemical Toxicology* 50, no. 2 (February 2012): 227–231. doi: 10.1016/j.fct.2011.10.070.

77. McFarlin, B. K., A. S. Venable, A. L. Henning, J. N. B. Sampson, K. Pennel, J. L. Vingren, and D. W. Hill. "Reduced inflammatory and muscle damage biomarkers following oral supplementation with bioavailable curcumin." *BBA Clinical* 5 (February 18, 2016): 72–78. doi: 10.1016/j.bbacli.2016.02.003.

78. Martin, R. C. G., H. S. Aiyer, D. Malik, and Y. Li. "Effect on pro-inflammatory and antioxidant genes and bioavailable distribution of whole tumeric vs. curcumin: similar root but different effects." *Food and Chemical Toxicology* 50, no. 2 (February 2012): 227–231. doi: 10.1016/j.fct.2011.10.070.

79. Wu, A., E. E. Noble, E. Tyagi, Z. Ying, Y. Zhuang, and F. Gomez-Pinilla. "Curcumin boosts DHA in the brain: implications for the prevention of anxiety disorders." *BBA Molecular Basis of Disease* 1852, no. 5 (2015): 951–961. doi: 10.1016/j. bbadis.2014.12.005.

80. Dong, S., Q. Zeng, E. S. Mitchell, J. Xiu, Y. Duan, C. Li, J. K. Tiwari, Y. Hu, X. Cao, and Z. Zhao. "Curcumin enhances neurogenesis and cognition in aged rats: implications for transcriptional interactions related to growth and synaptic plasticity." *PLOS ONE* 7, no. 2 (2012). doi: 10.1371/journal.pone.0031211.

80.b Xu, Y., D. Lin, S. Li, G. Li, S. G. Shyamala, P. A. Barish, M. M. Vernon, J. Pan, and W. O. Ogle. "Curcumin reverses impaired cognition and neuronal plasticity induced by chronic stress." *Neuropharmacology* 57, no. 4 (September 2009): 463–471. doi: 10.1016/j.neuropharm.2009.06.010.

80.c Sun, C.Y., S. S. Qi, P. Zhou, H. R. Cui, S. X. Chen, K. Y. Dai, and M. L. Tang. "Neurobiological and pharmacological validity of curcumin in ameliorating memory performance of senescence-accelerated mice." *Pharmacology Biochemistry and Behavior* 105 (April 2013): 76–82. doi: 10.1016/j. pbb.2013.02.002.

81. Martin, R. C. G., H. S. Aiyer, D. Malik, and Y. Li. "Effect on pro-inflammatory and antioxidant genes and bioavailable distribution of whole tumeric vs. curcumin: similar root but different effects." *Food and Chemical Toxicology* 50, no. 2 (February 2012): 227–231. doi: 10.1016/j.fct.2011.10.070.

82. Martin, R. C. G., H. S. Aiyer, D. Malik, and Y. Li. "Effect on pro-inflammatory and antioxidant genes and bioavailable distribution of whole tumeric vs. curcumin: similar root but different effects." *Food and Chemical Toxicology* 50, no. 2 (February 2012): 227–231. doi: 10.1016/j.fct.2011.10.070.

83. Beilharz, J. E., J. Maniam, and M. J. Morris. "Diet-induced cognitive deficits: the role of fat and sugar, potential mechanisms and nutritional interventions." *Nutrients* 7, no. 8 (August 12, 2015): 6719–6738. doi: 10.3390/nu7085307.

84. Labrousse, V. F., A. Nadjar, C. Joffre, L. Costes, A. Aubert, S. Gregoire, L. Bretillon, and S. Laye. "Short-term long chain omega3 diet protects from neuroinflammatory processes and memory impairment in aged mice." *PLOS ONE* 7, no. 5 (2012): doi: 10.1371/journal.pone.0036861.

84.b   Grundy, T., C. Toben, E. J. Jaehne, F. Corrigan, and B. T. Baune. "Long-term omega-3 supplementation modulates behavior, hippocampal fatty acid concentration, neuronal progenitor proliferation and central TNF-α expression in 7 month old unchallenged mice." *Frontiers in Cellular Neuroscience* 8 (2014): 399. doi: 10.3389/fncel.2014.00399.

84.c   Dong, S., Q. Zeng, E. S. Mitchell, J. Xiu, Y. Duan, C. Li, J. K. Tiwari, Y. Hu, X. Cao, and Z. Zhao. "Curcumin enhances neurogenesis and cognition in aged rats: implications for transcriptional interactions related to growth and synaptic plasticity." *PLOS ONE* 7, no. 2 (2012). doi: 10.1371/journal.pone.0031211.

85.   Siri-Tarino, P. W., Q. Sun, F. B. Hu, and R. M. Krauss. "Meta-analysis of prospective cohort studies evaluating the association of saturated fat with cardiovascular disease." *American Journal of Clinical Nutrition* 91, no. 3 (March 2010): 535–546. doi:10.3945/ajcn.2009.27725. Epub January 13, 2010.

86.   Harvard T.H. Chan School of Public Health. "Fats and cholesterol." http://www.hsph.harvard.edu/nutritionsource/what-should-you-eat/fats-and-cholesterol.

87.   Kris-Etherton, P. M., D. Shaffer Taylor, Y. Shaomei, P. Huth, K. Moriarty, V. Fishell, R. L. Hargrove, G. Zhao, and T. D. Etherton. "Polyunsaturated fatty acids in the food chain in the United States." *American Journal of Clinical Nutrition* 71, no. 1 (January 2000): 179S–188S.

88.   Milbury, P. E., C. Y. Chen, G. G. Dolnikowski, and J. B. Blumberg. "Determination of flavonoids and phenolics and their distribution in almonds." *Journal of Agricultural and Food Chemistry* 54, no. 14 (July 12, 2006): 5027–5033. doi: 10.1021/jf0603937.

89.   Chen, C. Y., and J. B. Blumberg. "In vitro activity of almond skin polyphenols for scavenging free radicals and inducing quinone reductase." *Journal of Agricultural and Food Chemistry* 56, no. 12 (June 25, 2008): 4427–4434. doi: 10.1021/jf800061z.

89.b   Jenkins, D. J., C. W. Kendall, A. Marchie, A. R. Josse, T. H. Nguyen, D. A. Faulkner, K. G. Lapsley, and J. Blumberg. "Almonds reduce biomarkers of lipid peroxidation in older hyperlipidemic subjects." *Journal of Nutrition* 138, no. 5 (May 2008): 908–913.

89.c   Rajaram, S., K. M. Connell, and J. Sabaté. "Effect of almond-enriched high-monounsaturated fat diet on selected markers of inflammation: a randomised, controlled, crossover study." *British Journal of Nutrition* 103, no. 6 (March 2010): 907–912. doi: 10.1017/S0007114509992480.

89.d   Mandalari, G., C. Bisignano, T. Genovese, E. Mazzon, M. S. Wickham, I. Paterniti, and S. Cuzzocrea. "Natural almond skin reduced oxidative stress and inflammation in an experimental model of inflammatory bowel disease." *International Immunopharmacology* 11, no. 8 (August 2011): 915–924. doi: 10.1016/j.intimp.2011.02.003.

90. Eyres L., M. F. Eyres, A. Chisholm, and R. C. Brown. "Coconut oil consumption and cardiovascular risk factors in humans." *Nutrition Reviews* 74, no. 4 (April 2016): 267–280. doi: 10.1093/nutrit/nuw002.

91. Bilton, R. "Averting comfortable lifestyle crises." *Science Progress* 96, Pt. 4 (2013): 319–368.

92. Ponte P. I., J. A. Prates, J. P. Crespo, D. G. Crespo, J. L. Mourão, S. P. Alves, R. J. Bessa, M. A. Chaveiro-Soares, L. T. Gama, L. M. Ferreira, and C. M. Fontes. "Restricting the intake of a cereal-based feed in free-range-pastured poultry: effects on performance and meat quality." *Poultry Science* 87, no. 10 (October 2008): 2032–2042. doi: 10.3382/ps.2007–00522.

93. Buettner, D. *The Blue Zones: Lessons for Living Longer from the People Who've Lived the Longest.* (First paperback edition.) Washington, DC: National Geographic, vii (April 21, 2009). ISBN 978-1-4262-0400-5.

94. Qin, J., R. Li, J. Raes, M. Arumugam, K. S. Burgdorf, C. Manichanh, T. Nielson, N. Pons, F. Levenez, T. Yamada, et al. "A human gut microbial gene catalogue established by metagenomic sequencing." *Nature* 464, no. 7285 (March 4, 2010): 59–65. doi: 10.1038/nature08821.

95. Sekirov, I., S. L. Russell, L. C. Antunes, and B. B. Finlay. "Gut microbiota in health and disease." *Physiological Reviews* 90, no. 3 (July 2010): 859–904. doi: 10.1152/physrev.00045.2009.

95.b Clemente, J. C., L. K. Ursell, L. W. Parfrey, and R. Knight. "The impact of the gut microbiota on human health: an integrative view." *Cell* 148, no. 6 (March 16, 2012): 1258–1270. doi: 10.1016/j.cell.2012.01.035.

96. Cryan, J. F., and T. G. Dinan. "Mind-altering microorganisms: the impact of the gut microbiota on brain and behaviour." *Nature Reviews* 13, no. 10 (October 2012): 702–710. doi: 10.1038/nrn3346.

97. Gulati, A. S., M. T. Shanahan, J. C. Arthur, E. Grossniklaus, R. J. von Furstenberg, L. Kreuk, S. J. Henning, C. Jobin, and R. B. Sartor. "Mouse background strain profoundly influences Paneth cell function and intestinal microbial composition." *PLOS ONE* 7, no. 2 (2012). doi: 10.1371/journal.pone.0032403.

98. Sekirov, I., S. L. Russell, L. C. Antunes, and B. B. Finlay. "Gut microbiota in health and disease." *Physiological Reviews* 90, no. 3 (July 2010): 859–904. doi: 10.1152/physrev.00045.2009.

99. Zimmer, J., B. Lange, J. S. Frick, H. Sauer, K. Zimmermann, A. Schwiertz, K. Rusch, S. Klosterhalfen, and P. Enck. "A vegan or vegetarian diet substantially alters the human colonic faecal microbiota." *European Journal of Clinical Nutrition* 66, no. 1 (January 2012): 53–60. doi: 10.1038/ejcn.2011.141.

100. Brown, K., D. DeCoffe, E. Molcan, and D. L. Gibson. "Diet-induced dysbiosis of the intestinal microbiota and the effects on immunity and disease." *Nutrients* 4, no. 8 (August 2012): 1095–1119. doi: 10.3390/nu4081095.

101. Cryan, J. F., and T. G. Dinan. "Mind-altering microorganisms: the impact of the gut microbiota on brain and behaviour." *Nature Reviews* 13, no. 10 (October 2012): 702–710. doi: 10.1038/nrn3346.

102. Sampson, T. R., and S. K. Mazmanian. "Control of brain development, function and behavior by the microbiome." *Cell Host & Microbe* 17, no. 5 (May 13, 2015): 565–573. doi: http://dx.doi.org/10.1016/j.chom.2015.04.011.

103. Quigley, E. M. "Probiotics in functional gastrointestinal disorders: what are the facts?" *Current Opinion in Pharmacology* 8, no. 6 (September 15, 2008): 704–708. doi: 10.1016/j.coph.2008.08.007.

104. Stilling, R. M., M. van de Wouw, G. Clarke, C. Stanton, T. G. Dinan, and J. F. Cryan. "The neuropharmacology of butyrate: the bread and butter of the microbiota-gut-brain axis." *Neurochemistry International* 99 (October 2016): 110–132. doi: 10.1016/j.neuint.2016.06.011.

CHAPTER 5: THINK CLEARLY

1. World Health Organization. "Mental disorders." Fact sheet 396 (April 2016). http://www.who.int/mediacentre/factsheets/fs396/en.

2. World Health Organization. "Mental Health Action Plan 2013–2020." http://apps.who.int/iris/bitstream/10665/89966/1/9789241506021_eng.pdf.

3. World Health Organization. "Mental Health Action Plan 2013–2020." http://apps.who.int/iris/bitstream/10665/89966/1/9789241506021_eng.pdf.

4. Kahneman, D., and A. Deaton. "High income improves evaluation of life but not emotional well-being." *Proceedings of the National Academy of Sciences of the United States of America* 107, no. 38 (September 21, 2010): 16489–16493. doi:10.1073/pnas.1011492107.

5. Repasky, E. A., J. Eng, and B. L. Hylander. "Stress, metabolism and cancer: integrated pathways contributing to immune suppression." *Cancer Journal* 21, no. 2 (March–April 2015): 97–103. doi:10.1097/PPO.0000000000000107.

6. Villarreal-Garza, C., B. A. Martinez-Cannon, A. Platas, and P. Ramos-Elias. "Specialized programs to support young women with breast cancer." *Current Opinion in Supportive and Palliative Care* 9, no. 3 (September 2015): 308–316. doi:10.1097/SPC.0000000000000155.

7. Repasky, E. A., J. Eng, and B. L. Hylander. "Stress, metabolism and cancer: integrated pathways contributing to immune suppression." *Cancer Journal* 21, no. 2 (March–April 2015): 97–103. doi:10.1097/PPO.0000000000000107.

8. Kiecolt-Glaser, J. K., H. M. Derry, and C. P. Fagundes. "Inflammation: depression fans the flames and feasts on the heat." *American Journal of Psychiatry* 172, no. 11 (November 1, 2015): 1075–1091. http://ajp.psychiatryonline.org/doi/full/10.1176/appi.ajp.2015.15020152.

9.　Zhang, M. F., Y. S. Wen, W. Y. Liu, L. F. Peng, X. D. Wu, and Q. W. Liu. "Effectiveness of mindfulness-based therapy for reducing anxiety and depression in patients with cancer: a meta-analysis." *Medicine* 94, no. 45 (November 2015): e0897-0. doi:10.1097/MD.0000000000000897.

10.　Avila, C., A. C. Holloway, M. K. Hahn, K. M. Morrison, M. Restivo, R. Anglin, and V. H. Taylor. "An overview of links between obesity and mental health." *Current Obesity Reports* 4, no. 3 (September 2015): 303–310. doi:10.1007/s13679-015-0164-9.

11.　Shomaker, L. B., M. Tanofsky-Kraff, J. M. Zocca, S. E. Field, B. Drinkard, and J. A. Yanovski. "Depressive symptoms and cardiorespiratory fitness in obese adolescents." *Journal of Adolescent Health* 50, no. 1 (January 2012). doi:10.1016/j.jadohealth.2011.05.015. Epub July 13, 2011.

12.　Rieck, T., A. Jackson, S. B. Martin, T. Petrie, and C. Greenleaf. "Health-related fitness, body mass index, and risk of depression among adolescents." *Medicine and Science in Sports and Exercise* 45, no. 6 (June 2013): 1083–1088. doi:10.1249/MSS.0b013e3182831db1.

13.　Patra, S., and S. Telles. "Positive impact of cyclic meditation on subsequent sleep." *Medical Science Monitor: International Medical Journal of Experimental and Clinical Research* 15, no. 7 (July 2009): CR375–381. http://www.ncbi.nlm.nih.gov/pubmed/19564829.

14.　Nagendra, R. P., N. Maruthai, and B. M. Kutty. "Meditation and its regulatory role on sleep." *Frontiers in Neurology* 18, no. 3 (April 2012): 54. doi:10.3389/fneur.2012.00054. eCollection 2012.

15.　Black, D. S., G. A. O'Reilly, R. Olmstead, E. C. Breen, and M. R. Irwin. "Mindfulness meditation and improvement in sleep quality and daytime impairment among older adults with sleep disturbances: a randomized clinical trial." *JAMA Internal Medicine* 175, no. 4 (April 2015): 494–501. doi:10.1001/jamainternmed.2014.8081.

16.　Innes, K. E., T. K. Selfe, D. S. Khalsa, and S. Kandati. "Effects of meditation versus music listening on perceived stress, mood, sleep, and quality of life in adults with early memory loss: a pilot randomized controlled trial." *Journal of Alzheimer's Disease* 52, no. 4 (April 8, 2016): 1277–1298. doi:10.3233/JAD-151106.

17.　Jayakody, K., S. Gunadasa, and C. Hosker. "Exercise for anxiety disorders: systematic review." *British Journal of Sports Medicine* 48, no. 3 (February 2014): 187–196. doi:10.1136/bjsports-2012-091287. Epub January 7, 2013.

17.b　Chu, A. H., D. Koh, F. M. Moy, and F. Müller-Riemenschneider. "Do workplace physical activity interventions improve mental health outcomes?" *Occupational Medicine (Oxford: England)* 64, no. 4 (June 2014): 235–245. doi:10.1093/occmed/kqu045.

18.   Hartig, T., R. Mitchell, V. de Vries, and H. Frumkin. "Nature and health." *Annual Review of Public Health* 35 (2014): 207–228. doi:10.1146/annurev-publhealth-032013-182443. Epub January 2, 2014.

19.   McGuinness, M. "What daily meditation can do for your creativity." *Behance*. http://99u.com/articles/6314/what-daily-meditation-can-do-for-your-creativity.

19.b   Colzato, L. S., A. Ozturk, and B. Hommel. "Meditate to create: the impact of focused-attention and open-monitoring training on convergent and divergent thinking." *Frontiers in Psychology* 3 (April 18, 2012): 116. doi:10.3389/fpsyg.2012.00116. eCollection 2012.

19.c   Colzato, L. S., A. Szapora, D. Lippelt, and B. Homell. "Prior meditation practice modulates performance and strategy use in convergent- and divergent-thinking problems." *Mindfulness* (2014): 1–7. doi:10.1007/s12671-014-0352-9.

19.d   Capurso, V., F. Fabbro, and C. Crescentini. "Mindful creativity: the influence of mindfulness meditation on creative thinking." *Frontiers in Psychology* 4 (2013/online January 10, 2014): 1020. doi:10.3389/fpsyg.2013.01020.

20.   Tops, M., M. A. S. Boksem, M. Quirin, H. IJzerman, and S. L. Koole. "Internally directed cognition and mindfulness: an integrative perspective derived from predictive and reactive control systems theory." *Frontiers in Psychology* 5 (May 20, 2014): 429. doi:10.3389/fpsyg.2014.00429.

21.   Dusek, J. A., H. H. Otu, A. L. Wohlhueter, M. Bhasin, L. F. Zerbini, M. G. Joseph, H. Benson, and T. A. Libermann. "Genomic counter-stress changes induced by the relaxation response." *PLOS ONE* 3, no. 7 (July 2, 2008): e2576. doi:10.1371/journal.pone.0002576.

22.   Yerkes, R. M., and J. D. Dodson. "The relation of strength of stimulus to rapidity of habit-formation." *Journal of Comparative Neurology and Psychology* 18 (1908): 459–482. http://psychclassics.yorku.ca/Yerkes/Law.

23.   Creswell, J. D., J. M. Dutcher, W. M. P. Klein, P. R. Harris, and J. M. Levine. "Self-affirmation improves problem-solving under stress." *PLOS ONE* 8, no. 5 (2013): e62593. http://dx.doi.org/10.1371/journal.pone.0062593.

24.   Legault, L. "Self-affirmation enhances performance, makes us receptive to our mistakes." *Association for Psychological Science* (October 24, 2012). http://www.psychologicalscience.org/index.php/news/releases/self-affirmation-enhances-performance-makes-us-receptive-to-our-mistakes.html.

25.   McGreevey, S. "Meditation's positive residual effects." *Harvard Gazette* (November 13, 2012). http://news.harvard.edu/gazette/story/2012/11/meditations-positive-residual-effects.